AVIS HUMPHREY

+1

AVIS HUMPHREY

A NOVEL

B.M. SIMPSON

AVIS HUMPHREY
A NOVEL

bmsimpson@LIVE.com
www.facebook.com/BMSimpson.author

ISBN- 10: 0-9863954-2-0
ISBN – 13: 978-0-9863954-2-0

PRINTED IN THE UNITED STATES OF AMERICA

Book Design by Mads Berg, Mads Berg Illustration

DISCLAIMER

Avis Humphrey is a work of fiction. Names, characters, businesses, organizations, places, events and incidents are either the product of the author's imagination or used in a fictitious manner. Any resemblance to actual persons, living or dead, or actual events or places is purely coincidental. The reader should consider the words on these pages to be as true as the stories told by old fishermen, which are typically tall tales about small or perhaps imagined fish which somehow grow a few inches longer with every sip of beer.

AVIS HUMPHREY

"Thankful for the air I breathe."

George

CHAPTER ONE

Having sex in the backseat of a 1982 Chrysler LeBaron was not as awkward as one might imagine, given enough practice and history. While the make and model often varied, Lindsey Beckham had mastered the art of a backseat orgasm prior to climbing into the LeBaron's backseat that hot and humid night in Watermill, New Hampshire in August of 1983. Thursday, August 18th, to be precise. It was just ten days before she wed Merle Humphrey and vowed to Merle, in front of God and friends and family who came to witness the holy ceremony, she would faithfully love and obey him "from this day forward." But, technically speaking, "this day" had not yet arrived on the Chrysler LeBaron night, and it was not Merle whom she was slip sliding around with on fake leather seats. While Merle had vowed to wait for their wedding night, Lindsey had simply vowed to wait until they were married before doing it, *with Merle*. Not yet being Catholic, and not having thoroughly discussed the minute details of the agreement, she had allowed herself a generous amount of flexibility on her pre-matrimonial commitment.

Being good at anything almost always entails a certain amount of talent, a love for what you are doing, and above all else, practice, practice, and more practice. In Lindsey's case, she had hit the trifecta. She had been an inexperienced rookie once upon a time, but her passion for what she did, inspired her to polish her talent the only way she knew how: practice, practice and more practice. Her training regimen was more stringent than one might have thought necessary as she honed her skills to near perfection.

As she perfected her passion, she came to understand the devil was in the details. First there was the clothing. As a novice, she went out on the prowl wearing tight jeans, snug-fitting sweaters, and high heels. She had the body for it when she was a teen, and at twenty-two she had only matured and improved. But through time and experience, she came to understand

1

shedding tight jeans and a sweater was more awkward than she anticipated. Between "him" trying to undress and her clumsily struggling to pull off tight jeans, panties, sweater, and a bra, without ruining the moment, was nearly an impossible feat. So, when she strolled into the bar at the Watermill Inn at 9:00 p.m. on that August 18th evening, she wore a light blue cotton sundress wrapped around her waist and tied with a matching blue cotton string. With a slight tug on the bow, she could gracefully drop the spaghetti strings from her tanned shoulders and almost instantly be completely bare and ready to do what she loved to do. Another improvement she had learned with time and experience was that while panties served a purpose in her day-to-day life, they served no purpose when she climbed into the backseat to steam up windows. Under the sundress, there was Lindsey and nothing more.

There were times when Lindsey went out into the night with no plan and simply left the night to fate. If the stars were shining bright and the love gods were smiling down, she would run into a friend, new or old, and the evening would go wherever it was destined to go. Typically to the backseat of *his* car. The backseat was her thing. It was her tacky little Xanadu. Her escape from getting out of bed and going to work every day. Her reprieve from being the sweet, polite, and intelligent woman with the pretty smile who said, Please and *Thank You*, and asked bank customers, "What brings you in today?" The backseat was Lindsey's escape and distraction from the humdrum reality of life in small-town Watermill, and the Ozzie-and-Harriet-like life she lived there. The backseat was Lindsey's good world, her reprieve from the real world.

She didn't like going back to anyone's place to do what they did. The awkward good-byes, or the expectation of spending the night, cast shadows on her good place. Sometimes the barking dog that greeted them as they tried to passionately work their way toward the bedroom was a deal breaker. "Hold on just a minute. I've got to let the dog out," were not words Lindsey considered heat-of-the-moment pillow talk, not that talk was needed all that much. In fact, no talk was almost always better than anything *he* had to say. And *he* never fell asleep after having sex in the backseat. She never had to lie in a dark room wondering what to do next. Finish and go was always the unwritten etiquette after backseat sex. Watermill was far too small for her to go to a hotel. If she was going to do that, she may as well have put up a billboard that said, "Lindsey's getting laid in 208." Besides, she liked the excitement of the backseat. She had attempted a few front seats, the reclining kind, but there was something about the front seat that just didn't work for Lindsey. She was a backseat girl.

A jazz band from Burlington was playing at the Watermill Inn for the week and the band had a bass player who would from this night forward be referred to, at least in Lindsey's mind, as *The Jazzman*. They played funked-up versions of Chuck Mangione and Herb Alpert music with a too-heavy bass and keyboards in place of horns. The band, which was on the dim end of their quickly fading 1970's flash of popularity, was playing out their last few months in smaller and smaller venues in front of fewer and fewer people. Lindsey sat at a table near the wall, just on the edge of the shadows of the tacky multi-colored stage. She strategically positioned herself to be in the line of sight, but not so much that she looked desperate in the hunt.

Tonight, was not her "no particular plan" night. She walked into the bar with purpose. She picked out her seat with purpose. She sipped her glass of wine with purpose and she gazed around the room with purpose. And shortly after sitting down and taking the first sip from her glass, she was certain, The Jazzman would be hers before the night was done. Two slow glasses of wine, a few smiles, some small talk with The Jazzman between sets, and then midnight arrived. As fate would have it, he had a rented car parked outside. With one last sip of wine, Lindsey stood up and asked, "Care to take me for a ride?"

Watermill was a small town, and Lindsey knew where to go without foolishly riding out into the middle of nowhere with a complete stranger or getting caught by a local yokel who would spread the news like the plague. Jazzman was surprised when she told him to take a left and then a right and then another left and they ended up in front of the police station. She pointed to an alley across the street and told him to pull in. For just a moment, The Jazzman thought he was being set up by some kind of country-bumpkin sting operation. He sat there parked directly in front of the lit sign that almost screamed, "Watermill Police Department," and he weighed out the risk-reward ratio.

3

"Don't worry. They cruise all over town every night, but they never think to look right under their noses."

"I don't know. It just seems..." As he searched for the right words, Lindsey gently tugged at the shoulder strap of her dress and almost, but not quite, exposed her entire breast that had already formed small beads of sweat. "My, it sure is hot out tonight. Hot enough to make me want to take this dress right off." Jazzman took a quick left and drove to the back of the alley and pulled into the narrow dirt driveway that hid them from the street and from the police station. There was no small talk. In less than a minute Lindsey stood leaning against the backseat passenger door with her dress string untied, her shoulder strings falling down to her elbows, and the rest of her body exposed in all its glory.

She not only considered herself to be the master of the backseat, but she was also a master at guiding her lovers through the process, from beginning to end. She had become somewhat of a sex guru who, out of social generosity, was willing to share her abundance of sexual wisdom and knowledge. For the experience to reach maximum pleasure, which was her goal, both participants had to overcome the awkwardness of being new to each other. They also had to manage being in the cramped quarters of the backseat with door handles, seat belts, and windows, with enough grace and dexterity to allow themselves to perform their respective duties without being so contorted that one or both of them experienced leg cramps, carpet burns, or a myriad of other backseat misfortunes.

Lindsey smiled, turned and opened the door. In a single fluid motion, she dropped her dress the rest of the way and rolled it into a small pillow. Her sandals fell off her feet as she climbed in and effortlessly rolled over and rested her head on the dress/pillow she had balled up against the driver's side door. It was all done in one graceful, effortless choreographed motion. Jazzman quickly leaned forward to join her, but Lindsey's long toes with dark red nails connected to her slender foot that was attached to her long leg which joined the rest of her flawless body, firmly planted itself against his chest, stopping him dead in his tracks. "Clothes off before you get in."

He obeyed.

Over the years, Lindsey had experienced not very good sex, okay sex, pretty good sex and every once in a while, damn good sex. As she would later recall, "Then there was *The Jazzman*." He was at an entirely new level she had never experienced, or ever even imagined possible. He undressed in a flurry, but not frantically. There was an excited calmness about him. Confident, but not arrogant. A boyish quality, but not juvenile. Their sweat level rose quickly and dramatically. Almost from the beginning, Lindsey lost track of time and to a certain degree she lost track of everything except her surreal existence in the moment. Her head swirled with every touch and every kiss. Before he had climbed into the backseat, she had thrown her left foot over the top of the front passenger seat; and when he arrived, she quickly wrapped her right leg loosely around the back of his legs. Her head rested on her right hand swaddled up in her dress, and the fingers of her left hand softly glided through his hair. Puddles of sweat were forming between her skin and the seat and between his skin and hers, but she liked it. She wasn't one of those girls who wanted things sterile and tame. This was backseat, hot-summer-night sex, not air-conditioned Holiday Inn frolicking.

She heard someone whisper in the distance and then the volume began to rise. "Oh my god. Oh my god. Oh my god," rang in her head at least three times before she realized it was her own voice. Her body tingled. It felt as if she were on fire and like warm melted butter all at the same time. The brick building just outside the car window blurred from view along with everything else her normal senses had picked up only a few moments earlier. The sounds of the crickets faded. The smell of the New England summer night was gone. The taste of the wine in her mouth was no longer detectable. When he first climbed in, she had felt his muscle-toned flesh in her hands, but that was gone too. External reality ceased to exist. For the first and only time in her life, Lindsey Beckham had a religious experience and it was while having backseat sex with The Jazzman.

Tiny lights began flashing in her mind and intensified to an almost unbearable level. She didn't notice her right arm tightly squeezing around The Jazzman's neck. She didn't notice her body tensing or her left foot pulling on the passenger seat headrest. Nor did she realize her right foot was pushing on the ceiling hard enough to dent the roof. Lindsey began to clench her jaw and she gasped for breath with her eyes tightly closed. If this was heaven, she wanted to die now. If this was what drugs were like, she was addicted.

At the very last possible moment before the explosion, before the rush of everything good in her world, and for no particular reason, her eyes opened wide and locked onto a rental car brochure hanging from the pocket on the back of the driver's seat. Centered on the top half of the brochure was a three-inch bright red square with bold white letters in the center of it. Suddenly, everything seemed to rush from all directions to the innermost point of her core. This time she heard her voice cry out one word. "AVIS!" Just as it was written on the brochure.

Nine months later, Avis Humphrey was born. Eight and a half months prior to his birth, Lindsey Beckham married Merle Humphrey, a devout Catholic who insisted they wait until after the wedding to share such a sacred moment. They had never climbed into a backseat together.

* * *

Two months before Avis's fifth birthday, a watered-down version of the Jazzman story found its way back to Merle. Watermill was small. The revelation was inevitable.

That very afternoon, four-year-old Avis Humphrey stood in the driveway in front of their apartment with his hands in his pockets and a perplexed look on his face. Merle and Lindsey had been yelling at each other inside the house while Avis sat on the front steps. When Merle stormed out with suitcase in hand, he glanced down at Avis and shook his head without saying a word. Avis stood up and followed him to his car. But before he could say a word, Merle had slammed his door and was peeling out, shooting dirt and dust into the air. Avis watched the dust swirls long after the car was out of sight. He watched as the tiny tornadoes spun up into the air and then disappeared into nothingness.

Merle, or "Daddy" as Avis had called him since he began to talk, never came back to hug his son or say goodbye to his son or to even acknowledge he had a son. He simply left without a word and never came back.

CHAPTER TWO

Ten-year-old Avis stood in the middle of the dirt road looking toward the dust swirls that had long since settled back down onto the road after the most recent car had driven off. His shorts were ragged and his T-shirt was too big. He wasn't crying. He never cried. He just looked and wondered.

"Hey Avis. Whatcha lookin at?" It was the first question he clearly recalled Leo asking him. There had been other questions before this one, and there would be countless more after, but that particular question was the first one that stuck out in his mind. It was the first one that Avis had no real answer for.

Leo lived two houses down from Avis's Gram and Gramps' home on Bunker Hill Road. The road was neither hilly nor Revolutionary War historic and was just one more thing Leo would eventually ask Avis about. "Hey Avis. Why's our road called Bunker Hill Road if there's no hills and no bunkers?" It was another question Avis could not answer.

Five years ago, Avis and his mom were living in an apartment they called home for a few months after Merle left. One day his mom sat him down and gave him a long, heartfelt, and overly detailed explanation of why they were moving in with Gram and Gramps. She told him about money and responsibilities and family and everyone helping each other out. He nodded as if he understood. Of course, he understood none of it. He was five. She didn't tell him she needed a live-in babysitter to look after Avis, especially on backseat nights.

* * *

Five years after that conversation, Avis shrugged at Leo's question. "Nothing, I guess." He wasn't looking at the long-gone car or the dust that had settled. He wasn't looking at the road. Even though he didn't realize it, he was looking at the empty space that was once his mother. He didn't think she would come back to fill that space again.

"Where's your mom gone?" Leo had seen the car drive off ten minutes ago with Avis's mom leaning out the window and yelling, *Good-bye* and *See you soon*, and waving while the new guy honked the horn. The last thing she yelled was, "Don't forget to mow the grass."

"Montana."

"Where's that?"

"I dunno."

"When's she coming back?"

"I dunno."

For a few minutes, there was no sound other than the leaves rustling in the breeze. They continued to look down the road as if they expected the car or the dust swirls to return. Leo eventually chirped in again. "Wanna go fishin?"

There was another long silence as Avis stood in the road and Leo sat on his bike beside him.

"Okay," is all Avis said. Leo got off his bike and followed Avis into Gramps' rundown garage. He dropped his bike in the middle of the floor. Avis grabbed two poles from the corner and handed one to Leo. They didn't talk much about his mother after that day.

CHAPTER THREE

Twenty-six-year-old Avis flipped the ticket through his fingers and looked at the back of it for a few seconds. He flipped it over again and looked at the numbers on the front. His eyebrows rose, and his forehead wrinkled as if he were surprised the numbers hadn't changed since the last time he read them.

"What the hell is this shit?" he mumbled out loud. He sat by himself at the kitchen table and ran his fingers along the scratches in the red Formica tabletop. He repeated the act of flipping and reading at least a dozen more times as he repeated the same question again and again, as if a great voice of the universe was going to answer him.

"This is insane, that's what it is. No way in hell do I want anything to do with nine hundred million dollars." As it turned out, it was nine hundred sixty-seven million dollars, before taxes. It also turned out that if he didn't want anything to do with nine hundred sixty-seven million dollars, he shouldn't have bought a Powerball ticket in the first place. The odds of winning may have been a near-impossible long shot, but winning became an unlikely, but realistic, possibility the moment he smiled at Carmen and slid two dollars across the counter.

After one or two more flips and deep sighs, he laid the ticket back down on the table and pressed it with his hand. Flattening out the wrinkles in the ticket was just one more nervous gesture he kept repeating as if he were going to lay his hand on top of the ticket and the ticket would magically disappear into the table. When it was as flat as it was going to get, he lifted his hand. The ticket was still there. He sat and stared at it as if he were watching TV and waiting for something to happen. Nothing happened. He closed his eyes, took in another deep breath, held it for a minute, and then slowly let the air escape from his chest. He repeated this pattern three more times before opening his eyes. The ticket was still there. He knew it would be, but he still felt a tinge of disappointment at seeing it.

"Damn…" he said in a long-extended word. "Son of a bitch," he whispered. Then he closed his eyes and took three more long, cleansing breaths.

After a few more rounds of breathing, Avis got up and walked to the dining room window and looked out over the wet, muddy yard and stuffed the ticket back into his shirt pocket, restoring the wrinkles he had just pressed out of it.

CHAPTER FOUR

Leo was lying flat on his back and casting his line almost straight up into the air without looking at the stream. He heard the splash, so he knew the hook and bobber landed somewhere in the water. For the moment, he was watching a helicopter flying so high above him, he almost couldn't see it and he could barely hear the chop of the blades through the air. Avis already had his line in the water and was well aware of where his hook was located. He glanced up at the helicopter too, a rarity to see in Watermill, New Hampshire, and wondered where it was coming from or going to. He glanced at Leo, still lying on his back, and shook his head back and forth as he returned to look at his line in the still water.

"Hey Avis," Leo blurted out, as he continued to watch the machine flying high up in the sky.

"Yeah, Leo."

"Hey Avis" was always a prelude to a question, and often a prelude to a question that would surprise anyone other than Avis. Leo was a walking, talking human version of Curious George. He wasn't academic in any real sense, or at least not in any conventional sense, but his curiosity and his questions were infinite. The first question Avis remembered Leo ever asking was about where his mom was going. From then on, the questions increased like snowflakes in a New Hampshire blizzard.

Like most of Leo's questions that followed over the years, there were rarely any discernible reasons for him to ask them. There was no conversation that led up to it, or even loosely tied it to the inquiry of the moment. Leo's mind was an enigma to Avis. Random thoughts seemingly stemmed from nowhere and led to questions and conversations that were often humorous, sometimes inspiring, and occasionally painful. So, on that spring day many years ago, Leo blurted out his first question for the day.

"Hey Avis."

"Yeah, Leo."

"Did you ever figure out why your mom left?" He didn't embellish or suggest any possible reasons why she may have left. He didn't hint as to why he was asking. It was just a random thought, like a cricket chirping or a twig snapping, or in Leo's case, a question appearing out of thin air. Perhaps it somehow came from the helicopter that he was not asking any questions about. He simply asked the random question and quietly stared at the sky and waited for a response from Avis, or for a trout to bite.

Avis sat on a moss-covered log that was like a cushioned seat and pondered the question as much as, or perhaps more than, he pondered the answer. He was thirteen when Leo asked the question, but only ten when she went away for a few days and never came back. At that age, how could he know why people did such things? How could a boy of his age know why a grown woman, his mother, would yell, "Make sure you mow the lawn," and then never return home? How could he know why grownups did anything? How could he have known that, with each passing day and month and year, he would ask himself the same questions over and over, and the deafening silence of his own response would haunt him almost as much as the memory of his mom waving goodbye as she rode out of his life.

"I guess it's what she wanted to do... I guess."

It was a life-changing moment for Avis. He had asked himself the same question more times than he cared to remember, and not once had he ever answered it. Nor had God or anyone else answered it for him. Not even with a bad answer. Each and every time he asked the simple question, "Why did my mom leave?", it was as if someone put a blank white piece of paper in front of him with nothing but the one question written on it. No good reason. No bad reason. Not even a reason he did not understand. Nothing.

For three years Avis had climbed into his bed and under his covers, repeated the question like a good Catholic boy reciting his Our Father and Hail Mary's. Over and over again, he would ask, "Why did Mom leave? Was it me? Was she supposed to leave? Did she have a better life and better family out there somewhere? Was it me?" He would always ask the first and last question more than all the other questions combined. "Why did she leave?" and "Was it me?" He wondered what he could have done that drove her away and what he could have done better to make her stay. Maybe he should have gone to bed on time without her yelling at him. Maybe he shouldn't have complained when he was hungry and she didn't fix lunch or supper for him. Maybe he shouldn't have worn his new sneakers out and played in the mud. Maybe. There were always a *maybe* this or *maybe* that, but there was never a definitive answer in his mind. The question, "Why did Mom leave?" was never answered. He always fell asleep with the punishing question and elusive answers flowing around in circles in his brain.

But when Leo asked the question, it only took a few moments for Avis to blurt out a response. It was a reflex response. He didn't over-think or contemplate all the what-ifs and the maybes. He didn't try to come up with the correct answer. Leo asked, and Avis's response flowed out of him as if it had been waiting inside for the right person to invite it out. And as vague as the answer may have been for some, the answer was a crystal clear, rock-solid explanation to Avis. His mother had left because she wanted to. There was nothing more to it than that.

She had left her hometown. She had left her family and friends. She had left her enemies, of which she had at least a few, even though Avis was too young to know about most of them. She had left her crappy job at the bank. She had left her past, and she had left the future she was supposed to have in Watermill, New Hampshire. And beyond any justifiable reason, she had left her one and only son to fend for himself. At ten, Avis Humphrey had no mother to go along with his no father. And at thirteen, he had a life-changing moment when he heard himself say the words, "She wanted to." At long last, he had an answer.

* * *

That question and that riverbank were a long time ago. On this particular morning, Avis and Leo were sitting on a different riverbank, and different fish were not biting at their hooks. It was barely seven a.m. and the mist was rising up over the still waters where their bobbers sat motionless waiting to be bobbed. Avis had his Red Sox cap pulled down, shielding th light out of his eyes. A crinkled Powerball ticket was almost falling out the pocket of his worn-out and faded orange T-shirt and he was mindlessly rubbing his fingers across the frayed tear in the knee of his blue jeans.

"Hey Avis," Leo blurted out, just loud enough to disturb any fish who were vaguely contemplating breakfast.

"Yeah, Leo."

"Do chickens have sex?" he asked while intently watching his bobber.

"Ahhh, yes," Avis said as if he were reminiscing about the taste of fine wine. "The cloacal kiss " He said it as if he were about to paint a picture of celestial poultry lovemaking. Leo was picturing chicken porn.

"The what?" Leo asked without taking his eye off his bobber.

" The cloaca. It's the thing that chickens have."

"Hens or roosters?"

"Both. They both have the same… *thing.*"

Leo's forehead wrinkled as he envisioned some sort of gender-neutral chicken lovemaking that somehow produced babies. It was only a momentary thought, though. "And then what?"

"Some rubbing. Not a lot to it," Avis mumbled and watched the water slowly flow past.

"Is that what makes hens have eggs?"

"Nope, but if they have red-hot chicken sex, the eggs can become chickens. If not, then they can only become omelets or pancakes or something along those lines."

"Hmmm. How often do they do it?"

"Roosters can do it like twenty times a day. Not sure about hens. I don't think they do it as much."

It fell silent again and Leo's brain went back to wandering.

Avis smiled, not so much at the question-and-answer period, but more that he suspected Leo had retained the biology lesson and moved onto a completely unrelated chain of thoughts.

Leo's bobber bounced a little and he instantly jerked his pole and scared the trout away. Avis shook his head and noticed the piece of paper 'bout to fall out of his pocket. He stuffed it down deep out of sight and mped back against the trunk of a leaning cedar tree. A small part of him wished the ticket had fallen out and drifted away downstream without him seeing where it went. Another part of him wondered if Leo would ever be quiet enough this morning for a fish to nibble on his hook.

His mind began to wander back to stopping by Alice Chin's house last night. The shock of holding the winning Powerball ticket had begun wearing off a few days ago. It was time to do something about it, and he hoped Alice would be able to help him out.

"Hey Avis," Leo called again.

"Yeah, Leo," he responded.

"Who do you suppose made the letter *Z*? It's kind of a funny letter, don't you think?"

CHAPTER FIVE

It was irony, really. Figuring out how to carry on while trying to figure out how to end it all. Savannah Gardener had been depressed for so long she had almost forgotten what it felt like to feel good about anything. Financial woes ate away at her like an inoperable tumor. One for which there was no cure, apparently, or at least not a fix she could afford. Untainted love was a distant and rapidly fading memory. Friends and family had become as faint as the sun had become over the past few weeks. And the gray, dreary weather was relentless. Rain that never came down hard, but the drizzle seemed eternal.

Her ability to make any decision had deteriorated over the past few months along with her will to carry on. Ending it all became more and more her obsession. What did she possibly have to live for, was the question she asked herself with ever increasing frequency. When the thought first came to her, she worked hard to come up with a list of reasons for why she should live. While the list was shaky, it was substantial enough, and the reasons were valid. She was young and relatively good-looking, or at least not bad looking. She was smart and educated and blah, blah, blah. That's how the list always seemed to end in her head: "Blah, blah, blah." With the passing of time, her will to live grew weaker and the list shrank. Then one morning when she asked herself what she had to live for, she came up with nothing to put on the list.

It was another cold, damp June day on a lonely side street in Biddeford, Maine, and Savannah sat at her kitchen table with her cat. She released an exaggerated sigh after making the long-overdue decision.

"That's it. I am going to end this misery," she announced to herself and her cat with confidence and conviction. She said it like a woman who knew what she was doing, but it was an act she performed in order to fool herself. She had no idea what she was doing, but she couldn't take it anymore. She had to do something.

The weather was dreary and gray. Just as the sun radiated through the windows on a bright summer day, the grayness now poured into the house and filled every nook and cranny. The rain had stopped, but this was Maine. When the rain stopped, it just stayed gray for days on end while Mother Earth prepared to drizzle some more.

When she made the decision to cash out, a tiny weight lifted, and she almost felt a ray of sunshine touch her face.

"My God," she said to Bruce, her cat. "Can you believe it? I finally made a decision." She gently rubbed his ears between her index finger and thumb. Now that *the decision* was out of the way, she knew there would be at least a couple of more decisions to be made. She hoped the remaining ones were easier than the first. "What to do? What to do?" she mumbled. "So, what do you think, Bruce? What's the best way for a woman to kill herself?"

He purred.

Creativity was never one of Savannah's strong points. She was a *facts* girl. Gather the facts. Put them in order. Let them explain themselves. She had never liked being the person who was responsible for gathering facts and making a plan of action. She was going to have to suck it up this time and step out of her comfort zone if she hoped to achieve her goal.

The truth was if she were better equipped to handle problems and could come up with reasonable solutions, she probably wouldn't have been selecting this option in the first place. As she sipped on her cup of coffee and considered the best way to kill herself, if there was in fact such a thing, nothing came to mind. Then she snuffed out her fifth cigarette of the still-young day and smiled. "If I keep smoking like this, I won't need a suicide plan," she said to Bruce as she reached for another.

Finally, after more than an hour of coffee and cigarettes and some minor chitchat with Bruce, she opened her laptop, clicked on the browser, and typed, "Suicide."

The page quickly filled with one heading after another. The most significant heading of all, even though it was the smallest print on the page, said *56,000,000 results*.

"Fifty-six million. Well, that's a big number, isn't it?" she asked the cat. Again, he didn't answer. "Hmmm. Guess I'll have to narrow this down just a bit," she mumbled and took another drag.

She typed "Suicide for Dummies" into the small box, and in the blink of an eye a new heading popped up. This time there were only 698,000. Mere child's play compared to the millions that had appeared minutes ago. She wondered what the other fifty-five million suicide-related sites referenced if not the topic, *How To*. There were less than a million sites to help people who were so hopeless they couldn't figure out how to kill themselves without getting instructions from someone else. Even worse, they were getting instructions from the Internet. "Seems we're not alone in our search, Bruce," she said to her friend, who lay contently in her lap. He looked up at her and she realized she had just included her innocent cat in her slowly formulating plan. "Sorry, Bruce. Don't worry. I'm not taking you with me," she said.

Savannah was done thinking about all the reasons she once had *to live*. Reasons that one by one, had slipped away. She had been engaged to be married just a few short months back. He didn't cheat on her. He didn't fall in love with another woman or decide to become a priest or announce he was gay or bi. He just stopped loving her and she stopped loving him. The fire had burned down to a flicker, then to a dim glowing ember, and finally, it simply went out. At just about the same time her love life was dying, her passion for being a freelance journalist had also faded. All through her college years and the three years that followed, she had loved investigating, researching, and writing. Then one day, it all started to feel pointless. She reported facts, details, and points of view to people who, for the most part, didn't care. Or if they did care, their attention span didn't last long, and the caring disappeared with their focus. A year ago, Mack, her ex, would have been on the list of her reasons to live. Her career would have been on the list. Making a difference in the world would have been on the list. Today, if she were being completely honest with herself, coffee and cigarettes would have been put on the list, and maybe Bruce. She didn't think they were enough to tip the scale and inspire her to continue to battle with the vast emptiness. They were barely list-worthy, if worthy at all.

She clicked onto the first site, but only spent a few seconds on it. The smartass who created the site thought it would be funny to write a blog that mocked people who surfed the net on how to commit suicide. Oddly enough, she chuckled at one of the comments where the blogger wrote, "My instructions may get overly detailed at times, but please keep in mind that my audience is largely made up of people who are unable to think of ways to kill themselves. I suspect that if they are going to succeed, I will have to leave no stone unturned and omit no detail." She cracked a slight smile, but quickly decided that being cheered up while trying to find a method to kill herself was a bit counterproductive. She saw a little less humor in it when it dawned on her that he was talking about her.

The next site was a compilation of suicide-related statistics, such as how many of any particular group called it quits and when they did it. What month they pulled the plug and how old they were. The information seemed to be important to whoever posted the article and contained a lot of details and data. Savannah read a few of the stats.

When she had made her decision earlier in the morning, a decision she had been pondering for weeks, she had felt a sense of resolution. She did not feel so much that she was giving up, but more like she was moving on. But as she read the staggeringly large numbers, she didn't get the feeling that the people these numbers represented had "moved on" at all. She felt more like she was reading stats about people who had given up all hope and killed themselves. It all felt cold and final. This was the moment when she began to realize that maybe she was hoping suicide was less quitting, less killing herself, and more like taking the step of discovering the big mystery of the universe. She wanted to believe she was searching for answers for questions like: What comes after life here on earth?

"Wow..." she whispered as she stared at the screen. "Thirty-eight thousand a year. That's a lot of people killing themselves." She continued reading to the cat. "Ten straight years of increasing numbers. More men offing themselves than women. More whites than non-whites. More non-whites than blacks." She sat and looked at the screen for a minute and pondered how non-whites and blacks were different categories, but then decided it didn't matter. She was on a mission and seemed to be drifting. Taking a deep breath, she refocused her energy and began reading again.

"Wow..." she whispered once more. "A lot of people shoot

themselves." Pulling the trigger and inflicting hot lead into the body or head was far and away the most popular way to go. Savannah had been a long-time anti-gun girl and instantly thought suicide this way was going to cause a moral or philosophical conflict for her. Just because she had decided to kill herself didn't mean she had to abandon all of her core values. One could argue tossing away her life should have rated quite high on her moral or philosophical conflict scale, but she didn't seem to see it that way. She just knew she wouldn't be using a gun. After shooting, suffocation and poison rounded off the top three. She was pessimistic about using any of these mainstream choices. Another couple of clicks took her to a new page.

The header on the next site looked promising. In big, soft blue letters the words, *Making It Happen* took up the top two inches of the page. She skimmed through the first couple of *Introduction to Suicide* paragraphs but as her eyes moved down the page, she became disappointed that the site discussed why people killed themselves much more than how people do it. Even worse, the page was written by a doctor who had apparently done research and had come to the mind-boggling conclusion that the number one reason people kill themselves, is because they are depressed.

"You see, Bruce. This is where I went wrong in life. I've always tried to be a good and reasonable woman. I'm hard working and honest, but I just can't seem to make ends meet. Can't pull my life together. And then guys like this shmuck write blogs and books and probably make a ton of money telling us people who want to kill ourselves we are doing it because we're not happy. Really? Did he think we didn't know people who kill themselves probably are NOT happy? It never entered my mind that people were killing themselves because they were just too damn happy and couldn't take feeling utopic anymore." She was on a minor tirade, and Bruce patiently listened while she vented. "He probably has a whole series of books that say things like, the reason people bleed is because they have cuts. Or…" Bruce stopped listening as she continued to ramble on between puffs on her cigarette.

She almost clicked off the site and moved to another, but at the last moment her eyes caught the rest of the list.

Reason #2, Psychotic. She pondered for a moment. No, she didn't think she was psychotic, but then she wondered if psychotic people would know whether or not they were psychotic.

Reason #3, Impulsive. Based on the fact that she had been pondering the issue of suicide for weeks and weeks, she ruled out being impulsive.

Reason #4, Crying Out For Help. Nope. She wasn't calling out. In fact, she had just about run out of anyone in her life she would want to call out to for help or anything else.

Reason #5, Philosophical. At first glance, she thought this would be the best fit. Philosophical almost made the whole damn business sound noble and enlightened, but there were problems with this category too. The writer explained that Reason #5 referred to those who are terminally ill or in extreme pain. They are making a conscious choice to end their pain and suffering. Even though Savannah's life had become pointless and her depression felt like it was a never-ending burden, she felt a tinge of guilt. She thought it was selfish to group herself with people who were suffering from agonizing cancer and other diseases that would certainly dwarf her current condition.

She moved on to *Reason #6, Mistake.* She didn't dare ponder whether or not she was making a mistake. That would take her right back to where she had begun well over a month ago. She couldn't bear the thought of wading through the whole process one more time. She stopped reading and clicked off the site. "Damn, Bruce. I not only cannot find out how to kill myself. Apparently, I can't even justify doing it. Guess I'll just stick with reason number one and leave it at that."

Bruce looked up at her as if he were waiting to be reminded of what reason number one had been.

"Depression," she answered his silent question.

She scrolled down the page and clicked onto another site that looked more promising. It looked more like a *How To* as opposed to a *How Many* or *Why.* Instantly a photo of a bloody corpse popped onto the screen. This particular woman, a woman who had succeeded—for better or worse—in discovering the answer to the question of what happens in the afterlife, had chosen to jump from the fourteenth floor of an office building. There were a few paragraphs written below the photograph, describing the supposed events that led to the woman taking such a bold step. Savannah did not read them. She sat with her mouth gaping open and her cigarette hanging between her fingers, as she stared at the bloody corpse. "Okay. I won't be a jumper," she said as she began to scroll down to the next photo.

It was of a guy who had hanged himself. "Jesus!" she said aloud and quickly closed the site. If she had scrolled down to the next one, she would have seen the gunshot photo. That one would have validated her opinion of guns. "Why would someone post pictures like that?" she whispered as she continued the conversation with Bruce. "Where would someone even get pictures like that?" she added.

Savannah closed her laptop, looked out the window, and watched a few cars drive by as she continued to scratch her cat's ears. She wondered if not being able to figure out how and why to kill herself made her more pathetic or less pathetic. Then she decided she didn't really care.

An old woman was walking down the sidewalk in front of Savannah's house. She used a cane as she gingerly stepped around puddles of water, being careful not to slip. Her coat was old and worn, her face even older and more worn, but she looked good. She looked old and worn and poor... and good. Somehow, despite having left the best years of her life well behind her, the old woman still seemed to be happy. Perhaps it was her posture, a small woman standing tall. Or maybe it was the look of concentration on her face that showed she still cared about what happened. She still cared enough to worry about slipping and falling down. Maybe it was just some sort of positive energy people could sense, a sort of positive radiance. There was an obvious visual difference between people like her who still had a sense of purpose, and a person like Savannah who had given up on life. The old woman continued her life journey, one feeble and purposeful step at a time. Savannah watched her until she rounded the corner and went out of sight.

"One step at a time, huh Bruce?" she asked her old cat. He blankly stared up at her again.

The thought of filling even one more empty day began to creep into her brain. It was eight minutes past ten and she rarely went to sleep before midnight. Fourteen hours with nothing to do and nobody, except for Bruce, to talk to. Thirty-seven minutes later, she was still sitting at her table, staring out the window, when the phone rang.

It rang three times before she picked it up. Looking at the caller ID, she presumed it was a telemarketer or a wrong number—there really wasn't anyone else. Her eyes widened a little when she saw the name on the screen.

"Steve. I didn't know you still had my number," she said.

"Well, Savannah, my better judgment told me to throw it out after you dropped the ball on the last story. But my instincts told me you might still make me look good for not giving up on you."

"Everyone else is busy, huh?"

"Now don't be like that, Savannah. You know you could use some rent money, and I need someone to write a story. It's even a good one." She had done decent work for him and showed promise right after college and the year or two that followed. But then she hit her life drought and her writing went down the toilet, right along with everything else.

"I've given up on finding good stories, Steve. Everyone's twisted these days."

"That's the spirit. Keep a positive attitude. Besides, I already found the story for you. You just need to go talk to some people and write everything down."

"Is that right?" she mumbled. She tried to sound like she was blowing him off, but her apathy was fading. The thought of having a reason to leave the apartment was refreshing.

"Got a great story for you to cover over in Watermill, New Hampshire. I'll email you what details I have. You'll have to let me know within the hour if you're interested and going to do it though. If not, I'll have to give it to someone else."

Savannah hung up her phone, lit a cigarette and opened her laptop. A few minutes later, the details came. She read the email, wrote, "Okay," and hit the Send button.

CHAPTER SIX

News spreads fast in Watermill. By the time Savannah and at least another two-dozen or so reporters had flocked to town, the locals had shared and re-shared so many details that *all* the details of the event had been shared. Some of the details were true, some were partially true, and some were just plain made up; but all were shared. Over the next few weeks, Avis and Watermill's finest would discover that most of the reporters didn't spend much time weeding out the truths from the untruths.

Avis had spent the weekend camping and hadn't heard any of the versions of what went down, but the onslaught was about to begin. He strolled back into his trailer about 9:30 in the morning and made a pot of coffee and plopped himself down on the couch that was nearly as old as he was. He reached down and pushed the power button on the remote and mindlessly waited for the lady newscaster to tell him some great news or tragic news that would almost certainly have zero impact on his life. But as soon as he turned on the TV he leaned forward, as if he thought he wasn't seeing clearly, and quietly whispered, "Oh shit!" Then he ran to the front door and saw a tall, square-jawed man talking to the cameraman while pointing toward his trailer. When the cameraman saw Avis's face peeking out through the small eyelevel window in the trailer door, he excitedly waved to let the newscaster know someone was at home. Avis quickly ducked down. Whether he realized it or not, he had taken the first step of going into hiding.

He ran back to the TV just in time to hear Square Jaw say, "This run-down trailer on the outskirts of Watermill, New Hampshire, is the humble home of Avis Humphrey, the man who purportedly has given away the Powerball ticket worth nine-hundred sixty-seven million dollars."

"Oh shit," Avis mumbled again. This time he looked through the living room window that had an obstructed view of the TV crew but allowed him to more or less see them. At his angle, he saw Square Jaw and company still standing right there. Not that he really needed to look. He could see him plain as day on his TV as he continued to fill in the airtime with the few things he actually knew, or had heard, about Avis.

"Locals say Mr. Humphrey was born and raised in Watermill and works as a mechanic at the Rusty Wrench Garage. And..." he added as if there were some newsworthy relevance, "locals say if you can't find Avis at home or at work, then you'll find him fishing at one of the area's lakes, ponds, or streams."

"What the hell is this crap?" Avis asked as if he were striking up a conversation with the guy on the TV screen. He felt a tinge of discomfort to hear that locals had been talking about him at all. He thought it completely unacceptable that the townsfolk would be telling complete strangers he liked fishing.

"When we stopped by the Rusty Wrench an hour or so ago," Square Jaw continued, "the owner said Avis was not scheduled to work today and he hadn't spoken to him since last Friday afternoon." The scene on the TV changed from Avis's driveway to the parking lot in front of the Rusty Wrench where Rick Allen, the garage owner, stood in a grease-covered T-shirt and baggy blue jeans. He was leaning up against a small sign painted on the front door that said, *Rusty Wrench Garage*. There was virtually no opportunity for free publicity in Watermill; Rick wasn't going to miss it while it was available.

"The fact he gave the ticket away is probably less surprising than that he actually bought a ticket at all. I ain't ever seen him buy anything other than his six-pack of Pabst Blue Ribbon, cigarettes, and fishing stuff. I guess you just never know." He trailed off and looked at the sign on the door, as if to say, *Come on down to the Rusty Wrench*.

The TV switched back to Square Jaw in the driveway, who repeated almost word for word what Rick had just said. "So, as you heard Mr. Allen say, he is more surprised Avis bought the ticket than that he gave it away." Avis felt another tinge of irritation and wondered how he and this guy who was making himself at home on his front lawn, suddenly got on a first name basis. Then the unthinkable happened. Square Jaw glanced over his shoulder and said to the camera, "It looks like someone is home. I'm going to go up and knock on the front door and see if we can get a comment from Avis."

The fifty-foot path from Avis's driveway to his front door had been crushed rock a half-decade ago. Since then it had become a muddy path sporadically filled with crushed stones. Square Jaw was trying to confidently walk toward the front door without stepping into the patches of two-inch-deep mud along the path. He nonchalantly kicked mud off his shoes as he stepped onto the two wooden steps that led up to the trailer. He knocked three times and called out, "Mr. Humphrey? Avis? This is Rex Tindal with WELX News. I was wondering if we could talk for a few minutes." He smiled back at the camera and waited a few seconds and then knocked again.

Avis sat and stared blankly at the TV and watched the guy knocking on his door five seconds after he heard the real-time version of the knocking. Just about the time he knocked on TV the first time, he knocked again in real time and called out to him again.

"Holy shit," Avis mumbled again. Rex stood on the front steps and turned around and looked into the camera.

"It appears Mr. Humphrey, Avis," he inserted as if they were old buddies, "is not ready to come out yet, but we'll keep you posted in the studio if we can get a word with him." Then the camera cut away to the news anchor who said, "Sounds like quite a story brewing up there in Watermill," and then she moved on to the next story. Avis hoped they moved onto the next story and didn't come back to his story, but he knew better. He reached down and picked up the TV control and switched stations just in time to see an attractive brunette, in a tight blue blazer and a blouse unbuttoned enough to show just a bit too much cleavage, sitting behind a Manchester news anchor set. "The big news in Watermill is the mystery of who won the Powerball last week. Rumor has it, a local man named Avis Humphrey won the nine hundred sixty-seven million-dollar Powerball and then, get ready for this, he gave the ticket away to his lifelong friend and teacher, Mrs. Alice Chen. The details are sketchy at the moment, but our own Rob Rogers is in Watermill right now talking with one of the locals."

"Holy fucking shit!" Avis yelled and threw himself back against the couch cushion and wrapped his hands around his head.

The TV instantly left the studio and landed inside Ernie's coffee shop where a short, round, nearly bald gentleman was sitting on a stool with a cameraman pointing his camera at him and Ernie. "We're here with Ernie Stump, owner of Ernie's Coffee & Stuff, to see what we can find out about this young man, Avis Humphrey, and what would make him give away over nine hundred million dollars." The camera zoomed in on Ernie, who smiled a halfhearted smile as he wiped the counter with a damp rag. "Mr. Stump, what can you tell us about Mr. Avis Humphrey?"

Ernie stopped wiping the counter and looked up at the man with a polite smile. "Oh, I don't know. He seems like a pretty regular guy here in Watermill. Good mechanic. Likes fishing." He stopped talking and hesitated before making his next move. He glanced over to a man sitting in the corner while Rob Rogers began asking another question.

"But why do you think he would give away so much money? And does it surprise you that he gave it away?"

Ernie nodded to the corner and said, "If you really want to get to know Avis, you probably ought to talk to that guy sitting over there." It was a win-win for Ernie. He was polite and fed the reporter what he wanted to hear; at the same time, he got the camera pointing at someone else, which is what he really wanted in the first place.

The camera panned to the right and quickly focused in on a guy with a long ponytail and an eye patch sitting at a table sipping coffee and nibbling on a biscuit.

"Who the hell is that?" Avis mumbled as Rob Rogers quickly got up from the stool and moved to the table and sat down in the empty chair next to the guy wearing the eye patch.

"Hi. Rob Rogers, Lakes Region News 28," he smoothly said as he slid into the seat next to the stranger and then looked back at the camera. A couple of generic questions later, Tom the eye-patch guy said, "Yeah. Avis and I go way back. Known him since we were kids."

"Who the hell is this guy?" Avis mumbled again as he switched stations. His mouth dropped open and he immediately regretted pushing the channel button. He sat in stunned silence as a tall blonde in a tight-fitting, low-cut dress stood next to Merle Humphrey. Avis had missed the beginning of the interview, but apparently Merle was either implying or outright claiming to be Avis Humphrey's father for the first time in over two decades. That was enough to make Avis hit the power button and watch the screen go blank. For the next fifteen minutes, he sat and stared at the turned-off TV and listened to three more people knock on the front door of his rundown trailer and introduce themselves through the thin metal door. It surprised Avis that the news had gotten out so quickly, but now that it was out there, it didn't surprise him how popular he was becoming. A wave of nausea hit him as he came to grips with the realization his popularity would only grow with each passing hour.

CHAPTER SEVEN

It was a discussion they had had a dozen times or more over the past few years. At least half of the exchanges had turned into a lot of name-calling shouting matches that nearly ended in bloodshed. The first battle stopped just short of blows when Denny was a sophomore in high school. He dropped the bomb on his parents that he intended to become a journalism major when he went off to Stanford. His sister and two brothers had all been accounting or business majors and had already established themselves as world-class players in their father's business empire. Seven years later, a week after graduation, Denny and his father were having one last battle in their ongoing war.

"For Christ's sake, Denny. Your grandfather worked seventy hours a week for forty years of his life and went from being a poor Irish immigrant to an American business owner. He was the American Dream come true. He was proud of what he accomplished and what he did for our family."

Denny had heard the legend of the Wilson family's migration to America a few hundred times, even before the battle over his career choice. His grandfather had left home by himself and finagled his way onto an ocean-freighter crew at fourteen years old where he worked harder than most of the grown men, riff-raff for the most part, who worked alongside him. Three years later he landed in New York where he once again outworked, outmaneuvered and outthought anyone and everyone who was in his way. From there, it took another five years of sleepless nights, back-breaking labor, fist fights and more than one near death experience, before he landed in Santa Cruz, California. The legend was inspiring and patriotic and likely exaggerated. It was a story Denny planned on one day putting into a book. But for now, it was just noise, designed to wear him down and force him to cave into his father's wishes and walk in his father's shoes.

"I'm not knocking Grandpa or anyone else, Dad." By *anyone else,* he of course meant his father. "It's just not for me. It's not the path I'm supposed to follow." In Denny's mind, *his path* was pre-ordained by a higher calling. Whether it was from God or the Associated Press, Denny did not know. All he knew for certain was he had a calling and he intended on answering it. There had never been a time when he hadn't wanted to be a journalist. He saw himself as a sort of guardian angel whose task was to make sure, the masses were being fed the truth. He hadn't yet fully grasped that in the news world, truth was a term relative to what people who owned the press thought—and it was typically slanted pieces of information.

"Not the path you're supposed to follow?" his father sniped back, half as a question and half in condemnation. "What the hell is that supposed to mean?" It wasn't a question he wanted an answer for, and Denny wasn't going to have the opportunity to even try to give one. "I took over the family company when I was only twenty-six years old and built it into a multi-million-dollar empire." This was another story from the Wilson family saga that didn't need retelling. "Do you know the kind of good we do for the community, for charities, and for our family? I didn't throw it all away because I wanted to run off and join the circus." There was nothing new in the dialogue. Both sides had laid all their arguments out for the entire family to hear, throughout high school and during Denny's four years at Stanford. In keeping with the family tradition of never giving in when the going gets tough mentality, neither of them budged an inch from the first fight until the last.

"I'm going to be a journalist, not a circus clown, Dad."

"Apparently you don't watch the news much anymore. Journalism is dead. It's all propaganda now. They're all clowns, or at the very least, puppets. Is that what you want to do with your life, Denny? You want to be a pitchman for somebody else's agenda? That's what you think God put you on this Earth to do? You think he put you here to be someone else's mouthpiece?"

The first four or five times James Wilson threw these over-the-top arguments at his son, Denny bit. The conversations quickly turned into heated battles that eventually became the family war. But over the years Denny had learned to maneuver his way through the minefields, and now he didn't take the bait. He listened and waited and still hoped, against the odds, that he would get his father's support.

"Dad, I graduated last week. We've got to stop this. I'm not following in your footsteps. It's not my path," he said for at least the hundredth time. Denny sat in the overstuffed chair in front of his father's desk and tried one more time to get his blessing. Despite their fights and differences, family meant the world to both men. This wasn't a revolt against his family or a condemnation of the family business. Denny was being sincere when he said business and accounting weren't his path to follow. He wanted to be a journalist.

And his father, despite what he appeared to be on the surface, was more supportive than Denny knew. He had already decided this fight would be their last. Either he would convince his son or not. But either way, he would support him, just as he had supported all of his other children. He reclined back in his chair and looked up as if there might be one more valid argument that could somehow sway his son to see his way of thinking, written on the ceiling. There was not.

"So, you're really going to do this?" his father asked as if he needed to hear it affirmed. It was the first time he had ever broached accepting Denny's wish to not join the family business and become a reporter.

"You don't really have to ask that, do you? I mean seven years of fighting kind of speaks for itself. Doesn't it, Dad?"

"Damn. You're one stubborn young man," he said as he looked down at the paper sitting on the desk in front of him. "You must get it from your mother's side." He handed the paper to Denny as he stood up and walked around the desk. "You'll want to call this woman," he said, referring to the name and number on the paper. "She's expecting you."

Denny took the paper and looked at the name and number written, along with the name of the online magazine the woman ran.

"Make me proud, son. Your mother and I raised our children to be good people and to give back to the family and community. Don't forget where you came from." Then he patted him on the shoulder and walked out of the office.

* * *

Reporters from New England and beyond were roaming around Watermill like lost dogs famished and sniffing hard for a bite to eat. So far, all they had found were scraps, but they kept sniffing. It wasn't every day some individual from a small New Hampshire town won a Powerball jackpot, and it was unheard of that anyone would give the whole damn thing away. So once the rumor leaked out, journalists from Boston to Burlington flocked in. They came from Portland, Maine and Hartford, Connecticut and Manchester, New Hampshire. They came from small-town papers in Belfast, Maine and an artsy publication from Providence, Rhode Island. A gray-haired woman even drove her Subaru in from Highgate, Vermont so she could get the big scoop to put in her neighborhood paper. It was delivered to eighty-seven homes each week, although it was not confirmed how many actually read it. A couple of ambitious reporters drove in from upstate New York. And last but not least, one, and only one, flew in from Miami, Florida.

Denny Wilson wasn't from small-town New England or small-town Florida or small-town any other state. A year ago, Theresa Babcock was sitting behind her less-than-flattering Chief Editor's desk at an underfunded online newspaper, called The Brickhouse Online, when she received a call from the owner of the company. He announced less than diplomatically that a kid from Los Angeles was arriving in a week and she was to give him a job. He said the recent Stanford grad was the son of an old college frat brother and if he were anything like his father, the Brickhouse would do well by having him on board. She briefly protested. The owner ignored her. The conversation was over. Denny arrived a few days later. Theresa gave him a small desk in the smallest cubicle in the office with no view, no perks, and even less guidance to go with it. For the first week, he sat in his cubicle and surfed the net, occasionally popping his head up like a prairie dog looking for something to eat, or perhaps to see if something was going to eat him.

It was debatable at first, whether or not Denny was an entitled silver-spoon kid who didn't know what it was like to go without things not earned. The truth was, at least in Theresa's mind, it didn't matter. She was forced to give him a job, but she had no intention of making him feel welcome or polishing his spoon, if in fact there was a spoon to be polished. According to what she had found out about the Wilson family online, he came from serious California money. That's all she needed to know. If there was a Pulitzer Prize in his future, there was no chance it would be won while he was working for her.

She ignored him most of the time, but it was a small office and it didn't take long for her to hear about all the things Denny had done in his short life and all the places he had been to. He rambled on to the other half-dozen reporters about various vacations in Aspen, as if everyone took vacations to Aspen. In the world he came from, everyone did. And he reminisced about sailing the Pacific on his family's 54-foot Beneteau, as if everybody sailed the Pacific over extended Christmas breaks. He asked coworkers if they had ever been to the South of France as if he were asking if they had gone to the beach over the weekend. Sometimes the other reporters sat in their seats and absorbed his stories with sincere interest. Sometimes they listened with a tinge of jealousy that this kid had done more in his life than most of them would ever do. And every once in a while, they got a little sick of hearing about his charmed life. He was the only rich kid at The Brickhouse Online. Theresa was sick of his stories before she had even heard the first one. The truth was that once upon a time, she had been married to a guy like Denny. So, Denny was screwed at the Brickhouse Online before he had even arrived.

During one of the lighter and less boastful office chat sessions, Denny had two reporters laughing to the point of tears as he mistakenly described in detail, right down to the grey skies, endless mud and black flies, the worst vacation he had ever taken one cold rainy July week at a friend's camp on Lake Winnipesauke in New Hampshire. Theresa had unsuccessfully tried to tune out the conversation, but from the moment she became aware of his loathing for New England, she was on a quest.

When word filtered through the Internet about a guy in New Hampshire who had won the Powerball, Theresa sat behind her desk and smiled. She pulled out a map to see where Watermill was located and felt a surge of satisfaction when she saw that Watermill was near Watermill and almost nothing else. From what she could find on Google, the town didn't have a mill and didn't have all that much water, other than a couple of small ponds and a few streams. There were no mountains in Watermill, no real nightlife—or much of a day life for that matter. From what Theresa could find, there was nothing to do other than slosh around in the mud beneath grey New Hampshire skies and swat at black flies and interview some local yokel who won the lottery. The icing on the cake came when she checked the Watermill weather forecast: cold and rainy for the next ten days.

"Denny, come here for a minute," she called from behind her desk.

He closed his laptop, stood and stretched as if he had been slaving on a story for hours. He hadn't been. Theresa rarely gave him stories worth covering. He covered a dog show last week because she heard him mention once he didn't like dogs. She gave the boat show coverage to Ann, the woman in the cubical next to Denny. Theresa had him cover town meetings, but only if they were meetings where little or nothing was expected to be going on. Scandals, major accidents, or tragedy stories all went to anyone else's desk other than Denny's. He may not have earned his job, but he was going to earn his stripes if he hoped to make any headway under Theresa's regime. Of course, if he hoped to make any headway, it was misplaced hope.

"Take a seat," she said without looking up at him. "I've got good news for you. You've been bugging me for a decent assignment, so here's your chance."

"Great," he said without enthusiasm. She had said the same thing when she sent him to the dog show. She had said the same thing when she sent him to cover a local selectman's campaign of a candidate who was expected to get less than five percent of the vote. He actually got one percent. Nobody knew who he was, and nobody cared who he was. His political past was non-existent, and his public future was non-existent. It wasn't likely that even a Pulitzer Prize-winning writer could have come up with an interesting storyline about the man. Denny was assigned to his campaign full time for nine weeks. He was the only reporter in the candidate's one-man press corps. Toward the end, even the candidate felt sorry for Denny.

"You're going to get to travel this time. Out of Miami," she added. Denny noticed the corner of her mouth turning up just a smidge on the left side of her face. It was her tell. As soon as he saw it, he knew she was shoveling more shit his way. Outwardly he showed no emotion, but inwardly he cringed. He wanted to call it quits and head back to Los Angeles, but despite what Theresa thought, he had burdens of his own to carry. She was correct, he lived a silver-spoon life, but it came with a price. His father had called in a favor to give his son what he wanted, but he wasn't happy about it. If Denny quit now, if he snubbed the favor his father had called in, there would be hell to pay. For the moment, all he owed his father was to do a good job and be grateful to his friend who gave him the job. Unless of course, he quit his reporting gig. Then he would owe an explanation, an apology, and a career to his father. Giving up was not a trait tolerated in the Wilson family. James Wilson had opposed his son's choice for years, but if Denny threw in the towel because Theresa was a bitch, a whole new issue would be on the table. The first disappointment of not joining the family business would pale in comparison to the shame of a Wilson man being run off by a woman in Miami. His grandfather would roll over in his grave and his father would make sure Denny was aware of it.

"You're going to Watermill, New Hampshire, Denny," Theresa said, finally looking up at him.

"Great," he said without hesitation. "What's going on up there?"

"Some guy, Avis something or other, won the Powerball and there's supposed to be a great human-interest story tied to the whole affair."

"What might that be?" Denny asked, still trying to pretend he cared. He didn't.

"That's what you're going to find out." Teresa said as she slid a boarding pass she had just printed across her desk. "You leave this afternoon. You should be up and back within a week. Just keep me posted every day and let me know how it's going." She could hardly wait to see his reports. She wondered if he would get creative and write something imaginative and positive. Or would he bitch and whine?

She didn't really care all that much. She was going to enjoy it either way.

He sat and stared at the ticket and ran the scenario through his head about how much shit his father would give him and how bad it really would be working for the family business.

"I'll shoot you emails," he said as he stood up and smiled at her. He knew the game they were playing, and he was more or less confident he could win. Not as confident as he had been a few weeks back, but still confident.

"Take your raincoat. Weather report says it's cold and rainy," she added as he neared the door.

He waved acknowledgment over his shoulder as he walked away. This time Theresa could see him cringe, even from the back. And he could feel her smug smile, without even looking back at her.

* * *

The Watermill Inn was full of reporters who had already beaten him to town and had taken the few rooms available. Denny parked his sub-compact rental in the dirt driveway and checked into a local B&B on the edge of town. It was more like some old widowed aunt's spare bedroom, with a kitchen where she served coffee and a Danish in the morning, than an actual B&B. And the Danish was the $2.79 package kind bought at the Shop & Save, not the French style pastries from a bakery Denny usually enjoyed. He arrived in town late and it was after seven p.m. when he finally found a place to stay. Ruth, the old woman who ran the B&B, didn't have Internet, and the cell phone reception was sketchy at best. There was no daily update sent to Theresa on the first day other than a text from his phone saying, "Made it here. No internet in my room. I'll update you tomorrow."

"Enjoy New England," is all she texted back as she sat at a sidewalk café in Miami sipping on her glass of sparkling wine.

On the first full day, Denny found himself with a dozen reporters camped out in front of Avis's trailer. The reporters more or less filled him in on the big-picture stuff. Of course, they were all there for the little-picture stuff. Someone had hung a wooden sign on the door that said, "Gone fishin,'" but it looked so rustic the reporters didn't know if it was part of the décor, or had Avis actually hung up a sign and gone fishing. It was almost ten p.m. when Denny finally gave up for the day. Earlier he had thought that maybe, just maybe, he could corner this Avis character and get a story out of him and hightail it back to Manchester to catch a flight all in one day. But as he pulled out of the muddy driveway, long after even the black flies had gone to bed, he began to think that this Avis guy had really gone fishing. Then it sank in that he wouldn't be driving to the airport or catching any flight anywhere for a day or two, or maybe more.

He stopped by the bar at the Watermill Inn on the way back to his room and sent an email. "No sign of Humphrey. Seems to be hiding out somewhere. Weather's great. Place is beautiful. Staying at a quaint B&B. Will update more tomorrow." Thirty seconds after hitting send he received a response. "Of course he's in hiding. You're there to find him. Good luck. Glad you're enjoying yourself." Denny read the response and mumbled, "Bitch." Trudy the bartender looked up at him. "Not you," Denny explained by waving the phone, and then returned to drinking his beer.

On day two, Denny was committed to getting his story. Perhaps not *the* story, but one way or another he was leaving Watermill sooner than later. It was drizzling off and on and he wondered if it rained perpetually in New Hampshire. It had rained the entire week he had come on vacation a few years back, and it appeared it was going to rain his entire stay again this time. Then he wondered if it had ever stopped raining since his first visit, or if any of the locals even noticed the rain.

Ernie, the guy behind the counter at the breakfast place, seemed bright and chipper. The grey dreariness didn't seem to have much effect on him or the local customers dressed in flannel shirts and smiles in July. The other reporters, almost all of them from New England, acted as if not seeing the sun for months was just another normal decade of life in this neck of the woods. But Denny was from California. He was from Los Angeles. When he left there, he moved to the Sunshine State, and that wasn't by accident. He liked sun, warmth, and blue water. It was one thing to give it up to ski in the Alps or climb a mountain, but this was unbearable. The hours passed like days and the days like weeks. In Denny's mind, or at least in his psyche, he had already been here far too long. *Get the story and get out of here. Today!* That's what he told himself as he sat at the counter sipping his coffee and eating a bagel fresh from the freezer and toaster. No Cuban coffee or fresh pastries here.

He looked around the nearly full diner for someone who might be able to help him on his quest. Half the customers were reporters and the other half appeared to be locals. The advantage most of the reporters had over him was they could relate to these small-town New England folks. Denny had nothing in common with them, but he presumed his advantage was that, as far as he was aware, nobody else in the diner was here from LA or Florida. He hoped that when he let people know how far he had traveled for the story, they would take an interest or have pity and be motivated to talk to him.

"Some weather you're having here," he said to the heavyset gentlemen behind the counter. Ernie, who had been behind the counter nearly every day since the diner opened twenty-two years ago, knew when a customer was trying to start a conversation. He presumed this kid was a reporter.

"Where you from?"

"Miami."

"Whoa! Miami's a long way from here. Must feel like winter to you."

"Nah," Denny said, shaking his head back and forth. "Miami doesn't get this cold. Not even in the winter."

"Well… welcome to summer in Watermill. You're here looking for Avis, I presume?"

"Yes sir. Any chance you could help me find him?"

"Hey, Betty. This guy here is all the way from Miami and looking for Avis."

"Miami! Holy crap. That's a long way from here," she said, as if she were Ernie's echo chamber.

A half-dozen customers looked up and over at Denny. With the exception of Betty and Ernie and a guy sitting at a table in the corner, none of them seemed to appreciate his presence or to be all that impressed about where he was from. Most of them were looking for the same story he was looking for, or they were friends of Avis. As far as they were concerned, if Avis didn't want to talk to reporters then the conversation should be closed. As far as the reporters were concerned, Denny was just one more guy competing for the same story they were searching for—and he wasn't even one of them. He wasn't a small-town New England guy who had covered all the same old lobster fests, clam festivals, county fairs, and high school football games that most of them had covered for years. He was a shiny kid who zipped in from Miami to grab their big scoop and then head back to the beach.

"So. What do you say? Is there anyone in town that might be able to help me? I'm under the gun to get a story into my boss," he said as he leaned halfway across the counter, as if looking for Avis were some sort of big secret.

Ernie looked around and acted as if he had a secret of his own to share, but only with Denny. He handed a plate of eggs to a guy at the end of the counter and then wiped his hands off with a dishtowel before leaning his elbows on the bar in front of Denny. "You see that guy sitting in the corner?"

"The guy with the eye patch?"

"Yeah. The guy with the eye patch. He's probably someone you might want to talk to. He'll help you with your Avis story."

"Who is he?"

"Just go talk to him."

CHAPTER EIGHT

Merle Humphrey was one of those people who always made sure there was a shred of truth in everything he said. It was his built-in conscience cleaner. In Merle's mind, he was an honest man. That was his mindset in life in general, and it was certainly his mindset while sitting in his living room sipping coffee with the reporter from the Manchester Chronicle.

"So, I'm a little confused, Mr. Humphrey," the reporter said as she sat across from Merle with her pen and pad ready. "Of course, my knowledge of your family is only what I've heard from rumors around town. I mean, I'm not from here so that's all I really have to go on for now."

Merle shook his head back and forth as if he were speechless that such shameful allegations had been made about him, even though she hadn't yet made any such allegations. He had asked, 'for family privacy reasons,' that the interview not be recorded. By family privacy, he was referring to not being able to be sued later down the road and losing any of his 'private' money for telling stories that likely rated quite low on the truth scale.

"I heard years back," she continued, "When you found out that Avis was not your son, you disowned him. Now you're reversing that position? How would you respond to those who say you're just doing this for the money?"

Merle forced a smile. It was the same forced smile he always had on his face. It was the smile of a politician or a grifter, or in this case, a used-car salesman, who would one-hundred-percent say any partial truth to close a deal. Wanting to adequately respond to her question, Merle began with his best closing-the-deal smile. "Well, Ms. Thompson, you know how small towns can be. A lot of stories can be spun out of one story. My ex-wife and I don't like sharing our… oh, dirty laundry, I suppose you'd call it, for lack of anything better. In a place like Watermill, folks will fill in the blanks if you don't fill them in for them. We didn't feel the need to let everyone in on our family business." When he stopped talking his teeth immediately flashed his used-car-salesman smile once again as he waited for the next question.

"Well, given the situation. Given Avis's newfound fame and fortune, you can understand how people would love to have some of those blanks filled in by a reliable source, such as yourself. Especially since, according to some folks around town, the timing of your relationship change with Avis makes you seem somewhat opportunistic." She stopped talking without posing an actual question and waited to see where he would go with it.

Merle took a deep breath and rolled his eyes, as if he didn't want to share any of the information that was hanging on the tip of his tongue.

"Ohhh... I suppose I can understand that people would like to know more about Avis... and our family." He stopped talking and shook his head back and forth as if the conversation was too difficult to continue with, and he was beside himself that friends and neighbors would want to pry into his personal life. Of course, they were Avis's friends and neighbors, too. And Avis was likeable.

"So, how do you respond to those who say you disowned Avis when he was a small boy, or more importantly, when he was poor?" Now it was her turn to paste a forced smile on her face—and pretend her questions were not offensive.

"It wasn't really like that," Merle began as the smile dropped off his face and his eyes welled up. He seemed appalled that his dearest friends were saying such unpleasant comments about him. "The truth is Lindsey and I were very, very young and things just didn't work out for us. Not hardly unusual in today's world. And neither of us handled our divorce with much decency. Young and dumb and all that nonsense." His smile popped back onto his face as naturally as breathing in and out.

"So, you didn't abandon Avis?" she asked with one raised eyebrow.

"Nah," he said and waved his hand at her as if her question was the silliest thing he'd ever heard. "It wasn't anything like that. The truth is when we split, Avis lived with his mother and we, Lindsey and I, weren't speaking." That part, of course, was the truth and there was always a thread of truth in everything he said. "After we split, Avis and I saw less and less of each other." Again, he was sort of speaking the truth. In fact, they didn't see each other, period for Avis's entire childhood, which was a near impossibility in Watermill, New Hampshire. "It wasn't like I announced he wasn't mine or anything like that. We didn't have much of a bond when he lived with me, being I worked so much back in those days. After a while we just didn't have any bond at all." That part was a lie. The last words he yelled at Lindsey before storming off was, "I'll be damned if I'm spending my time and money raising some other son of a bitch's kid." Then he stormed out the door, jumped into his car, and tore down the road, leaving behind a young mother who screwed a lot of guys, and a young boy who hadn't done anything to anyone and couldn't possibly understand what was happening as he watched the dust swirl up in the air and then die back down to the ground with the words, "some other son of a bitch's kid" ringing in his head.

"So, Avis is your son then?"

"Absolutely. No doubt about it."

"Well. Forgive me for being forward and I suppose perhaps a little rude, but don't you think it may appear to be... a little self-serving to reach out to Avis now, after all these years?"

"Ms. Thompson, it's all right for you to come right out and ask. You want to know if I'm after the money?" He was prepared for the question like a politician addressing an extramarital affair the whole world already knew to be real.

"I suppose that is what I'm asking then."

"Look. I've done pretty well in Watermill. Businesswise I mean. You know I own six local businesses, and if there's one thing I don't need, it's more money." Again, a shred of truth. What he didn't say is that although he didn't need it, he damned sure would love to get his hands on some of it. There were only two things in the world that Merle Humphrey truly loved. Merle loved Merle, and Merle loved money.

"Then what's your motivation in reaching out now?"

The forced, fake smile stayed glued to his face as he preached his sincere concern for his long-disavowed son. "Like I said, I'm a businessman. Avis is a mechanic. I hear he's a pretty good one at that, but there's a big difference between knowing what to do with a sputtering engine and what to do with over nine hundred million dollars. I know how the vultures flock in when news of money breaks. I've dealt with my share of wheelers and dealers over the years and I'm just concerned for my son's well-being." He took another sip of coffee and waited patiently for the next question.

"There's a rumor around town that at least four local men are taking paternity tests in hopes of matching up with Avis's DNA, not that I've heard he's willing to participate. Do you have any plans to take a paternity test?"

With the smoothness of the used-car dealer that he was, Merle answered with complete confidence, like he was telling her the first owner of the vehicle was an old Christian lady who only drove the car to church on Sundays. "Oh, I don't think there's going to be any need of that. I mean, Avis was born almost exactly nine months after our wedding night." By almost nine months he meant eight months and two weeks. "I think that speaks for itself," he added.

"So, you would not be willing to take a paternity test?"

"Now I didn't say that either. I suppose if it came down to it, you know, just to calm people's suspicions, I'd do what needed to be done." This was a no-brainer. The worst thing that could happen is a test would be negative and he would act like a wounded and outraged father, again, and then continue on with his life as it was before the Powerball drawing. Although, there might be some sort of lawsuit for personal damages. A reasonable person would never be able to see how Avis could be responsible, but Merle knew how the game was played. You only sue people who can pay up, then hope for a settlement. But that would only be if the test turned up a negative match. Against all odds, he knew there was an outside chance he actually was Avis's dad. In the unlikely event the test showed he was the father, he would still act wounded and outraged that Lindsey had told him all those years ago he was not the boy's father. Either way, he had already saved all the expenses of raising a son and anything he made off the Powerball thing would be pure profit. "Pure profit" sounded like sacred words to Merle Humphrey.

CHAPTER NINE

Savannah sat on the trunk of her old green and rusted-out Corolla and swatted black flies in vain. Her willpower held her in check for several seconds at a time as she passively ignored them, until she could no longer take the irritating little bastards buzzing and biting at her from every direction. Then her hands frantically flailed around as if she were sporadically losing her sanity or having some sort of weird hand dysfunction. Blood seeped from bites behind her right ear, the back of her neck, and the top of her head. Her current dilemma paled by comparison with the debate the cat witnessed her having with herself two mornings ago, but everything is relative. She swung wildly again at the flies and screamed out in frustration. It helped for about five seconds and then the little bastards returned, undeterred and still hungry. Just as she presumed things couldn't get any worse, a single drop of rain landed on her cheek.

Steam rose from beneath the car's raised hood for almost thirty minutes as she flailed and screamed and not so patiently waited for someone to drive by and help her. At least that's what she hoped for, as opposed to someone lugging her off into the woods in the middle of the no-man's land where she currently sat. When the car first broke down she was worried about the wrong type of character coming along. It hadn't dawned on her that it was entirely possible that no type of character would be coming along any time soon. This was Watermill and no traffic was just as likely as a little traffic. The only impossibility was a lot of traffic and no black flies.

Avis and Leo chugged down the road toward where she was parked. They stopped and pulled over in front of the broken-down Corolla. Both doors creaked loudly as they opened them up and got out. Two years ago, and almost daily since, Avis had made a mental note to fix the doors, but they creaked louder today than they had back then. Savannah sat ready to hop off the trunk and greet whomever came along to save her… until she saw them.

She had thought it possible the black flies would pick her to the bone before she was found. As she looked toward the two men, she thought the bugs might have been the better way to go. The twenty-something-looking year-old guys dressed in faded, worn-out T-shirts and even more faded and dirty jeans, old work boots, and wrinkled baseball caps strolled over and stuck their heads under the hood of her car. Leo's hair was almost shoulder length. It had been neatly styled the last time he had gotten it cut three years ago. Avis's was only slightly shorter and a lot curlier and it was sticking out from under a Boston Red Sox cap. The two looked like a New England version of frontier outlaws from the Alaskan outback—or perhaps New Hampshire's version of the cast from *Deliverance.*

"Better be careful or Deputy Souder might come along and give you a parking ticket," Leo said with a big grin on his face as he poked his head up and out from underneath the hood. Savannah feigned a smile and tossed her cigarette on the ground as she slid off the trunk.

"And littering," Avis added as he eyed the cigarette and her car. It wasn't clear which litter he was referring to.

"If you won't tell I won't," she answered. Their appearance didn't seem quite as bad as she approached them. Hair seemed to be recently washed. She could smell aftershave, too much aftershave, on Leo. Both looked to have a mouthful of teeth with no black or half-rotted teeth in the front. And other than their strong New England accents, that
sounded normal to Savannah, they both seemed like regular local guys.

"Car broke down?" Leo asked with his head back down under the hood.

Savannah didn't respond, but gave Avis a puzzled look, not sure if she was supposed to actually answer his question or not. Avis smiled at how familiar Leo's questions were to him and how everyone else was regularly caught off guard.

"Yeah, Leo. Her car is broke down."

"What's wrong with it?" he asked, again without looking up.

She again looked at Avis, who answered for her. "I think she's hoping we might be able to tell her what's wrong with it, Leo."

"Ohhh. That makes sense, I guess. It looks like the radiator hose is broke. That's probably the problem."

"It started steaming and then just died and I pulled off and parked here. Possibly illegally parked. Before I littered. Anyway, I was hoping you could give me a ride to town, so I could find someone to come out and fix it."

"Well, you've got a bucket full of problems today, lady." Avis grimaced and looked back at his truck as he tried to figure out how he was going to break the bad news and slip away. "First, other than your car being broke down, I'm not heading into town. I'm heading out of town, as you can see by the direction my truck is pointing. We're going fishing. Second, I'm the mechanic the guy from the garage would send out, but I'm not there, so you see... taking you to town to get the mechanic just won't work."

"Is there any chance you could take me in, so I could at least get a hotel room until you get back from fishing and fix my car?"

"Ooooh. It's still just not your day," Leo chirped in with a wide grin. "Hotels are all booked up. Everyone is here to do his story." He gestured toward Avis.

"You're Avis Humphrey?" Savannah asked. She stepped forward with her hand extended as if she were certain he would want to shake it.

Avis glared at Leo without saying a word. Leo made a silly face and acknowledged he probably should have held onto that information and then stuck his head back down and under the hood as if there were something else to find besides the leaking radiator hose. Her hand was left hanging in the air without being taken ahold of or shaken.

"And who are you?" Avis asked, already knowing her answer. He was undecided how to deal with Savannah. As far as he knew, she was the only twenty-some-year-old, attractive woman who had shown up to get the Avis story. On the other hand, his life had kind of gone to shit over the past week or so due to the hordes of strangers who showed up to write about The Life and Times of Avis Humphrey. He presumed they were all going to be disappointed when they got to the final version of his story. Either way, there was a reason he'd stocked up and was headed out of town to go fishing.

"I'm Savannah. Savannah Gardener," she said, sticking her hand out once again as if she had suddenly become a power broker within the news world. He liked her better when she was a discouraged, black-fly-ravaged, attractive woman sitting on the trunk of her broken-down car looking as if she didn't trust the two knuckleheads pulling up in their beat up old red pickup-truck.

"Hey," Avis mumbled and gave a halfhearted wave and left her hand once again hanging in midair. He felt his jaw clench and he unintentionally stepped backwards. It had been a rough week. He knew there would be publicity, but he wasn't prepared for everything that had come. The story had gone "viral," as they say, and it seemed the entire Northeastern journalistic world thought there was a story to be had. He didn't agree. Perhaps more importantly, he didn't want to *be* the story.

Savannah dropped her hand and reached into her front pocket and pulled out her cigarettes and held them out to Avis. It was so cliché that he laughed and waved her off. "No, I don't smoke, but thanks." It was a lie, but he didn't feel compelled to be honest with her. "By the way, I think I saw that move in an old movie. You know, offering a cigarette to buddy up. Bit obvious."

"I was just being polite, but..." Her words trailed off as she momentarily reconsidered her suicide plan. "So, you're not leaving me out here, are you? I mean, is there someone you could call and have them come pick me up?"

"Damn. Not your luck again," he mumbled and shook his head back and forth.

"You won't even call someone for me?" she snapped.

"Well... I don't do the iPhone thing and even if I did, the only person I could call is Leo. He's under your hood right at this moment and his phone battery is dead about ninety percent of the time. I think he just carries it around because everyone else has one."

She looked past Avis, down the road to the corner about a quarter-mile back and hoped another car would come around the bend. No car came as they stood in silence while she smoked.

"So, you're just leaving me here or what?" Savannah snapped.

"You know, most women get to know me a bit before they decide to get all snippy."

Leo leaned against the front of the car and watched as if he had a front row seat to a boxing match. He sort of did.

Savannah took a deep sigh and closed her eyes and pulled herself together. "Look, I'm really sorry. I've been on a bit of a downhill slide lately." She didn't know why she was explaining herself and was quite certain there was no reason for a redneck fisherman to care. But the words just kept pouring out. "Coming here to do this story was supposed to be a turning point, you know? I was supposed to be picking myself up and getting back in the game and all that crap." It had been so long since she had talked to anyone new, anyone who wasn't someone from her past who had grandiose expectations of her and even more grandiose disappointment over what she had become. "Then the car broke down and the black flies from hell and now, now I can't even get a ride to town. Not that there's any rooms to be had in town, according to the two of you." Leo smiled with pride that he had been the one to break the hotel news. "So, with all that said, any suggestions?"

"Man. Do all reporters share that much information with people they're supposed to be interviewing? Because it was really more than I needed to know." Savannah shrugged. Avis stood in front of her, not knowing if he should give her a hug and tell her it's going to be all right or get back into his truck and leave her standing on the side of the road without saying another word to her. Leo just watched with anticipation of who would say what next.

"So?" is all Savannah said; she continued to look at Avis.

"Lady, I just want to go fishing. So, unless you want to go fishing, I got nothing."

There should have been an awkward silence. There should have been that moment when Savannah pondered what to do and then resigned herself to walking to town, even though she had no idea how far away the town was. There should have been the moment when Avis and Leo walked back to their truck and drove away, leaving Savannah standing beside her car while Leo grinned and waved.

But at that moment when Avis blurted out, "So unless you want to go fishing, I got nothing."

Savannah didn't hesitate and said, "Okay," and opened the door to her car and reached inside for her purse.

"Okay, what?" Avis asked. His forehead scrunched, and his head tilted, and he clearly didn't have any idea of what was happening.

"I'll go fishing."

"You didn't see that one coming, did you?" Leo said with another grin.

"Aw, lady. You don't look like the fishing type. Let's just slow things down a bit."

"You don't know what type I am, but I assure you, I'm not the 'sleeping in my broke-down car on the side of what will eventually be a dark country road' type of woman. Besides. I've been fishing before. My father took me fishing a bunch of times when I was a kid." It was a lie. She had never been fishing in her whole life, but her options were limited, and she was climbing into a truck with Avis Humphrey.

"Well then. It sounds like we're going fishing," Leo said. He had already made his way back to the truck. The door squawked open like a dying rooster. He stepped back and motioned for Savannah to climb in and then he slid in beside her. The door squawked again as he closed it and she and Leo sat in the truck and waited for Avis to climb back in.

"I hope you don't mind, but I'm going to call someone to let them know who I'm with."

"You can try, but you can't actually call. Not much signal around here. You might get lucky, though. You never know."

She pulled out her phone and waved it up in the air as if she were trying to catch a rogue signal floating around the cab of the truck. "Of course there isn't," she mumbled.

Avis finally climbed in and started the truck without saying a word and without looking at her. Since his news got out, the onslaught was relentless. He thought he had come up with a solution, an escape.

"Well, nice to meet you, Avis." She patted him on his arm as he drove. "And you too, Leo."

"Beer?" Leo asked. He reached into the bag sitting at his feet and pulled out a Pabst Blue Ribbon.

"Don't mind if I do. It's been one of those days, don't you know."

Avis drove in silence. Everything had changed. The locals acted as if Avis had turned down an invitation to heaven and they couldn't wrap their minds around the concept of someone saying, No thank you to the Powerball jackpot. Others acted nicer than normal. Some were put off by his decision, as if they thought they had any kind of say-so in the matter. And outsiders, they were the worst. The morning after the news began to spread, there were four or five of them already sniffing around town. A couple of them even found Avis, but he wouldn't talk to them. He wouldn't even tell them he wouldn't talk. When they approached him he just put his head down and walked straight toward his truck and drove off. By the end of the week there were at least a couple dozen. And they were still arriving.

So, he had come up with a plan. He was just going to slip away and go fishing. They'd never find him.

But instead of them finding him again, he had found one of them.

CHAPTER TEN

It struck Savannah as odd that just a couple of days ago she had gotten over her brief obsession with killing herself and today here she was in an old beat-up pickup truck, driving down a dirt road in the middle of nowhere with two complete strangers. *Seedy-looking* was one of the nicer phrases that popped into her head as she glanced at her two new companions. She had never considered "Get yourself kidnapped, raped, and murdered by two New Hampshire derelicts" as a way of committing suicide. It hadn't come up in her Google search.

They drove down the paved road away from her car, where she could have stayed, climbed inside, and locked her doors and waited. After driving a good ten miles, Avis swung his truck off to the right onto a well-traveled dirt road. Less than a mile later he turned right again onto a lesser-traveled dirt road and followed it around a few curves and over a little hill and then down through a small valley, until he eventually reached a stretch where grass sprouted up in the middle of the road between the paths worn by the very few tires that had made it this far. She smiled and listened to Leo as she discreetly kept an eye on Avis. Leo was an easy read. A wide-open book who was willing to share everything. In fact, he was not only willing, he insisted on it.

Avis was more difficult. He was quiet and for the moment a little irritated that this stranger, this reporter, this woman named Savannah Gardener, had somehow finagled her way into his truck. Worse yet, he was well aware he had accidentally invited her.

"So anyway," Leo said, as he rambled on about why they were going fishing today. "Avis usually works on Tuesdays, but since this whole ticket thing broke, there ain't no damn way he can work in the garage. Between reporters showing up to see him, and Rick, that's his boss, trying to jump into the spotlight and get some free advertising, there just weren't no damn way

51

to work." He periodically came up for air, but all in all, Leo talked so much, and Savannah was garnering so much information, she didn't want to interrupt him to ask the only question that was on her mind at the moment, which was, "Am I safe coming out into the middle of the woods with you guys?"

"And then the locals. My gawd! Everybody is loving on Avis this week. Hey Avis, ole buddy. Hey Avis, drop over for a beer tonight. Hey Avis, stop by the house. Shit. Rusty York even invited him to go fishing with him. I don't think Rusty has ever fished a day in his life." Savannah smiled at him and then glanced at Avis once again. She got nothing from him. He was either not in an information-sharing mood or he felt Leo was sharing enough for both of them. Or, it was possible he was planning out her murder in his head.

"You know what's the worst part?"

She didn't respond for a moment, presuming it was a rhetorical question and Leo would simply continue. He stared blankly at her and waited for her response.

"Oh. I'm sorry. What is the worst part?"

"Old boyfriends. Can you believe it? Old boyfriends are coming out of the woodwork." With that he stopped talking and looked out the window at the passing trees. Savannah stared at him and tried to piece together what was going on. It hadn't dawned on her that these two country bumpkins were gay. Her head cocked to the side a little bit like a confused puppy. She glanced over to Avis again, who, for the first time since she'd climbed into the truck, had a slight grin on his face. He didn't add anything to the story. He just drove down the grassy dirt road in silence and let her imagination wander.

"Ummmm. Avis's old boyfriends?"

Leo was momentarily speechless and stared at her before blurting out, "What?"

"Are you referring to Avis's old boyfriends?"

"What?" Now it was Leo's turn to sit with a cocked head like a confused puppy.

"You said old boyfriends are coming out of the woodwork. I guess I'm a bit confused about whose old boyfriends you're talking about and how they come into the picture."

"Lindsey's old boyfriends," he snapped. "What would make you think that Avis is gay?"

Avis could have given him a hug.

She waited again for an explanation of who Lindsey might be. When none came, she glanced at Avis again, who offered nothing but a ride to the fishing stream.

"And Lindsey is?"

"Yeah," Leo said in a drawn-out pronunciation that made it clear that Lindsey was not spoken of in high regard. "Lindsey is Avis's mom. She got around a bit, back in the day. She liked riding the sausage, if you know what I mean. There's a pretty heavy debate of who might be Avis's dad." He looked back out the window again as if he had shared a bit of nearly worthless trivia.

Savannah's eyebrows rose; she sat speechless and looked at the back of Leo's head. He was looking out the window once again. She waited for more, but more did not come.

"Whoa. Hey Avis. Did you see that hawk back there?" Leo blurted out.

"Yup. Big one, huh?"

Savannah said, "I'm sorry. I don't mean to pry into your personal life, but I'm just trying to get a clear picture. So, you don't know who your father is?"

The grin dropped back off Avis's face. "You don't mean to get personal? You came down here from... where did you say you are from?"

"Biddeford."

"You climbed into your old piece-of-shit car and drove down here from Biddeford, Maine, and then somehow worked your way into my truck and into my fishing trip in order to ask me god knows what, and you don't want to get personal. Just what are you looking to do, then?"

"Technically you invited me to go fishing with you. I just accepted."

Avis stopped talking. She was right, and it kind of pissed him off.

"So, your father?"

"Maybe we'll talk about that stuff later. First, I'll have to see if you can fish. In fact, that's the deal I'll make with you. I'll answer a question or two if you can catch a fish." Leo was in a talkative mood, so it wasn't likely any of them would catch any fish today.

"So, what do these boyfriends want?" she asked, looking back at Leo.

"I'm guessing after twenty-six years of nobody wanting to be his dad, now half the town wants to claim him and the cash."

"Don't you think it might bother Avis to hear you talking about his mother and his father like this?" Savannah asked as if Avis couldn't hear her.

"Lindsey's reputation is old news in Watermill. The only new thing is how many guys are suddenly admitting to being a part of it. Used to be most of them denied it and didn't acknowledge it. Ain't no damn way any of them wanted to be the father of her kid."

Avis lit a cigarette and took the conversation in stride. Leo was right. It was old news that he had long ago come to terms with. The only one in the truck uncomfortable with all of it now, was Savannah.

"I thought you didn't smoke," she said, hoping to at least get an answer about that.

"I lied," was all he said.

"Here's the best one I've heard so far," Leo blurted out. "Rumor is ole Paul Harris is throwing his hat into the ring. He's been the high school principal for almost thirty years and is suddenly claiming Avis might be from his sperm pool."

Savannah's forehead wrinkled at the phrase *sperm pool*, but Leo continued unfazed.

"He and Melissa would have been already married at the time he's claiming to have, you know, knocked Lindsey up, and he's still married to the woman. Seems like having a shot at Avis's millions might soften the blow of him screwing around on Melissa way back then. Someone told me that Melissa is the one who insisted he should lay his claim."

"Where did you hear that rumor?" Savannah asked.

"Well, it's just a Watermill coffee-shop rumor. Sounds like there's four or five real contenders," he said, as if he were talking about who may have won a local raffle. "Ernie said he heard at least a couple of them are getting tested to see if Avis might be their boy."

"You mean DNA tests?" Savannah asked and wrote more notes.

"Yup. That's what I hear."

"Doesn't this make you even a little uncomfortable?" Savannah asked Avis.

"Lady. I'm just a guy that's going fishing. I tuned the two of you out awhile back." The truck slowed and Avis eased off the road onto a grassy patch before coming to a complete stop. Savannah looked around wondering if anyone else actually came out this far. It didn't seem likely there was any need for Avis to pull off the road. Then she glanced to both sides of the road but didn't see any water. Avis shook his head back and forth as he opened the truck door. "Don't worry. The water is just over there," he said, and motioned to the other side of a patch of alder trees. You're safe, other than Leo might talk you to death or the black flies might eat you alive."

Leo climbed out on his side and started up again. "Avis is a lot better at fishing than I am. Personally, I think he's just luckier. You know, just like the Powerball thing. I'd never win. He plays one damn time and wins. Same with fishing. He always gets lucky."

"You've only played the Powerball one time?"

"You gotta catch a fish before you can ask questions," Avis said and handed her a pole. "That's the deal."

Chapter Eleven

"You want me to put the worm on the hook for you?" Leo asked. Savannah looked into the coffee can full of dirt and worms and contemplated her answer. Then she glanced over at Avis and recalled telling him how much she loved fishing with her father.

Avis looked back at her with one raised eyebrow, as if he also wanted to remind her of what she had said. Surely a good father would have shown his little girl how to put a worm onto a hook.

She fought back any outward sign of gagging and reached into the can and pulled out one small red worm and held it between her thumb and index finger. With the hook in her other hand, she tried to gently poke the pointed hook through the poor thing, as if the torture would be less painful to the wiggler if she slowly and methodically jabbed it with the razor-sharp point. With one final push, the hook shot in through one side of the worm and out the other before poking into her own outer layer of skin. She and Leo both simultaneously flinched. A small drop of blood formed on her finger. Her eyes began to tear up as she pulled the hook out and dropped the worm onto the ground. Avis smiled and said nothing as he tossed his bobber into a small pool on the edge of the stream and made himself comfortable on the moss-covered bank.

"I guess I'm a bit out of practice," Savannah mumbled to Leo as she handed him her pole, wiped a tear out of her eye and watched a drop of blood drip down onto her shorts. Leo put the worm onto the hook, adjusted the bobber on the line, and showed her where to toss it into the stream. She tossed the hook and bobber and nearly missed the entire stream, never mind where he had instructed her to aim. Leo looked puzzled at where she chose to throw her line. Savannah looked relieved that she had hit the water at all. Avis looked as if he were going to enjoy being part of this fiasco in the making.

Avis sat and thought about the last time he and Leo had taken anyone fishing with them. It surprised him when he realized that in all the years of them fishing, it had almost always been just the two of them. They went with Avis's friend George once in a while, but that was when they were kids. Back then it was George and Avis, and Leo was the tag-along. Now that there was someone new, he wondered if Leo would say, "Hey Savannah," instead of "Hey Avis."

"It's best if you keep your line real still, so you don't scare the fish away," Leo said, as if he ever kept his line still or caught many fish. Savannah made a mental note to jiggle her line as often as she discretely could to hopefully scare any fish away from her hook. She needed to catch *a* fish to ask questions, but she thought it might be best if she took things one-step at a time.

"So, you guys fish a lot, huh?" she asked Avis as they both sat and watched the water flow by.

"You catch a fish yet?" he responded without looking toward her.

"Excuse me?"

"The deal was if you catch a fish, you can ask me some questions. You catch a fish yet?"

"I was just being polite. It wasn't like an interview question," she defended.

"Catch a fish, ask a question. That's the deal," he said without looking at her.

"What if we don't catch anything?"

"Then it's going to be a quiet and peaceful day."

"Hey Avis," Leo chimed in and reminded Avis that silence was unlikely.

"Yeah, Leo."

"Where did the state of Kansas get its name?" he asked. He gave his fishing pole a little jerk and made the bobber and hook bounce up and down.

Avis sat without answering for a few moments, and watched Savannah process the question and try to make some sort of connection between their day and the word *Kansas*. There was none.

"Well," Avis answered slowly, "The short version is a Sioux Indian tribe whose people were called Kansa by some of the Frenchmen who were *civilizing* the country a few hundred years ago. Then someone started calling the area Kansas, and there you have it. The short version."

"What's the long version?"

"You gotta read a book to get the long version, Leo. Always got to read the book for the long version." It was a canned answer Avis had given Leo a thousand times over the past two decades. He typically gave the short answer and told Leo to read a book to learn more. Leo was always satisfied with the short answer, but Avis held out hope that one day Leo just might pick up a book and read.

"What made you ask about Kansas, Leo?" Savannah asked in hopes of stirring up more conversation.

Leo stared at her blankly, as if he didn't understand what she was asking. Then his face contorted as he tried to make sense of her question. Wasn't the answer obvious? It all seemed rather obvious to him. He thought of the name Kansas and didn't know what it meant, so he asked Avis.

"I was just wondering, that's all," he said as he tossed his hook back into the water.

"But something must have made you think of it. Right?" she asked.

"I'm sure something did make me think of it. And then I asked where it came from."

Her mouth began to open, but she didn't know what to say. If Avis wasn't going to talk to her, she wanted to at least keep chatting with Leo. "Do you know where New Hampshire's name came from?" she asked Leo. She presumed if he didn't know, he would appreciate her little history lesson. Leo shrugged and stood up and walked twenty yards upstream before sitting back down by himself. Before she had time to consider what had just happened, she felt a bite on her line, and before she had time to jerk her pole to scare the thing away, a fish chomped down and impaled the hook into its mouth. Savannah jumped up to her feet as if she were preparing for a mighty fight with a blue-water tarpon. She yanked upward on the pole, expecting a fishing battle of epic proportions. A second later her bobber, the hook, and a five-inch trout shot twenty feet up and dropped over a branch of the birch tree directly behind her. Avis and Leo sat and looked up toward the fish that was dangling and likely going to spend its final moments of life looking down at the stream where it had peacefully lived only moments earlier. Savannah frantically spun around and looked on the ground for her catch. After glancing at the ground and then at both Leo and Avis, she looked up and saw her fish hanging up in the air.

"So, you guys fish a lot?" she asked Avis while all three of them continued looking up toward the treetop.

"Yes. Yes, we do," Avis answered as he stared at the dying trout.

CHAPTER TWELVE

Savannah nibbled on a small piece of trout while Avis turned another one over in an old aluminum frying pan that sat on the small fire he had built. She scooped a spoonful of baked beans from the can and plopped them onto her paper plate and began to wonder what she was supposed to do when the sun went down.

As usual, Leo hadn't caught any fish, but this time not only had Avis out-fished him, a good-looking reporter from Biddeford, Maine, with no apparent fishing experience, had also caught three more fish than he had. One was still hanging in a tree six hours after it had died there.

"So, Avis, I've been with you now for almost an entire day and I caught three fish, but you haven't really answered any questions yet." Savannah stuck another piece of trout into her mouth and spit out a small bone onto the ground.

"I answered what you asked," he said and plopped another trout onto her plate.

"You answered most of my questions with questions," she said, looking over the top of her plate as she scooped up more beans with her spoon.

"What do you mean?"

"I mean just that. I said you answered most of my questions with questions and you said, 'What do you mean?' I asked why you gave the ticket away and you said, 'Why not?' I asked, couldn't you have used the money yourself and you said, and I quote, 'For what?' So, as I said, you have answered almost every question I have asked you with another question."

"You think so, huh?" he said without looking at her. He thought his latest answer was funnier than she did.

"I think she's right, Avis," Leo added, as if Avis wasn't aware that he was avoiding all of Savannah's questions.

Avis looked at Leo and scooped a spoonful of beans into his mouth and shook his head back and forth.

"Look," Savannah said. "I'm out here in the middle of nowhere with two guys I don't know. My legs are all bit up from black flies and mosquitoes." She scanned a half-dozen bloody dots on each leg. "I caught the fish you required me to catch, plus two more."

"You're not actually counting that one, are you?" Avis asked, nodding his head up toward the sky.

"Damned right I am," she snapped and continued. "My car is dead on the side of the road fifteen miles or so away from here and I guess I'll be sleeping on the wet ground or in the truck tonight. The least you could do is let me interview you and, if it's not too much trouble, answer some questions."

"Think so, huh?" he said again, while scooping more beans into his mouth while not looking at her.

"And I have to pee!" she yelled and looked around as if she might discover a restroom somewhere nearby.

Leo sat back against a tree with a Pabst Blue Ribbon in his hand and waited for Avis to respond. Avis held the pan of fish toward Leo.

"Nah. I'm good," he said with a grin and waited to hear what question Avis would ask Savannah next.

"Well?" she snapped.

"Well what?" he asked.

"Where do I pee?"

"Gotta pee, huh?" he asked for no particular reason other than to irritate her that he had asked another question without answering hers. It worked. She threw her plate onto the ground and stormed off behind the truck and squatted down out of sight. When she came back, Avis and Leo both stood next to the stream with beers in their hands and grins on their faces.

"What the hell are you grinning about?"

Avis shrugged without answering. She looked toward Leo.

"What are you looking at me for?" Leo asked, looking like a deer caught in the headlights.

"An answer."

"I just think you guys are kind of funny," Leo said, and kicked a rock into the water.

She reached into her pocket and pulled out her cigarettes and lighter and lit one. Avis watched her take a long drag and blow the smoke into the air as if she were blowing out ten pounds of frustration.

"Leo," Avis said as he continued to watch her, "Why don't you drive Savannah to your mom's house for the night. Stop by her car first and get her stuff. Let her crash in a bed tonight. I'm guessing she doesn't really want to sleep on the ground and I've only got one sleeping bag…

"Unless you want to share it with me," he said as he looked at Savannah with a mock expression of optimism on his face.

"Thanks, but I'll pass on the offer." She was momentarily caught between relief that she wasn't going to be sleeping on the wet ground in the woods where it might start raining any minute, with two strange men she didn't really know, and disappointment that she wasn't getting any of her questions answered for her article.

"To your mom's house it is," he said to Leo as he headed to the truck to get his gear.

"So, I presume this means you're not actually going to answer any questions?"

"Leo can bring you back out tomorrow and we'll talk," he said as he walked to the truck and tossed a rolled-up tent and sleeping bag onto the ground. "I mean, you did catch a fish and all."

"I caught three."

CHAPTER THIRTEEN

Steve sat behind his desk and reread the text he had received from Savannah an hour earlier. He couldn't quite decide whether he should offer her some sort of mini-Pulitzer Prize or have her head checked out. But this was Savannah. She was always either all in, or all out. He had sent her to find Avis Humphrey and get his story. An average reporter would have gone to Watermill, talked to a few people, written a nice human-interest story, expensed out a good meal or two, and driven back home. He wasn't surprised that she took it to another level.

> *Steve...*
>
> *I'm in Watermill. Well, actually I've been just outside of Watermill and you won't believe my luck. While the whole world is looking for this guy, my car broke down and guess who stopped and helped me out. AVIS HUMPHREY and his buddy, Leo. These guys are characters like you won't believe. I'm putting together a story for you, but it's going to be a few days. (Don't get in a tizzy about expenses because I think I'm going to be camping out in the woods with the two of them.) I think it's safe. Seems safe anyway.*
>
> *I'll be back in touch in a couple days. This is unbelievable.*
>
> *Thanks for watching my Bruce for me. Take care of him.*
>
> *Savannah*

Steve glanced in the general direction of the litter box in the corner of his office and then looked up at the cat sitting on top of his file cabinet. "Your owner is camping out in the woods with two strange men. I'm not sure who's more at risk, her or them."

Bruce stared back at him as if to say, "I don't have an owner," and then looked back out the window without feigning the least bit of interest in the memo or in Steve.

CHAPTER FOURTEEN

Denny Wilson picked up his coffee cup and the last half of his bagel and walked over to the table in the corner. The eye-patch guy put a forkful of pancakes into his mouth and smiled at Denny as he made his way toward him.

"How you doing?" he said with a mouth full of pancakes and a strong New England accent. Denny smiled at him and thought to himself that the man looked a little like someone who would live in a run-down trailer on the outskirts of town with a mangy dog and a collection of broken-down cars and trucks in the yard. Then he realized he had just described Avis's trailer and he wondered if he really wanted to find Avis.

"I'm doing well. How are you?"

"Pancakes, coffee, nice people, and it ain't snowing. Can't say it's heaven, but it's pretty damn close."

"Mind if I join you?"

"Hell no. Have a seat." He shoveled another half a pancake into his mouth and took a big gulp of black coffee.

"The guy behind the counter said you might be able to help me," Denny said, motioning his hand in Ernie's direction.

"You mean Ernie? Hell of a guy. Known him for a damn long time."

"Yeah. Ernie. He said you might be able to point me in the right direction."

"I suppose you're looking for Avis. Everyone's looking for him lately. Not that I mind. Quite a story and all. That's a shitload of money, don't you think?"

"Yes. It is a lot of money. A bunch of money, in fact. So, are you the guy who can help me find Avis?" Denny hadn't yet developed the skill of small talk and chitchat.

"Where you from?" Eye Patch asked and took another gulp.

"I flew in from Miami a couple of days ago."

"Miami! Holy shit. That's a long way from here."

"Yes. It is," Denny said with a smile. He wondered if everyone in Watermill was working off one giant mind. He had told three people where he was from and all three gave the identical response.

"Hey, Ernie!" Eye Patch called out loud enough for all the customers to hear. "Did you know this kid came all the way up here from Miami to get the Avis story?"

"Yeah, Tom. That's what he told me." Ernie nodded and answered without looking up and continued to pour coffee for his customers.

Everyone in the diner looked over at Denny for a minute, and he felt as if he, not Avis, was the minor local celebrity who would probably be on the front-page story of the Watermill Post: "Miami Reporter Comes To Town!"

"So... Tom. That's your name, I presume?"

"Tom Palmer. That's me." He grinned from ear to ear with one eye sparkling.

"So, Tom. How do you know Avis?"

"Hell. This is Watermill, New Hampshire. Everyone knows everyone."

Denny raised his eyebrows and smiled in acknowledgement that he understood that everyone around here would know everyone else.

Eye Patch continued, "Plus, he's my cousin. Third or fourth or something like that. You know how it is. It's tricky figuring out second or thirds or fourths. A first cousin is easy because his parents would be my aunt and uncle. Once it gets further than that.... Shit. Who knows then?"

"That's true," Denny answered. He didn't really find it all that hard, but he could see how this Tom character might struggle with such a complicated puzzle. Around here, Denny was thinking, maybe a second cousin could actually be a sister or an aunt, too. Maybe both. That was more than he wanted to consider. "So, are you and Avis close?"

"Oh. I guess so. Not like we're brothers, but I suppose we pop a top now and then. But he's into fishing. Doesn't really do anything for me. Hooks and worms and sitting in the damp woods with mosquitoes and black flies.

Doesn't do it for me. Now I like lake fishing now and then, but that's different. You know... out on a boat, enjoying the lake and all. On a good summer day, you might even see a bikini or two. Now that's fishing."

Denny was beginning to think this could be a time-consuming process if he didn't keep Tom focused on Avis. "I've been out to his trailer. There's a sign that says he's gone fishing. Don't suppose you would know where he might be fishing? I mean, if you don't really like fishing and all."

"In New Hampshire? Damn, man. There's like a million lakes and streams."

"Yes. That's true. I looked on the Internet and there is a lot of water in New Hampshire. But there must be some place the locals like to go to, isn't there?"

Tom smiled and shoveled the last forkful of pancakes into his mouth and washed it down with more coffee. He sat back and swished the coffee in his mouth and then cleaned his front teeth with his tongue and patted his full stomach.

"Miami, huh? I went to Florida once. A long time ago. Didn't turn out so well." He stopped talking and drifted off and looked at the ceiling and waited for Denny to chime in.

Denny didn't have years of experience as a reporter, but he didn't need it. Tom wanted to talk about Tom before they talked about Avis. If Denny wasn't interested in Tom's story, then Tom probably wasn't interested in sharing anything about Avis.

Tom continued, "Didn't go all the way down to Miami though. Only made it as far as Daytona. Spring Break, you know." He stopped talking and waited again.

"Ahhhh. I hear there are a lot of rough Daytona Spring Break stories."

"Not like mine," Tom said. This time there wasn't any smile.

"What happened?" Denny asked, feigning concern. He presumed it included too much drinking, a bar fight, or a flight off a balcony or something along those lines.

Tom just pointed to the eye patch and took another drink of coffee.

"You know, Tom, the editors always like a local connection. We all know Avis is from here, but if he's got a cousin who has a tragic Florida connection, well, Floridians are consumed with the Florida connection. News people love it. That's if you want to tell me your story."

"Really. You think they might like me in the Avis story?" he said, as if he hadn't expected it.

"Well, it depends what your story is."

"I'm thinking you're probably not going to be able to use this one."

"Well. I'll tell you what. Let's give it a shot and I'll see what I can do with it." Denny waved to the waitress and held up his mug for more coffee and leaned back in his seat to hear what the New Hampshire Pirate had to say and how he likely got drunk and poked his own eye out.

"I've never been much of a drinker," was how the story started, surprising Denny. "A few of us took a road trip to Daytona about twenty-odd years ago to do some Spring Break stuff. My buddies mostly drank the whole time we were there, but I spent all of my time on the beach, swimming in the waves, checking out bikini babes, and just taking in all the beach stuff. I've seen the ocean in New England a bunch of times, but it wasn't nothing like Florida. The beach was softer and flatter and went on for miles. The water was bluer. It's almost black up here. Not to mention the water feels just a notch warmer than ice but almost like a bathtub down there. And the birds were the coolest. All we got up here are mostly seagulls. But down there, there were all kinds of birds flying and walking on the beach. They had long legs and long beaks. All kinds of different colors. I really liked looking at them Florida birds."

"So, you didn't lose your eye in a drinking escapade?" Denny asked, still a bit surprised.

"Nope. Didn't drink a whole six-pack the entire week I was there."

"So, what happened?"

"To be honest, I can only tell you what I've been told, because I didn't see it coming."

"Didn't see what coming?" Denny was beginning to feel a bit like a rat in a lab that had to push a buzzer to get more cheese. Tom gave a bit of information and then Denny had to push a buzzer, or in this case, ask the obvious question to prompt Tom to talk more. Denny kept pushing the buzzer.

"It was almost sunset and I had spent the entire day swimming and laying in the sun. The beach was packed all day, but most everyone had already gone back up to their rooms. You know, to clean up and get their second wind or whatever." He sat back and drifted off for a few seconds.

"And?" Denny pushed the buzzer for more cheese.

"And I stayed on the beach. I walked for a long time. Looking for shells mostly. I probably walked a couple of miles and then turned around and headed back. It was kind of dusk and the sun was just setting, but it wasn't dark yet. Man, the sunsets are awesome in Florida." He drifted away again and looked like he was picturing a Florida sunset.

"And?" Another buzzer. More cheese, please.

"Anyway, I kept strolling along, looking down toward my feet. Seeing what seashells I could find. And then it just happened. Like I said, I can only tell you what I've been told."

"Well, I guess we'll just have to go with the eyewitness account of what happened." Denny prodded.

"I glanced up every once in a while and was amazed by the pelicans. You're from Florida. You must have seen how they fly in that formation just a couple feet above the water."

"Oh yes. See them all the time."

"Well, like I said. I was walking along, looking for seashells, and glancing up now and then to watch them pelicans flying. Amazing how they do that. They look like a squadron of B-29's skimming just above the waves and they move along like it's something they practice every day. Anyway, some kids on the beach said there was a lone pelican zipping along just a few feet from the shoreline where I was walking. You know how them things like to fly for miles without hardly flapping their wings?"

"Sure do," Denny said. Buzzer pushed again.

"Well, I guess as it got closer to me, it started fading away from the water and flew closer and closer to the shore. I don't really remember what happened, but they tell me someone screamed just before the collision. That's probably what did me in. Without the warning, my head would have been down and I would have only gotten a cut on my forehead. But when they yelled, I looked up to see what the commotion was all about, and Bam!" he blurted out and slapped his open palm on the table. "Pelican beak right in the eye."

Denny sat speechless. On the one hand, he thought it wasn't possible for this story to be true. On the other hand, the one-eyed man, who didn't skip a beat or crack a smile while sharing his story, didn't look smart enough to make up a story like that.

"Get the hell out of here. You're telling me a pelican ran into you and took your eye out. You're serious?"

"Serious as a heart attack. But it gets better. Some bird-lover woman on the beach was all upset and was as worried about Peter Pelican as the paramedics were about me. She rushed the thing to the vet and the vet saved its life and all. Here's the kicker though. The vet said the pelican was blind in one eye and that's probably why it flew crooked and didn't see me. Ironic, huh? A one-eyed pelican turned me into a one-eyed guy."

"Come on man. You've got to be making this up."

"Man, you can't make this shit up. Why would I even want to? I'd just like my eye back."

Denny momentarily lost his one-track thought of leaving Watermill. This was the first time since arriving in Theresa's office that he had been part of an even mildly interesting interview and he wasn't quite sure what to do with it.

"So, you think you can use my story? You know. As the Florida connection?"

"I don't know. You think you can point me toward Avis?" Tom smiled from ear to ear and Denny felt like he was getting the hang of this whole reporter thing.

* * *

Even Theresa didn't know what to think of the 'Tom the Pirate' story when Denny sent it to her later in the afternoon. She read it twice and then responded with, "What are you waiting for? Go find A. Humphrey."

On day three, Denny spent the better part of seven hours sloshing up and down the shores of a remote stream about fifteen miles north of town where he found no sign of Avis. It was a cold, drizzly day, and the only thing worse than the rain were the black flies and Denny's hunger. Finding Tom and getting directions gave him the false illusion that finding Avis would be easy. After four hours of trudging through the wet forest, his water-resistant jacket had stopped resisting water and he was soaked to the bone. Every inch of his body from his head to his toes was wet and cold. The two power bars he had stuffed into his pocket were long gone before lunchtime and he had lost all track of time. Halfway through the day he realized how far he had hiked. Even worse, he realized how far he was going to have to hike to get back to his car. He nearly jogged, as best as he could on the log-and rock-covered bank of the New Hampshire stream, all the way back to his car.

Yesterday's journalistic excitement had slipped away and was once again replaced with dreams of doing some real reporting—in Miami. At four in the afternoon he sat in his car with the heat blasting on high while he shivered and tried to piece together a story that would be interesting enough to send to Theresa without giving her the satisfaction of savoring the pure hell he was going through.

For the first time in months he seriously considered just how bad it might or might not be, working for his father. Then he wondered if it could possibly be any worse than this.

CHAPTER FIFTEEN

Things got quiet in the Beckham house after Lindsey left for Montana. Two senior citizens and a ten-year old boy might have been an all-right situation had the seniors not been Frank and Judy Beckham. Judy liked things to be just so, even when they were not. According to Judy, Lindsey was doing well out west and was always coming back home to get Avis, *soon*. At least that's what Judy said. And Frank shuffled off to work, shuffled back home, watched the news, and cussed about politics or the economy or something else that, as far as Avis could tell, was responsible for everything bad that happened in Frank and Judy's life. Even at ten, Avis was pretty sure the Beckhams would have exhaled a cosmic sigh of relief, if by chance he quietly slipped out the back door and did not return. And that was pretty much how it all went down. Avis slipped out the back door and landed at the Schnells.

The first time Avis said, "Hey, Gram. Can I spend the night at Leo's tonight?" Gram's eyes got big and a smile spontaneously landed on her face. She didn't even try to contain her excitement as she jumped at the opportunity for her and Gramps to have their house to themselves, even for just one night. And for the first week, it was just one night. The next week it was two. After that, Avis was spending half of his time at Leo's and half at the Beckhams. Slowly and steadily his clothes and books and toothbrush migrated two doors down the road. Eventually even his fishing poles moved from Gramps' garage to Leo's porch. None of them could say exactly what day the official move-in took place, but at some point in time, Avis began telling Tina Schnell when he was staying with the Beckhams, instead of the other way around.

A few months later, eleven-year-old Avis Humphrey stood again in the middle of the road looking at the dust swirls settling back down onto the dirt road long after the car had driven off and out of sight. A little over a year had passed since Lindsey said she was leaving for a little while, but would

71

be back to get him as soon as she was settled in. She apparently never settled in, because she definitely never came back. Frank and Judy were, Avis supposed, just as deceptive, albeit in a different manner.

After Judy's uncle died and left them a condo in Clearwater, Frank promptly retired from his job at the county appraiser's office and set in motion a plan to winter in Florida. Much like Lindsey's discussion, they sat eleven-year-old Avis down and had a full-blown adult conversation with him. They explained how Frank had worked hard his entire life and how he deserved a break from the grueling task of loafing about at his government job and how they'd both earned a reprieve from the New Hampshire winters. Then they went on to explain why an eleven-year-old boy could not go with them. This point wasn't made as clearly as the work and winter points. From what Avis could gather from their explanation, not many children lived in Florida—other than at Disney, he presumed. They then explained he would be much better off staying with the Schnells. Well, they didn't so much explain it, but simply said, "You'll be better off staying with the Schnells," especially since he already pretty much lived with them full-time. Last but not least, Judy said his Mom had called yesterday and swore she would be back soon to get her son. Even Avis knew better than that. He had overheard one end of the conversation more than once. What had likely happened was this: Judy called Lindsey. In order to get the rigid, plastic-covered-couch woman, who only believed whatever was convenient for her to believe, off the phone, her daughter likely said, "I'll come back to get him, Mom, as soon as I can." In Judy's world, "I'll come back as soon as I can," was best translated into "I'll come back soon." That was the version that worked best for Frank and Judy, so that's the version Judy shared with Avis.

"Hey Avis," Leo mumbled.

"Hey, Leo," Avis said, still looking off in the distance with no expectation of the car returning.

"Watcha looking at?"

Avis shrugged. "Nothing, I guess."

"Where did Gram and Gramps go?"

"Clearwater."

"Where's that?

"I dunno, but I guess they don't have many kids there."

"When they coming back?"

"I dunno."

For a long time neither of them said anything.

Avis was looking at nothing but the ghosts of his family who had all driven down the road. Leo looked to see if he could see whatever it was that Avis was looking at.

Avis said, "They'll probably come back when my mom comes back."

The sarcasm was lost on Leo, but the scars of life had already begun to form on Avis, even at eleven years old. Avis often hoped, with low expectations, for one of them to come back. But eight months later Frank and Judy had still not returned.

Growing up in Leo's house was a free-for-all. Leo had a brother and two sisters, all older than he was. Tina, Leo's mom, worked at the school cafeteria. She headed out the door each morning as the rest of the herd crawled out of bed to get ready for school. So at 6:30 a.m. the Schnell kids and Avis all scurried around; fought over the one bathroom; grabbed cereal, Pop-Tarts, or left-over pizza from the night before; and then all ran to the bus that was sitting and honking in front of the house—except for Avis. He always managed to be the first one out of the door and standing on the side of the road waiting for the bus to arrive.

The morning ritual was unwavering. The driver gave him an indifferent "Morning, Avis," as he lugged his oversized, over-stuffed book bag onto the bus. Avis rarely said anything. Just a sleepy nod, and then he went to the first row with two empty seats for Leo and himself, always on the right-hand side of the bus. Two houses after they pulled away from the Schnell's home, Avis always looked to see if there was any sign of Gram and Gramps at the house. There never was.

Then one morning, after winter had ended, and the school bus was passing the house two doors down from the Schnells, and Avis sat in the window seat on the right side of the bus with his face pressed against the glass, he saw it. Gramps tan Ford Taurus sat in the driveway as if it belonged there. As if it had never gone away. Avis looked at it and sat up straight and elbowed Leo. "They're back, Leo. They're back." He couldn't believe it. Gram and Gramps had come back. Merle had somehow disappeared and never returned, while still living in Watermill. Lindsey went to Montana and stayed as if she didn't have a son back in New Hampshire. But Gram and Gramps hadn't permanently abandoned him.

That school day was eternal. Each class dragged on and on as if time had nearly stopped. All he could think about was someone from his family had come back to get him. He wasn't alone in the world. He wasn't a stray dog living with the family who had taken him in. He liked Leo's family, but they weren't his. Even at his age, Avis knew that the Schnell family was better than his family. But better or not, they still weren't his.

When the school day ended, Avis was the first person in line to climb onto the bus. He sat in the very first row by the door on the left side, so he could see Gram and Gramps if they were in the yard when the bus pulled up in front of their house. He had a plan to ask the driver to stop and let him out two doors earlier than usual. Avis was excited to see someone from his family and it was a new emotion for him. He felt the bond of family calling, and it felt like home. He couldn't wait to run up and hug them and tell them how much he had missed them. They had never really been the comforting touchy-feely type, but he didn't care. He was a kid with no father and a missing mother and he had thought his Gram and Gramps had gone for good, but they came back and that was all that mattered. When the dust swirl finally settled, someone from his family had finally come back for him.

The bus slowly accelerated away from the school and headed down Oak Street and began its route. The bus, like the classes, seemed to go slower than usual and the ride felt eternal. Kids dragged their book bags in slow motion and stopped to say things to their friends, and they slowly climbed from their seats and nearly crawled to the door. He wanted to scream, "Hurry up!" But he sat and squirmed and rode along with a grin bursting on his face. When they finally reached Bunker Hill Road, they chugged down through a long valley and then around the sharp corner that led to the straightaway where a handful of houses sat with their dirt driveways.

Avis looked to see if the car was still in the driveway as soon as the house came into view. He didn't see it, but there was something red on the front lawn. He squinted and tried to figure out what it was. They came closer and it hit him like a spear in his chest. The car, along with Gram and Gramps and whatever stuff they had loaded from the house, had already come and gone. The only indication that anyone had been there earlier in the day was a red 'For Sale' sign in the front yard. They had come back to sell the only home he had ever known. And little did he know, that wasn't the worst of it.

* * *

Frank and Judy Beckham had called Tina Schnell a few days earlier to let her know they were moving to Clearwater permanently and they wanted to know if she would become Avis's legal guardian. "Just temporarily, mind you," Judy had said as if she were still telling lies to Avis.

"Jesus Christ, Judy. He's eleven years old and everyone keeps abandoning him."

"I know it seems harsh, Tina. You must understand that Frank and I are not equipped to take care of a little boy. And we're optimistic she's coming back, but just not sure how soon."

Tina understood with absolute clarity what *soon* translated into. Lindsey was perhaps the most self-absorbed woman she had ever met, other than Judy Beckham. The apple hadn't fallen far from the tree. In fact, it had possibly cloned itself when it came to the two women. Judy Beckham had probably taken up golf or shuffleboard or bridge, or mall walking; and her grandson would be an imposition, an inconvenience, a distraction from the make-believe world they had retired to. They were not about to be the first people in the family to put Avis's needs in front of their own.

"Are you and Frank going to break the news to him?" she asked when Judy called.

"Well... we aren't really that close to him. We thought it might be better if you explained the situation to the boy." That's what she called him, *the boy,* as if he didn't really have a name and he wasn't a real person or part of their family.

* * *

The bus drove past the Beckham house and slowly came to a stop, two doors down. Avis walked down the steps with his head hung low and his chest crushed under the weight of being abandoned, again. For the first time in his life he thought he should just get rid of his family. It didn't matter, though. They had already gotten rid of him.

Leo had seen his mom in the cafeteria and told her about the car. Then he told her about how excited Avis was. Tina's heart sank, but she just smiled and didn't let on about her news. When Avis walked through the front door, Tina, who was always busy doing something, was standing in the middle of the room waiting for him. He looked at her with watered-up eyes. He was not quite crying on the outside, but he was dying on the inside. She opened her arms wide and when he got to her they wrapped around him and he was hugged like he had never been hugged before.

"You're part of our family now, Avis."

Avis hugged her back and wanted to stay in her arms forever. He didn't want to talk about "family." It wasn't something that had ever worked out too well for him. He just wanted to stay wrapped up and safe in Tina's big mom-hug and pretend the rest of the world didn't exist. The Beckham/Humphrey world had left deep scars on a small boy that were invisible but cut to the bone. The wounds would alter his world for far longer than the foreseeable future.

CHAPTER SIXTEEN

Leo and Savannah drove up in Avis's truck at 10:40 in the morning and pulled into the same grassy spot as yesterday. Avis wasn't surprised they were so late. In fact, he would have been surprised if Leo ever showed up anywhere when he said he would. Still, he felt the need to remind him, just like he reminded him every other time, that he was late.

"What the hell happened to bringing me some breakfast?" Avis snapped with one hand stuffed into the pocket of his ragged jeans and the other hand waving in the air toward the two stragglers.

"Hey... we brought you breakfast," Leo barked back with a cigarette hanging from his mouth. "Besides, it's her fault we're late. Had to stop at pretty much every damn place in town."

"Why is that?" Avis grumbled with his face scrunched into a scowl.

"Well, first she had to go back to her car and get something. Then I thought we were heading here, but after that she wanted me to go back to town to get some stuff from the store. And then she saw Ernie's and wanted to stop and grab coffee and stuff. And—"

"So, pretty much, you guys had breakfast, stopped for coffee and had a nice leisurely morning while I sat here on a log waiting for you to bring me back my truck along with something to eat. Am I getting it right?" he said and shot another dirty look at Savannah.

"Man. Ernie's is packed," Leo continued as if Avis hadn't spoken. "Every damn table was full. Counter was full. There were people standing outside waiting to get in. Reporters. TV crews. And a few guys who look more like prospectors than reporters. Not sure what they're planning on doing, but I think they're looking to strike gold."

Avis shrugged and hoped that when all was said and done, the conversation taking place would eventually lead to a cup of coffee and something to eat.

"Turns out it pays to have a local connection," Savannah said as she climbed out of the driver's seat holding a carrier with two cups of coffee and a couple of doughnuts on it. She handed a cup and a doughnut to Avis, who did not feel the need to thank her. "I thought we were going to get mugged when Leo walked in and called out for coffee and doughnuts and he got served in front of all the out-of-town folks."

"It's called taking care of your own," Avis mumbled, without looking at Savannah as he took the carrier out of her hand. "It's not like we invented it here in Watermill. I presume they get better service where they're from. They should consider going back."

"They can't," she answered. "Avis Humphrey is the big story, and everyone wants a piece of it. They can't go away until they have something to take back."

"Good gawd," Avis snipped, and then sipped the coffee. "Ahhhh."

"Good gawd? You gave away over nine hundred million dollars, Avis. And you drive a piece of shit truck and don't think anyone should be curious?"

"Yeah? What the hell were you doing driving my truck anyway? I gave the keys to Leo. And I like my truck, thank you very much."

"She asked if she could drive and I said okay. Ain't nothing she could do to hurt that pile of shit. And I got to eat my doughnuts and drink my coffee," Leo said, holding his coffee cup up for Avis to see. "Everybody wins."

"I didn't win. While you two socialites were out bouncing around town, I was sitting here on a log waiting for breakfast," he mumbled one more time. He took a bite of his jelly doughnut. "And you couldn't have at least gotten me a muffin or a biscuit? Seriously? A jelly doughnut?" He stuffed the last half into his mouth in one bite and showed no sign, other than his grumbling, that he didn't enjoy jelly doughnuts.

Leo looked curiously at Avis and thought about asking what all the bitching was about, but it wasn't exactly a Leo question. A more likely question would have been, "Hey Avis. Who came up with the word *zebra*?" Besides, Leo was pretty sure he knew what was going on.

The problem was Avis really wanted to dislike Savannah for being a nosy, intrusive news reporter who was looking to pry his life wide open. She was at least partly to blame, as far as Avis was concerned, for the return of all of his ghost from the past. But the truth was, he felt good she had returned, and it irritated him.

He took another sip and gave dirty looks, first to Leo and then toward Savannah. After he made sure they both knew how disgusted he was, he shook his head and walked back toward the stream. Savannah followed, completely indifferent to his wrinkled feathers, with a little cellphone-size recorder in her hand. When he sat down on the bank of the stream, she sat down beside him.

Before they got settled in, Leo called out, "Hey Avis."

"Yeah, Leo."

"Who invented the ice cream cone?"

"Some say it was Ital Marchiony, but others say they were in Paris almost a hundred years earlier." Avis answered.

"Really?" Leo answered matter-of-factly. He didn't say anything more, as if he were considering the accomplishments of a man he had never heard of. He wasn't. His mind had already moved on to something else.

Savannah watched him for a second or two, but she wasn't all that caught off guard by Leo's questions anymore. When Leo didn't say anything else, she turned back toward Avis. She still struggled to understand how Avis could know things like, Ital Marchiony or that some Parisian made the first ice cream cone, but for the moment she had questions of her own to get Avis to answer.

"So, are you going to answer any questions for me today with something other than more questions?" Savannah asked.

"No recorders," he answered without looking up at her.

"Why not?" she snapped back, as if she were entitled to dictate the terms of the interview.

"You can either interview me with no recorder or you can record the beautiful sounds of the babbling stream. Your call." He continued pushing her buttons and it felt good to Avis that he was starting the interview off on the right foot.

"Give a guy nine hundred and sixty-seven million dollars, and suddenly he thinks he's hot shit," she moaned. She shut the recorder off and pulled a small tablet and pen out of the leg pocket of her cargo shorts.

Avis hid his smile behind the coffee cup. He and Savannah had started off in some sort of verbal competition from the moment he had pulled off the road to help her with her broken-down car. It didn't seem like the battle was going to let up anytime soon.

"So, where do we start?" she asked.

"You're the reporter. You tell me." Another small point scored.

Leo walked over and set down a plastic cooler that, from the way he was struggling with it, appeared to be full.

"What's in that?" Avis asked, knowing Leo rarely had any money, and even when he did, he was too irresponsible and cheap to get them something to eat or drink.

"Savannah stocked you up. Beer. Sandwiches. Snacks. Oh, and there's toilet paper and some other stuff in the truck."

Point for Savannah.

Avis showed no sign of gratitude and only a slight sign of irritation. He wondered what other stuff she could have brought that was not food, drinks, or toilet paper. Then he wondered if he wanted to know.

"Well," Savannah said as if she were doing a live interview on TV. "Everyone already knows you won and that you gave the ticket to Alice Chen. So, I guess I'll ask the next obvious question. Who is Alice? And why give it to her?" She waited for a moment and then interrupted him before he could speak, "And, *Why not,* is not an acceptable answer." Avis's mouth was half open when she blurted out the new rule. He closed his mouth and searched for a different response that would not adequately answer the question, but would technically qualify, at least in his mind, as an acceptable answer.

CHAPTER SEVENTEEN

Alice Chen had a habit of gently rubbing students on their heads as she greeted them good morning. There was a mixed bag of reactions from the children of Watermill. Most would smile and say, "Good morning, Mrs. Chen," and keep walking. Some would blush and zip along. And every once in a while, a student would sort of pull away and shrug off the human contact. She was okay with that. Not everyone liked to be touched, especially by someone they didn't really know.

Avis was only in kindergarten the first time her fingers ran through his hair as he walked past her on his way to his classroom.

"Good morning, Avis," Alice said with a smile and kept walking. Avis stopped dead in his tracks and turned around and looked at her without saying a word. He stood expressionlessly as he looked her up and down and tried to figure out why this woman had rubbed his head and why she was saying good morning to him. He tried to figure out why she acknowledged him at all. His mother barely acknowledged his existence; his grandparents never shared encouragement or love, and they certainly would never rub his head.

"Are you all right, Avis?" Alice asked as she stopped, turned, and looked back at the little boy in the baggy jeans, sneakers, and Red Sox T-shirt.

"Ah-huh. You rubbed my head," he answered matter-of-factly.

"Yes, I did," Alice answered as she turned and walked back toward Avis. "Are you okay with that?"

"Ah-huh. I washed my hair last night, so my hair is clean," he said, as if that might have been of concern.

"I'm glad to hear that, Avis," she answered with a broadening smile. "I washed my hands, too. So my hands are clean."

"Good morning, Mrs. Chen," he finally answered after he rattled his way through a long thought process, searching for an appropriate response to her greeting.

She rubbed him on the head again and they both smiled and headed off in different directions.

It was a pivotal moment in both their lives. It was an anchoring moment for Avis. Neither of them could have known that Lindsey would abandon him, or that her parents would abandon him a short time later. But when they did, Avis had Alice Chen. She was steady. She was loving. She felt a connection to him. And perhaps as important as anything else, she would never leave him. She was a third-generation Watermiller, who wasn't going anywhere. She rubbed his hair and she was his rock, or at least one of them, through thick and thin.

As other teachers complained over the years that Avis Humphrey was lazy or didn't apply himself, it was Alice Chen who would defend him and explain that Avis was a fly-under-the-radar kind of kid. He was a boy who fed on solitude but enjoyed one-on-one company with people he was close to. Whether he had the talent to be the brightest boy in school, or star of the basketball team, or a rock-and-roll star was irrelevant. His early childhood had set the stage for solitude, a few close friends, books, fishing, and no desire for the limelight. Alice may not have seen all of that on the first morning when she rubbed his head, but through the years she watched him grow and evolve into a young man who was much more brilliant than anyone—with the exception of herself and Leo—could possibly understand. One thing she did know was Avis Humphrey was the first kindergarten student who had ever stopped and contemplated why she rubbed his head. At five years old, he stopped and mentally processed and questioned what was going on in his world. *Why is Mrs. Chen rubbing my head? What does it mean? Why would she rub my head when nobody else has ever done that to me?* Alice saw that he was different from other children, but her observations paled in comparison to his. For perhaps one of the few times in his young life, five-year-old Avis Humphrey felt the touch of someone who was kind and caring, and in time he would come to know this is how kind and loving and compassionate people treat others. Their bond was immediate.

Avis couldn't say she had become his mother figure, exactly. He held her in high esteem—and that was counter to every motherly trait he had ever experienced in his own family. His mother and grandmother, who were the only two mothers he ever really knew, did not inspire any warm, loving, or encouraging connection. Lindsey oozed of superficial physical love and she reeked of sexuality. In time Avis would realize she was simply a weak woman who gave in to her every personal desire, no matter the consequences, especially the consequences to other people. And her mother Judy was as hard and loving as a rock. He supposed that as much as she and Lindsey appeared different on the surface, they were cut from the same cloth. Both took care of themselves first and last, and they both went after whatever it was they wanted. Both had left Avis behind to fend for himself.

Alice he decided when he was in the fourth grade, was his guardian angel. She and Burt Chen had been married for six years and they had yet to have any children of their own. Avis became her surrogate son. She rubbed his head from kindergarten through eighth grade, when he headed off to high school. Even then, if she saw him around town she either fought the urge to rub his head, or she rubbed it as if he were her eternal little boy.

After he won the Powerball drawing, he sat on the ticket for a couple of weeks without telling anyone. Once he finally accepted that he was going to have to ask for help, he knew there was only one person to go to.

So, when Savannah asked, "Why Alice? And why give it to her?" it was perhaps the easiest question Avis had ever answered.

"She's my guardian angel. I knew she would know what to do with it."

"And what makes her your guardian angel?" Savannah asked, presuming there was a story to be told.

"God, I suppose. I mean… that's where angels come from, right?" he answered and asked, almost as if he were giving a Leo response.

Savannah jotted a note and looked at the scruffy guy in front of her with the messed-up hair and the T-shirt wrinkled from sleeping in an old sleeping bag under the open sky, who was talking about God sending him an angel. She looked to Leo to see if he seemed intrigued or surprised by the conversation. He didn't. He chomped on another doughnut while tossing rocks at empty beer cans on the ground and paid no attention to either one of them.

"Next question," Avis blurted out as if he were in a hurry or had a schedule to keep. He didn't. Questions and fishing were the only two items on today's schedule. The first task was almost complete, as far as he was concerned.

CHAPTER EIGHTEEN

"So, tell me something about yourself that people would like to know," Savannah said. "Anything that might catch a reader's attention other than a country bumpkin who won and then gave away millions."

"I like to fish," he said with a shrug.

"Yeah. I was watching the news last night. The whole world knows you like to fish. There's got to be something more interesting than PBR and trout fishing."

"No, not really. I'm a pretty basic guy." Avis shrugged again and watched the water go by. The whole world was so obsessed with him being an interesting character. It never dawned on anyone that he might just be who he was: boring, dull and mundane, and nothing more.

It was possible that Avis Humphrey was simply a small-town bumpkin who was in over his head and wanted to get rid of the winning ticket, but Savannah was beginning to doubt it.

"He's real smart," Leo threw in as he aimed a rock at another beer can. "Bulls-eye!" he yelled when the rock knocked the can over.

"Compared to who?" Savannah asked without making any attempt to mask her skepticism. Avis was content to let her doubt it, and hopefully get started with fishing.

"Everyone," Leo said, shaking his head back and forth. His next rock missed. He didn't bother to tell her that other than himself, and Alice, and perhaps his friend George, most folks considered Avis to be a pretty regular guy.

"Why don't I tell you about George?" Avis said, steering the conversation in another direction. "He's an interesting guy."

"Oh. George. That's good," Leo said. "You'll like George. He's cool."

"Okay. Who's George?"

"George was the first guy to take me fishing. He taught me how to fish when I was a kid. In fact, other than Leo, he's just about the only other guy, I've ever gone fishing with."

"And me," Savannah said.

"You don't count. You just kind of forced your way into the truck. You weren't really invited to fish with me."

"We've already had this discussion. You invited me." Point for Savannah.

Avis cringed when he was again reminded that he did indeed invite her to join them.

"More, please," she mumbled as she jotted.

"When I was six, there was this old black guy who walked by our house early in the morning just about every day, carrying a fishing pole. He always nodded at me and I always waved at him from the front steps of my grandparent's house. One day I got off the steps and followed him to the stream."

"How far was that from your house?"

"Oh… about a half-mile. Maybe less."

"Nobody cared if you wandered away like that?" she asked. "I'd have thought a six-year-old wandering off with a stranger would have been frowned upon." *Even in the Beckham house.*

"Shit," Leo chimed in. "It would have taken them a week to notice he was even gone. And then they would have just been mad, not worried." Savannah made another note and looked at Avis to continue.

"Anyway, I followed him for two or three days in a row and he never said more than a couple of words to me."

"What did he say? Do you remember?"

Avis laughed a bit. "I think the first thing he ever said was, I should go home before someone got worried about me. I still remember shaking my head and telling him that nobody ever worried about me." Avis looked toward the stream and smiled to himself as if he were recalling a life-changing moment. "Then he said, 'My name is George. What's yours?' I still remember looking up at him and announcing, 'I am Avis Humphrey.'"

"Damn…" he trailed off, lost in his thoughts for a few seconds. "I think it was the first time a grownup had ever asked me my name.

"I am Avis Humphrey," he said again, remembering how proud he had been to tell someone who he was.

"And he let you fish with him?"

"Oh. After about a week of following him to the stream and watching him fish, he walked past one day and nodded at me. I hopped off the steps and walked beside him without saying a word. I didn't walk behind him anymore. As we were walking, he handed me a fishing pole and asked if I could take care of it if he left it with me. We fished just about every day that summer, except for Sundays. George did church on Sundays. Still does."

"Did you bring home what you caught?"

Avis shook his head again. "Only once. Not a mistake I made twice. I thought the Beckhams would be impressed that I caught a thirteen-inch trout. That's big for around here. They got mad that I had brought home a stinky fish and made me throw it away. After that, I always gave them to George to take home. Or once in a while, on a Saturday, he made a little fire and we ate them right after we caught them. He taught me how to clean 'em, and then he taught me how to put them on a stick and cook them over a fire without a pan."

"How come he only cooked on Saturdays?"

"He had to be at work by noon or so on most days. We just fished for an hour or so and then he'd head off to work. On Saturdays, we made a day of it, most of the time."

"And what ever happened to George?"

"Still in town. He's old now, but we still go fishing every once in a while. Still cook 'em over an open fire."

"Do you suppose George would talk to me if I went to see him?" she asked while scribbling more notes and not looking up.

"He hangs out in the park most afternoons. Likes to listen to the Red Sox on his radio. If Leo introduces you, he'll probably talk to you," Avis answered. But he was beginning to lose interest in the Q & A session. He glanced toward his pole leaning against the tree, and then glanced at Leo who was still throwing rocks.

"And what if I introduce myself to him without Leo?"

"Then he'll probably politely ignore you. He's a loyal friend in a small town. Not likely to run his mouth like some of the other folks have."

Savannah scanned her notes and pondered what to ask next. Avis stood and stretched and looked at Leo.

"Who else are you close to?" she asked, ignoring that he had stood up and appeared to be done.

"Time to fish. You gotta catch another fish to ask more questions." He grabbed his pole and walked upstream. Leo hit one more can with a rock and jumped up, grabbed his pole and walked toward the water's edge too. His chatter started almost the exact moment his hook hit the water.

"Hey Avis."

"Yeah, Leo."

"What do you like better, Velcro or shoelaces?"

"Shoelaces. They're quieter," he answered softly and watched his line. Leo pondered the answer without making the connection.

Savannah sat and scanned her notes. She was already anxious to meet this George guy and get his version of the story. She wrote down a couple of questions to ask later and stuffed the notepad back into her pocket and stood up and looked at her pole.

She was determined to bait her own hook today. After two or three minutes of fighting with a squirming worm and jabbing her finger two more times, she finally decided it was more or less on the hook good enough to throw into the water. Two hours later she reeled in a six-inch trout. This time she did not hang it up in a tree. But while she may have mastered getting the worm on the hook, she had not yet mastered the art of getting a fish off a hook. She reeled it in and lifted it out of the water. It flopped around and gasped for oxygen on the three feet of line on the end of her pole. After staring at it for a few seconds while Avis watched her out of the corner of his eye, Leo went over and helped her take it off the hook.

"Seems like you got Avis luck," Leo said. "You both caught fish today and I haven't got a thing." He had been talking almost non-stop since he sat down. Savannah smiled and thanked him and walked over to the cooler and got a beer. Fishing was growing on her. She sat down on the soft, mossy bank of the stream and watched the water flow by, and smoked a cigarette while Avis continued to fish, and Leo continued to do whatever it was that he was doing. It couldn't really be called *fishing*. Savannah decided it probably wasn't Leo's talking that kept him from catching fish. It was more likely because he moved his pole around so much, the fish couldn't keep up with the ever-bobbing hook and worm. She wondered how many times over the years, fish had tried and failed to bite his moving hook. She smiled and watched her new friend and then turned and watched Avis. He was different. He was.... she couldn't quite put her finger on it. Avis Humphrey struck her as someone who, well, someone who might give a Powerball ticket away simply because he didn't want to be bothered with all the headaches that would come with the money. He sat and quietly watched the water and his line. He listened to the light breeze blow through the branches. He looked like a guy who was content with life. He was okay with his old truck. He was okay with his job as a mechanic. He was okay with his best friend who couldn't catch a fish at Sea World. About the only thing he was not okay with, was that he had to find a way to get rid of nine hundred sixty-seven million dollars, and to get rid of all the people who wanted to attach themselves to it.

Savannah took one last, long drag off her cigarette and then snuffed it out on a rock that was on the ground beside her. She tossed it onto the ground and began to stand up when Leo yelled at her.

"Pick that up!" Leo snapped. Savannah looked at him and froze halfway between sitting down and standing up.

"Pick it up," he snapped again and motioned toward the cigarette butt.

"Oh. I didn't—" She didn't get a chance to finish before he cut her off.

"Don't look like a dumpster here, does it?" he blurted out. She reached down to pick it up.

"Don't look like an ashtray, either, does it?" he added.

Avis smiled and watched her pick up the dirty butt and stick it into her pocket. Littering in his beloved woods of New Hampshire was one of the few things that got Leo riled up. That and paying too much for beer at the All American.

"What the hell are you doing?"

Now Savannah was completely confused.

"Who the hell puts a cigarette butt in their pocket?" Leo continued.

"Well, what would you like me to do with it?" she snapped back, finally regaining her balance.

"Throw it into the fire," he answered and shook his head back and forth.

Avis smiled and cast his line back out into the middle of the stream.

"Lunchtime and question time," she called out toward Avis. She reached into her pocket and threw the butt on the smoldering fire. He acted as if he hadn't heard her and ignored her call for more questioning. Her fishing ability had surprised him. He was going to have to come up with a better way to stave off her questions. At the very least, he was going to have to make her work harder. This was just getting too easy for her. He never meant for her to enjoy the process. Or at least he didn't think he had.

CHAPTER NINETEEN

Ernie suggested to Jeremy Higgins that he should go over and ask a few questions of the eye-patch guy, who seemed to be homesteading at the corner table where he had planted himself for the past week or so. Tom fiddled with his eye patch just enough to make sure nobody missed the fact he was wearing it, and then ran his fingers through his long, slightly greasy, dirty-blonde hair before taking a sip of his coffee and acknowledging the arrival of his next audience.

Jeremy was a twenty-something year old reporter who was less than worldly but slightly full of himself. He was getting paid little more than an internship from a small e-zine publication somewhere up near Syracuse. Ernie repeated his canned story about Tom being a cousin or something to Avis, and how he was probably the guy a smart reporter should be talking to. Jeremy took the bait and in less than fifteen seconds, he found himself sitting at the corner table with the small-town pirate.

"So, the guy behind the counter over there says you and Avis are pretty close. He thought you might be able to help me out." Jeremy had walked over, sat down, laid his notepad on the table and begun asking questions without so much as an introduction or a polite request to sit down at the table. Tom took it all in stride. He was becoming experienced at talking to reporters, so when Jeremy plopped his chubby ass in the wooden chair and dove headfirst into questions, the Pirate presumed he would be less skeptical than some of the old salty-dog reporters he had previously spoken with.

"Close? We're practically brothers," Tom answered matter-of-factly to the pudgy kid wearing the *Walking Dead* T-shirt under his wrinkled corduroy blazer with suede patches on the elbows. Tom glanced over at Ernie as if he were offended he hadn't let on how close he and Avis really were. He gave a wink to assure Ernie he'd get his $20 referral fee before he left.

"Oh. I didn't realize. Then I guess you *are* the right guy to be talking to," Jeremy added and flashed an unwarranted cocky grin. Tom shrugged and took another sip of coffee as Jeremy leaned forward and scribbled a note on his small pad. "Were you raised in the same house?" There was no small talk. No easygoing segue from, "Nice to meet you" to "Can you give me the big scoop?" In fact, there was no "Nice to meet you" at all, but Tom loved talking to the *Walking Dead* kind of guys. They were a captive audience who gobbled up everything thrown their way like giant pandas mindlessly chomping away on bamboo leaves.

"Nah. We lived in different homes, but we go way back."

"Did you go to the same school?" he asked as he scribbled. He barely looked up at the guy he was interviewing.

"Well, Avis is a few years younger than me, so we weren't ever in the same classes or anything like that."

"How much younger is he?" Jeremy continued with his barrage of questions as if he were playing a timed game of chess. Tom could almost see the kid's hand shoot out and smack the timer each time he blurted out another of his questions.

"Ohhhhh...." Tom began to intentionally slow down his already slow pace of talking, to build Jeremy's anticipation. "I guess he's, what?" He stopped talking and looked up at the ceiling with his one good eye and pretended he was trying to recall how old Avis was. "Twenty-six? I'm six years older than that." He reached up and adjusted the eye patch again. "Damn thing gets a little irritating sometimes," he said and looked over at Jeremy, hoping he would take the hint he wanted to talk about his eye, or lack thereof.

"Does Avis have any brothers or sisters?" Jeremy was not one who would have been referred to as having keen investigative instincts, and the clue as to where the conversation was being steered, was a wasted clue. Tom took another sip and looked at the kid who was still scribbling notes and not looking up. After five seconds of silence, Tom began to speak at the speed of a sloth.

"Sometimes I wear a glass eye, but not all the time. Never quite figured out why it irritates me on some days and not on others. Doesn't seem to have anything to do with the weather or anything like that, but it just kind of pains me to wear it… some days." He said this as he reached into his pocket and pulled out a small dark-green felt bag and began to tug at the silky drawstring. He poured the glass eye into his palm and showed it to the dull pudgy kid sitting at his table. He stretched out his hand as if he wanted Jeremy to take the glass ball that was sometimes inserted into his head.

Jeremy stared at the piece of glass without responding. Tom sat quietly with his outstretched hand, awaiting the appropriate response. After a few seconds of awkward silence, Jeremy's eyebrows rose as if to say, "Ooohhh. He wants to talk about his eye?"

"So, do you mind if I ask you about your eye?" he asked without reaching for it. "You know, how did it happen?" He was a bit slow, but the light in the attic was coming on and he realized the path to Avis was going to be through Tom. More specifically, it was going to be, through the story of Tom's eye.

"Well, I don't typically like talking about it all that much," he said with a ring of insincerity. "But I suppose everything tied to Avis is news these days. Least that's what the guy from the New York Times told me."

"Only if you feel comfortable," Jeremy added, with the words "New York Times" ringing in his ears.

"You ever been to that restaurant, Tavern on the Green?"

"The one in Central Park? No. Can't say I have. Though I've heard it's pretty legendary. At least it was before it closed."

"Heard it opened back up."

"Ahh," was the only thing that came to Jeremy's mind and he wondered if they had just wandered off track and were talking about something completely different now. Or was this somehow related to the eye or Avis or anything relevant.

"Shit. Everybody who was anybody ate there back in the day. You wouldn't believe the celebrities and politicians and such who used to come in and rub shoulders. Man, I could run a whole list of folks who I got pictures taken with back in my early twenties."

"Did you work there?"

"Mr.… what did you say your name was?" Tom had a captive audience and was feeling the moment.

"Jeremy," he said as he leaned forward.

Tom stopped talking as he opened a pack of Camel cigarettes and slowly peeled the foil back, pulled out a cigarette and put it into his mouth.

"No smoking in here, Tom," Ernie yelled from behind the counter.

"I'm not lighting it," he mumbled back and tossed the pack back onto the table. He had intended on lighting it before Ernie spoke up. "Yeah. I worked there for just over six years," he said, referring to the Tavern on the Green. He shook his head in disgust and stuffed the cigarette back into the opened pack. "Can't believe we can't smoke inside anymore," he mumbled and stared at the full pack sitting on the table.

"And what did you do there for work?"

"Me? Oh… I was a pastry chef," he said as if he had almost forgotten what they were talking about, or that they were talking at all.

"You were telling me about your eye?" Jeremy said, reminding him that they had been having a discussion.

"Oh yeah," he answered and took a deep sigh before starting back into the conversation. "My eye. Well, we used to create this fancy dessert pastry sort of thing that was dropped into hot oil while it was still frozen solid. Kind of a signature dessert that had a crunchy hot pastry crust on the outside and was still almost frozen in the center after it was cooked. Then we topped it with different sauces, depending on the time of year and such. Man, it was good." He picked up the cigarettes again and looked as if he were pondering lighting one up despite what Ernie had told him.

"And your eye?" Jeremy added in an effort to keep him focused.

"Well, one night I was cooking up a storm. The place was packed, and the kitchen was going crazy and I was out straight like a madman from hell. I don't know if maybe the oil was too hot, or if there was maybe a chunk of ice on the pastry or something. You can't just be dropping ice into a deep fryer full of boiling oil without being careful, you know."

"I presume not," Jeremy answered as if he could find his way around a kitchen. The truth was he didn't actually presume anything about cooking since he was a microwave oven and pizza-ordering kind of guy.

"So, I had about fifteen desserts in one stage of preparation or another, and I dropped the pastry into the fryer, and that was that." He pulled the same cigarette out of the pack and put it into his mouth one more time and shot a scowl toward Ernie. By this time even Jeremy wished he would just light the damn thing and be done with it.

"I'm sorry. I'm not really knowledgeable about cooking stuff. What was what?"

"Jesus Christ! It exploded!" he snapped loud enough for the entire diner to momentarily look toward their table. Tom glanced around and slid down in his chair a bit. "Sorry 'bout that," he said, a bit more reserved. "The pastry...," he said with a shrug. "The pastry exploded. The oil exploded. Shot all up into the air and went all over the place. Got some burns here on my arm." He pointed at his arm but didn't roll up his sleeve to show the scars. "Got some pretty bad burns up on my head, but they're hidden now by my hair. And worst of all, one big boiling drop of hot oil splatted right into my eye, and that was that. I lost my eye and Brad Pitt didn't get his pastry."

"Damn, man. That's horrible," Jeremy said. He felt himself squirm in his chair as he pictured the hot oil hitting Tom's eye. Then he glanced down at the glass eye still sitting on top of the pouch on the center of the table.

"Damn shame all the way around if you ask me. I lost an eye. He lost dessert. I didn't get a picture to add to my wall of fame, and the Tavern on the Green closed down for a short while after that. Damned shame all the way around."

"Do you still cook?"

"Nah. Got a pretty big settlement. Now I've got an emu farm just outside of town." They sat in silence for a few more seconds as Tom allowed Jeremy a few moments to absorb the story about the restaurant, his eye, and most importantly, the emu farm. "Damned shame," he added and took another sip of his coffee. Jeremy had stopped scribbling and sat looking at the glass eye. He shuddered at the thought of the oil and the damage it had caused.

"Well, I don't mean to be insensitive, but do you think you could get me in touch with Avis?" he asked, feeling guilty about diverting from the tragic saga. "You know, so I could be the guy to break the big story and all?" In his mind, he thought he had demonstrated a completely smooth and acceptable transition.

"I could probably give you a little assistance, but you know what?"

"What's that, Tom?"

"I sure could use a little publicity for my emu farm, if you know what I mean. We could kind of do each other a favor, so to speak. PR for me. A big story for you. What do you think?"

"Emus huh? I'll have to run it by my editor, but it sounds reasonable." The truth was the editor would print anything that was fairly well written and was interesting enough that someone online might read it. She'd probably print anything about Avis Humphrey, period. He was *the* big human-interest story of the moment.

Two hours later Jeremy had everything he needed for his story about Tom, the tragic chef/emu farmer and most importantly, cousin to Avis Humphrey. That afternoon the story was written and submitted. It came out before nightfall. The following morning, he met Tom again and got directions to a bait shop on the west side of New Found Lake in Hebron, New Hampshire. The drive would be less than two hours and when he got there he was supposed to ask Paul, the proprietor, for directions to the Rearick camp. That's where he'd likely find Avis Humphrey.

"And who are the Rearicks?" Jeremy asked again, as he stood up to leave the Pirate's table.

"They're probably the closest family Avis has ever had," he answered. "Other than me," he added without looking up while he buttered his biscuit.

CHAPTER TWENTY

When he first met Savannah a few days ago, she was just another reporter. A young and attractive reporter, but nonetheless, she was just one more person looking to stick her nose into his life with no regard for him or his friends. He presumed if she had her way, she would turn his world upside down to see what shook out. Then she would write a story that would likely be only half-truths. Once she had bled him for all of the details she could find or make up, she would climb back into her broken-down piece-of-shit car and head back to wherever it was she had come from. That was his initial reaction to her and he didn't like it, or her, one little bit. Worming her way into his fishing trip hadn't helped her case either. Last but not least, the final straw was that she was beginning to grow on Avis—and it happened so quickly he wasn't sure how it came to be, or how he felt about it. He still clung to the theory that she had forced her way into his truck, and he couldn't bring himself to admit he had accidentally invited her to join them. What bothered him the most was that he was in the midst of an internal battle as to whether he should send her packing or ask her out on a date.

"So, Leo said this was the first time you ever bought a Powerball ticket. Obviously, you don't want the money, so why would you buy a ticket in the first place?" Savannah asked the question as she sat on a log and munched on a cheese stick. There was no recorder and no notepad in her lap. To be honest, she didn't think he would give her anything worth writing. He had barely given her anything to write about up until now.

Avis sat on his log directly across from her and pondered how to best answer her question.

Leo sat on the tailgate of the pickup and watched both of them. He had never been with someone while they were being interviewed, and he found the question-and-answer sessions to be more entertaining than he would have thought. He was usually the one asking all the questions.

A smile came to the corners of Avis's mouth as he pondered Savannah's question.

* * *

It had all started off innocently enough. On the day Avis bought the ticket, he had worked until noon. When he got off work, he swung by and picked up Leo from his mom's house and the two spent the afternoon fishing. Nothing out of the ordinary. Avis caught four trout, but they were all small and so he threw them back. Leo was on a question binge the entire time they fished. Perhaps more accurately said, the whole time Avis fished. Leo almost always went home empty-handed when he was in his Curious George mode, and that particular day was no exception to the rule.

"Hey Avis. Who invented the first gear sprocket?"

"Hey Avis. What do you think happened to the first guy that tried to fly?"

"Hey Avis. Why do you suppose some folks like big houses and shiny cars and others like old trucks and cabins in the woods?"

"Hey Avis. What do you think the first cheese tasted like?"

"Hey Avis. This whole evolution thing, how did we get from being polliwogs to people and why are there still polliwogs if they evolved into people?"

"Hey Avis..."

Leo's questions had become a sort of white noise in Avis's world. White noise that required a response. It was a comforting sound that had been a part of Avis's world for almost as far back as he could remember. Most of the time Avis knew the answers. Every once in a while, though, Leo would hit him with a question he had to give serious thought to. Or even do some research on when he got back home. The research was for Avis, not for Leo. Leo always forgot unanswered questions just as quickly as they came into his head. Question asked, question answered or not answered, question gone. Either way, Leo moved onto the next thought and didn't carry unanswered questions along with him.

After fishing they headed to Avis's trailer, but first they stopped by the New All-American Market. When the owners named the market back in 2001 they thought the name sounded good. Now, over fifteen years later, the word *New* no longer fit, but it was on the sign and license and all that stuff, so the *New* remained, even though almost all the locals just called it, The All American.

Avis did not call it The All American, new or old. He called it Carmens and he was well aware he paid at least a dollar more a six-pack to buy beer at Carmens than he paid at the Shop & Save a mile up the road. But Carmen did not work a mile up the road and he gladly paid the extra dollar many, many times over.

Leo got why he did it, being that Carmen was... Carmen, but he wasn't sure if he would pay extra for beer just to see her. The upside for him was he rarely paid for the beer whether they bought it at the Shop & Save or at Carmens.

Avis pulled the truck in front of the store and shut off the engine. The truck sputtered for another twenty seconds before going silent.

"Gonna pay the big bucks again, huh?" Leo asked, shaking his head back and forth.

"You know... I imagine she's like fifty-year-old scotch."

"What's that supposed to mean?"

"Dark and sweet and raspy and probably more than I could handle," Avis said as he looked through the advertisement-laden window to catch a glimpse of her.

"You ever had fifty-year-old scotch?"

"No. But I will someday. Just to see what's it's like."

"And Carmen."

"Hmmm. Not yet, but life is full of surprises. You just never know, do you," he mumbled as he continued to peer between the stickers that read "Budweiser on Sale" and "Fresh Coffee Every Day" In reality though, Avis did know, or at least he suspected. The scotch was a maybe. But Carmen? He just never saw it happening. It's not like he'd never been with good-looking women or anything like that. It wasn't even as if he hadn't been with at least one or two who were out of his league. He had a one-nighter with Betty

Dochery after she left her husband. She and Mr. Dochery eventually reconciled, but not before she and Avis had some fun times together. Then there was Renee' Abachaun. They spent a few months together before parting ways. She eventually married an attorney, but again, not before she and Avis wrinkled some sheets together. And of course, there was Agnes. She was beautiful and sexy, but so bat-shit crazy she kept Avis constantly vigilant for her rapid and drastic mood swings that could lead anywhere from her moving out, to the two of them having hot wild sex. They had an on-again, off-again thing going for a few years now. Leo was just plain scared of her.

Then there was Carmen. She was in a whole different league from the "good-looking" women of his past. Avis was pretty sure if he had closed his eyes before they met and tried to picture the perfect woman, physically speaking anyway, he would have envisioned Carmen Marden. She was small, but a strong-looking woman with brown eyes that sparkled, and shoulder-length black hair that flowed like a river of silk. Mostly, she just had "it," whatever that might be.

The first time they met, she took his breath away. He walked into the store a couple of years back and she said, "Hi. Welcome to The All American," in a raspy voice that stopped him dead in his tracks. After he had grabbed his beer and chips and wandered to the counter, her perfume swept over him like a warm breeze on a cold day. Carmen looked at him and waited for him to say something, but only incomprehensible stammering came out of his mouth.

"You okay?" she asked, as if this had been the first time this had ever happened to her. It wasn't. There had been plenty of young men over the years who were awe-struck with her. Avis was just the latest in a long line.

"Uh-huh," was all he managed to mumble.

In time, he came to understand that her voice, her looks, and her perfume were just tangibles. Those were the things that could be heard and seen and smelled... and touched, if he were ever so lucky as to touch her. But they were not what drew him to her. Two years later, he still could not adequately explain the magnetism, but it had only grown stronger in time. He had come and gone hundreds of times since that first visit. Each time he left as hopeless as a seventh-grade boy falling in love for the very first time. Carmen couldn't decide if his infatuation was incredibly romantic or extremely pathetic.

"Avis. Where's your shadow?" Carmen asked, glancing up from the receipts she was flipping through as he entered the store.

"Out in the truck. Making sure nobody steals it."

She laughed out loud at the absurdity that someone would steal his truck. She doubted they would take it if he had left the keys in the engine.

"You think that might happen?" she asked with a raised eyebrow.

"Anything's possible." He was implying, as Carmen was well aware, that Avis and Carmen were possible. It was much more likely his truck would be stolen than the two of them being a couple. Carmen didn't see it in the stars either. Or the bed, or anywhere else. Avis couldn't get the thought out of his mind.

He grabbed a twelve-pack of PBR and set it on the counter. His outward composure had improved with time even if his inner demeanor was still hopeless.

"That going to be all?" She leaned forward and planted her palms onto the counter so he couldn't help looking directly down her shirt. She couldn't help herself. He had been in love with her since the moment they met, and she knew it. She was so naturally flirtatious that she felt compelled to keep the bait on his hook. Her perfume swept over him one more time and he felt his knees go weak.

"What else you have in mind?" Avis asked, not expecting a response.

"You're going to buy a Powerball ticket, aren't you? Over nine hundred million tonight."

"I dunno. You think I might get lucky? You know, if I buy a Powerball ticket."

"You just never know, Avis. You just never know," she said with a wink as she tapped the back of his hand with the tip of her index fingernail.

Avis did know, but he bought the ticket anyway. A Quick-pick. Carmen finished ringing him up and he picked up the ticket and his beer.

"Hope you get lucky, Avis," she called out to him as he pushed the door open. He walked back to the drivers-side door looking at the ticket and calculating his odds.

"You're pathetic, man," Leo said as Avis threw it into reverse. "Pathetic."

Avis just smiled and drove away with the Powerball ticket sticking out of his T-shirt pocket.

* * *

Savannah was still waiting for a response as Avis sat on the log with a smile on his face.

"You okay?" she asked as she nibbled away on her cheese stick and waited for his answer. "Why did you buy the ticket in the first place?" she asked him again. Avis sat with a widening grin on his face as he stared down at his beer.

"Carmen," Leo called out from the back of the truck. "Carmen Marden is the reason why that pathetic sap bought the ticket. Couldn't help himself."

"And who is she?" Savannah asked and reached into her pocket for her notepad. She surprised herself when she felt her face flush at the thought of Avis and Carmen, whoever she was, being together.

"Leo will take you by the store to meet her on the way home tonight." He didn't elaborate further. He pretended he didn't notice she had looked irritated about him and Carmen, but he had to admit, if only to himself, what he was feeling for Savannah was something he hadn't experienced before. He had never known a woman who got under his skin and made him want to spend more time with her, both at the same time. He thought she was a bit like red pepper. No matter how hot the last bite was, he still craved another. Whatever was happening, he was glad Savannah was becoming a part of his life. And if she was trying to conceal her jealousy, she wasn't doing a good job at it.

CHAPTER TWENTY-ONE

Tom the Pirate had become a minor celebrity at the diner, with a little help from Ernie. Nobody seemed to be paying attention that he had shared at least a half-dozen different versions of what had happened to his missing eye. On the upside, any reporter who ventured to his table, sat down, and eventually asked about the eye patch was fortunate to get an original story. None of them had felt the need to verify whatever eye tragedy he had shared with them. The truth was most of the stories had been published online in small e-zines, and they were happy to have anything to report, other than Avis Humphrey liked to go fishing and was apparently on an extended fishing trip somewhere out in the woods of New Hampshire. Either nobody noticed, or nobody cared about all the mismatched versions of Tom's eye tragedy. All that most of them knew, was they had all been sent to Watermill to get a story on Avis Humphrey and for almost an entire week, Avis had been hidden away from the world. There was a somewhat substantiated rumor that the winning ticket had been given to Alice Chen, but she also seemed to have fallen off the face of the earth. For the moment, other than half of Watermill suddenly claiming to be Avis's potential father, Tom was about the most interesting thing going.

"How'd you lose your eye?" Gia asked as she sat down at his table, with her cameraman positioned with his back against the window to get the best lighting. Gia Thompson was the same woman who had pressed Merle Humphrey for Avis information five days earlier. In her mind, Tom's sincerity rang truer than Merle's. His story seemed genuine, with no hidden agenda and no quest to rake in millions.

"Got attacked by a cat," he blurted out and then left the statement hanging in the air as if those five words painted a clear picture for all to see.

"Really?" she answered, as if she expected to hear something like "Got shot out with a BB gun when I was a kid."

"You mean like a bobcat or mountain lion kind of cat?" she asked with her head slightly tilted, and with a fake look of concern on her face. Her blonde hair perfectly framed her Botoxed face and her ultra-white straight teeth, popped against her ruby-red-painted lips. Her skin was flawless and had been made up to perfection. And she had long ago mastered the art of feigning concern—to the same skill level that Lindsey Beckham had mastered backseat sex.

"Nah. It was just one of them fluffy white Persian cats. Damn thing always laid around on the back of the sofa at an old girlfriend's. About as worthless as most cats, I suppose."

Gia momentarily froze and searched for where to go with "a fluffy white cat took out the eye of her small-town idiot" story. She looked at her cameraman, who shrugged, and then she pulled herself together. "We'll edit before sending," she said and turned back to Tom, who was stuffing an oversized biscuit into his mouth in the middle of the interview.

"Biscuit?" he asked, blowing crumbs from his mouth. He held the plate up to Gia; she pretended not to hear him.

"Well, that sounds terrible. How did it take out your eye?"

"I kept blowing puffs of air into its face because it just kept staring at me."

All Gia could think was, *Ahhh. A battle of wits and the cat won.* She silently held the microphone in front of Tom's face.

With biscuit crumbs stuck to his whiskers, he said, "The woman I was dating... we were already on the skids, and I wasn't trying too hard to stay on her good side. Anyway, she kept saying, 'You better stop blowing in Tabby's face.' Tabby was the thing's name. Anyway, she said to stop, which just made me do it more—and the damn cat just sat there and stared at me like some furry little statue."

"Oh. This doesn't sound good," Gia added, knowing nothing else that could be said.

"Anyway, I looked at the woman with a big old shit-eating grin on my face and then turned back to blow another puff and that little piece-of-crap cat took one quick swipe. Then it just sat there like a statue again. Happened quicker than shit."

"You're joking, right?" She presumed this small-town hick was pulling the leg of the pretty little newsgirl.

"Wish I was. At first it just hurt and then after a while Darlene, that's the woman I was on the outs with, said we'd better go to the hospital. So we did, and the doctor did all kinds of stuff, but in the end, I wound up with a glass eye and a patch."

"What happened to the cat?" Gia asked. It sounded like a pointless question, but the truth was there was simply nothing else left to ask.

"Darlene and the furry little fucker went one way and I went the other and that was that."

"Does she live here in Watermill?" The truth was Gia had given up on the interview, but Watermill was small. She didn't want to be known as the bitch that snubbed Avis's cousin, so she continued as if she thought there was something to be salvaged from the conversation.

"Nah. I was living in Kansas City for a couple of years. That's where we met. Suppose she's still there making some guy miserable, and the cats probably still sitting on the back of that sofa being as worthless as ever, maybe staring at some other unsuspecting victim."

Gia motioned for the cameraman to shut off the camera and sat and looked at the weird guy with the eye patch. She wasn't quite sure what to do with the story. She certainly wasn't going to try to confirm the story with some woman up in Kansas and she couldn't air the profanity-laden recording. In the end, she stood up and shook his hand. "Thank you for that amazing story, Tom."

"Did I tell you I have an emu farm?" he added as she turned and walked away. She pretended once again she didn't hear him.

On the six o'clock news she stood in front of Ernie's and gave the scoop of how a small army of reporters were searching for Alice and Avis. She mentioned how Merle had come out of the shadows, for those who had missed yesterday's news, and then she brought up Avis's cousin, Tom, with a picture of him in the corner of the screen. She referred to him as "Avis's cousin who lost his eye in a tragic accident with a wildcat and who now owns an emu farm," and said nothing more about him.

CHAPTER TWENTY-TWO

The Watermill Inn Hotel was marketed as the best 2-Star hotel in Watermill, New Hampshire. It was also marketed as the only hotel in Watermill, New Hampshire. Back in Syracuse, Jeremy Higgins wouldn't have normally stayed in anything less than a 4-Star, or in a jam, maybe a 3-Star. His first night in the Watermill Inn, the alarm clock started buzzing loudly at midnight, and again at 1:00 a.m. and then one more time at 2:00 a.m. At 2:01, he had a flash of brilliance and unplugged the clock. At 3:00 he took the batteries out. At 5:15, as the sun began to sneak through the thin linen curtains covering the eastern wall window, a rooster in somebody's backyard, maybe in the Inn's backyard, began to crow.

The hotel was one of those places where the mattresses weren't dirty, but they were cheap, lumpy, and uncomfortable. The blankets were not quite thick enough to take the chill from out of the room and when Jeremy turned up the heat, the room quickly warmed up to a toasty 85 degrees and kept climbing. Once he realized the thermostat didn't work, he got out of bed and shut it off. Twenty minutes later he was wrapping himself up as best as he could, with the skimpy blanket and fighting off the chill once again. After three nights of pure misery, he hoped he had just spent his last night in the chilly-hot, lumpy, clock-less room with sketchy Internet… and a rooster.

Yesterday's meeting with Tom the Pirate was, at the least, entertaining. At best, Tom had provided a promising lead. Today, Jeremy felt a sliver of hope that he might actually find a story worthy of publication for the first time since arriving in the nearly sleepless town. He felt optimistic that he would get enough information, from either Avis or the Rearicks, to piece together something interesting enough for him to submit and use as a hall pass out of this town so he could return to New York. Three days in Watermill had been the slowest three days of his life.

Even in his exhausted state of mind, Jeremy was one of those people who believed he created his own positive energy. In fact, he read daily positive-attitude blogs that made him certain of it. So, as he stood in the parking lot with drizzling rain falling down onto his pumpkin-like head, he focused on cleaning yesterday's black flies off his windshield while he listened to *Florida Georgia Line*, '*Cruise*' through his ear buds. He danced in place and wiped the driver's side windshield with a rag and then danced to the other side of the car and repeated.

Fifteen minutes later he was headed up the highway with *Bruno Mars* cranked up on the cars stereo as he embraced what he was certain was going to be *the day*. The road wound through the hills and woods and along the banks of a stream that sometimes-splashed white water onto the river rocks and at other times was as serenely calm and glassy as a mirror. He drove and sang and ate his way along, and occasionally glanced over and imagined what Avis was going to look like. He pictured him standing on the riverbank, reeling in trout with a fly rod in his hand, all the while looking attractive and manly like some fisherman on the cover of a Trout Fisherman magazine. That was at 9:30 a.m., when the day was young.

He got lost twice along the way, not because the directions were all that complicated, but because Jeremy, was Jeremy. He lost himself in the music. He ate, gobbling down a half-dozen doughnuts, washing them down with coffee that had as much cream in it, as coffee. And when he occasionally had cell reception, he made calls to his gamer friends back in Syracuse to discuss the next epic battle between the make-believe electronic warriors they had created in their make-believe electronic world. It was almost 2:00 in the afternoon before he finally found the bait shop tucked into a hidden cove on New Found Lake.

He thought it was wise to not share why he was looking for the Rearick camp and tip anyone off that the now legendary Avis Humphrey might be hiding out in the area. So, with the same sharp wit that got his journey going in the first place, he came up with the brilliant story that he was trying to find his cousin's camp but was unclear on their directions.

"If they're your cousins, then why don't you just give them a call and get directions from them?" the old guy in the flannel shirt and khakis asked with his pipe hanging out from his mouth. Jeremy looked blankly at him and said nothing but "Uhhh…"

"You all right there son?" he asked and blew a puff of smoke out from his pipe. Jeremy couldn't tell if the old geezer was just giving him a hard time or was he actually curious about why he just didn't call the Rearicks. Either way, he didn't have an answer.

"Uhhh…" he responded again.

The flannel-shirt old man stood behind the counter without saying another word and watched the chubby kid in the corduroy blazer with elbow patches walk back to his car mumbling something to himself as he closed the car door.

Two hours later, after stopping at a small general store in the middle of nowhere and a gas station that may or may not have been further into the middle of nowhere, and then finally after knocking on a couple of camp doors, Jeremy pulled into the driveway of an old rundown camp. A Subaru wagon and a Mini Cooper were parked at different angles in the eighteen-inch-tall grass, as if the drivers had no idea where the driveway was when they pulled in and abandoned their vehicles at least six months ago. Then there was a 1990-something Chevy station wagon. It was the only car that looked as if it had been driven recently and was actually parked in the dirt, not the grass. As usual, it didn't stick out in Jeremy's brain that the two newer vehicles looked broke down while the dinosaur one looked like it was the go-to car.

He climbed out of his car and stretched out the kinks after his almost full day of driving around the New Hampshire wilderness. Then he brushed off the remnants of the last doughnut he had just eaten a minute or two before he had finally discovered the Rearick's camp, a camp Jeremy thought looked to be hidden away as if someone never wanted it to be found in the first place.

He wandered up to the porch, looked down at the rotten wooden steps, hesitated, then raised his head and looked around. The only thing missing from the porch seemed to be a warning sign telling visitors to, "Enter At Your Own Risk." He stepped over the bottom step that looked rotten enough that it might not hold his weight. As his foot touched down on the second step, it almost went through the wood, and he quickly climbed the last three steps hoping he wouldn't fall through. The porch looked in no better condition than the steps he had just climbed. Once he reached the front door, he took a deep breath, stood up straight, and knocked on the wooden frame. Then he waited as he listened to what sounded like a pack of dogs scurrying, yapping, barking, and stampeding from every corner of the camp toward the front door. Like a pack of lemmings running toward a cliff, the first couple of barking dogs reached the door and stopped. A split second later another batch arrived and plowed the first dogs into the door. More followed repeating the running, plowing and colliding routine.

A woman who looked to be somewhere between seventy and a hundred and five opened the door with a cigarette hanging from her mouth. At least ten dogs of varying sizes were stacked up behind and around her clamoring for the screen door to be unlatched. She opened the door and looked at him through the rusty screen without saying a word. Jeremy looked at her and then down at the pack of dogs. He waited for her to say something, but she just stared at him without uttering so much as a syllable. Then she glanced at his car with a curious look, as if it were the first car, other than the three already parked there that had ever shown up in her driveway. She looked back at him, at his messy hair and chubby face. She inspected his wrinkled corduroy jacket with elbow patches and his Walking Dead T-shirt that still held remnants of the six doughnuts he had stuffed himself with. Then she blew a long stream of smoke from the side of her mouth that wasn't holding the cigarette, and still said nothing.

"Mrs. Rearick?" Jeremy finally managed to mutter.

"Yeah," she gruffly answered, with the cigarette hanging from her lips and looking like it was about to fall to the ground.

"Mrs. Rearick, my name is Jeremy Higgins and I'm doing a news story on Avis Humphrey."

"Who?" she snapped, and once again blew smoke out the side of her mouth.

"Your nephew? Avis Humphrey?" he asked, as the first inkling of doubt began to creep into his sugar- and caffeine-filled brain. For the first time since he had sat down with the Watermill Pirate, it began to dawn on him that perhaps pirates were not to be trusted.

"Never heard of him," was all she said as she turned and swung the door closed with a slam. Loud coughing came from inside the door and faded away as she walked through the camp with the pack of yapping wolves following her. Jeremy stood like a statue and stared at the light-blue door with chipped paint and a faded Christmas wreath hanging at eye level. Then he glanced down at the worn-out grey welcome mat with faded orange lettering and pondered the irony of its message. Two minutes later he was still staring down at "Welcome," while wondering what to do next.

Just as he took a deep breath and looked up at the ceiling in resignation at his failure to gather Avis information, the barking, rumbling stampede sounds from inside surged toward the front door once again. He was still frozen in place when the door swung open. This time the dogs did not stop inside. This time they charged past the unlatched screen door, banging it up against him as they squeezed, pushed, and climbed over each other to get out and onto the porch to greet the clueless stranger who continued to stand stupidly in the same spot. All the dogs, except for one short, fat, grayish-black one, took a quick sniff and headed out into the yard. The short, fat, grayish-black colored one stopped at Jeremy's feet, looked up at him, momentarily inspected him, and then lifted his left leg and peed on Jeremy's red high-top Converse sneaker before waddling his way out into the yard to join his friends.

Jeremy was no longer staring at "Welcome." He was looking down at his wet shoe when Mrs. Rearick's hoarse voice snapped him out of his trance.

"You still here?" she asked.

"Uh-huh," he mumbled back, when nothing else came to mind.

"Not really your day, is it?" she asked, looking down at his wet shoe.

"No. Not having a good day... week." He added "week" when he thought about how the past few minutes hadn't been all that different from the way the rest of the week had gone for him.

"So, you're looking for Avis Humphrey, huh?"

"Uh-huh," he answered again, not able to snap out of his dazed trance.

"And someone said he would be here?"

"Uh-huh," he said, finally looking up at her. "Tom Palmer sent me here."

"Never heard of him," she said, just as she had said about Avis.

"Tall skinny guy? One eye? Wears an eye patch?" Jeremy rattled out hoping something would ring a bell.

"Ohhh yeah. Saw him in the paper yesterday. Seems like quite a character," she said, finally giving Jeremy a ray of hope.

"So, you know him?" Jeremy asked, perking up with aspirations of getting his story and then getting out of New Hampshire.

"Nope," was the one-word answer she blurted out as she lit another cigarette and stuck the lighter into the back pocket of her baggy faded blue jeans. There was no way for either of them to know that Tom the Pirate had picked the Rearicks name and address at random from the phone book. He needed to send the kid somewhere to find his story. New Found Lake seemed as good a place as any. And the Rearicks camp was likely just as good or bad as any other address.

The door slammed, the dogs barked, and Jeremy turned to leave. That's when he noticed an old guy sitting in an old wooden lawn chair in the middle of the un-mowed yard. The dogs were yapping all around him as he gulped on a Corona. He leaned down and mumbled something to one of the dogs. A flash of hope reignited in Jeremy's mind and he scooted down the steps and out into the yard. Halfway between the porch and where the old guy was sitting, he stopped dead in his tracks. The dogs had chased each other to the backside of the camp, but the old guy was still sitting and mumbling at something. That's when Jeremy realized he was talking to a broken-down lawnmower that was sitting in the deep grass directly in front of him.

On his way back to Syracuse, Jeremy pulled into Starbucks for another cup of caffeine. He asked for a Double Chocolate Chip Frappuccino with a double shot of expresso and whipped crème and wandered to an empty table. Other than the pirate story he had submitted, he was heading back home empty-handed, so he decided to cheat and Google *Avis Humphrey,* to see what he could plagiarize. He read what the entire world already knew. Avis won the Powerball, he apparently gave the ticket to a woman named Alice Chen whom nobody could find, and he liked fishing. There was almost nothing else written. That is, there was almost nothing else written, unless

Jeremy counted the nine stories about Avis's cousin who had lost his eye in the Gulf War, or while cooking with hot oil, or when he was attacked by a pelican in Daytona, or when his neighbor tried to shoot an apple off his head with a slingshot, or when he got hit with a broken beer bottle in a biker bar fight somewhere in Arkansas, or when he was gored by a bull in Pamplona, Spain, or when something went terribly wrong while scuba diving and the depth pressure somehow caused his eye to pop out. And last but not least, while Tom visited the Philadelphia zoo when he was eleven years old, and a monkey threw feces at him and caused a severe infection, eventually leading to the loss of his eye. The only thing the stories all had in common was Tom had only one eye, and he was very close to his cousin, Avis Humphrey. And of course, there was his emu farm on the outskirts of town. It was likely becoming the most publicized emu farm in the nation, if not in the entire world.

"Aw, man...." Jeremy said in one long, drawn-out word as rain began to pick up outside and he sucked on the straw of his whipped-crème-topped coffee.

Twenty minutes later he was back on the road to Syracuse with one wet shoe and no story to turn in. The sleepy little town of Watermill, New Hampshire had defeated him in less than a week. He surrendered in shame and went home to do battle with an animated princess warrior who threw lightning bolts and could kill other warriors with toxic kisses.

Chapter Twenty-Three

The press pool at Ernie's surged at first, then thinned, but over the past day or two it seemed like it had rejuvenated, as more and more reporters arrived as replacements for the ones who had recently left. They all asked the same questions and got the same answers. A few had heard reports that Leo and Savannah were hanging out with Avis, but they didn't have any luck getting information on the where. A couple tried to follow Leo around town, but he always took them on a wild-goose chase, usually to nowhere. Sometimes after an hour or two of driving around the outskirts of town, they ended up back at the diner where their original journey had started. Things were a bit quiet today, and nobody was bothering Leo and Savannah for the moment.

"Don't let his run-down truck and worn-out clothes fool you," Leo said, presuming Savannah hadn't yet been convinced of who Avis Humphrey really was. "And don't think he's a mechanic just because he doesn't know how to do anything else; he's a mechanic because he likes fixing things. And mostly, don't think because he's quiet, he doesn't know stuff. Avis is flat out, the smartest guy I ever met. That includes the smart kids from school and the teachers who thought they were smarter than he was. I'm guessing that includes you, too," Leo added as he nodded his head toward Savannah.

She smiled and nodded back and tried to hide her look of skepticism. She believed Leo thought Avis was smart, but she doubted he was anywhere near the Einstein level Leo was praising him to be.

"Do you know he got straight A's in every class until high school? That's when he decided to stop doing it."

"Stop doing what?" Savannah asked, still not buying into the boy-genius story.

"Making the grades and studying things so he could grow up to be an accountant or cellphone-store manager or something like that," he said, apparently believing those were jobs held by intellectual elites. "One day when we were freshmen, he looked at me and said, 'I think I'm going to stop getting straight A's.' And he did."

Savannah listened and took notes as she and Leo sat at the table a few feet away from the eye-patch guy at Ernie's and ate hamburgers for lunch.

"What did he get for grades after that?"

"C's. He got straight C's, on purpose. Not one A. Not one B. Not one D. Not one F. C's, C's and more C's."

"Maybe high school was just harder than middle school. Do you think it's possible he just couldn't keep making good grades?"

Leo smiled and recounted a time when he was sitting on the couch watching a rerun of the original Terminator movie. The cyborg version of Arnold was crushing everything in sight and while Leo stuffed popcorn into his mouth, Avis sat in the corner of the living room with headphones on and read a thick book from one of his classes. In the three hours it took Leo to watch Arnold Swatchzenager destroy half a city, Avis had read about two hundred pages in his American history book. "And when I say he read two hundred pages, I don't mean he skimmed over it," he told Savannah. "He read it and he remembered it." A few days later, when they went fishing, Leo asked him about what he had read, and Avis nearly recited the text, at least all the important parts. The following Monday he took the test and got a C. Always a C. Leo got a C too, but only because Avis had told him what he needed to know for the test.

"What do you suppose makes him so smart?" Savannah asked, still not buying into Avis being as smart as Leo claimed.

"Well, I asked Avis the same question a few years back." Leo tried to talk and swallow his hamburger at the same time. "He said he must have inherited it from his father, because he damn sure didn't get it from Lindsey. His exact words were, 'I damn sure didn't inherit it from Lindsey.'"

"So, Merle Humphrey is smart, too?"

"Shit. That miserable old fucker is about as smart as he is nice. And he kicked Avis to the curb and made sure the whole damn town knew Avis wasn't his kid, back about twenty years ago. Never gave him the time of day since then. Merle made sure everyone in town knew he didn't owe Lindsey or Avis a damn penny. Well... that's the way it was up until the big news broke. Then lightning or something must have struck him and all of a sudden, he grew a big heart and believed maybe there was some sort of family resemblance between him and his long-lost son, after all. Nah. Ain't no way in hell that dumb old tub of lard is Avis's dad."

"You sound pretty sure about that," Savannah said, and glanced up from her notepad.

"I was born and raised here, Savannah, and Avis and me... I suppose we're like brothers, but even better, because we chose to be. Avis will tell you that blood family isn't exactly anything to brag about."

"Does he know who his father is?" she asked, since Leo was certain it wasn't Merle.

"He told me once he hasn't ever given it much thought."

"Do you believe him?"

"I dunno," Leo said and shrugged. "If it were me, I'd be thinking about it a lot, but Avis is smarter than me. Maybe he just decided it didn't matter. I mean, it's not like anyone in town has laid claim to him. At least not before now."

"Do you have any idea who it might be?"

"From the stories I've heard over the years it would be pretty hard to narrow down Lindsey's list enough to pick one guy. Heard it was a pretty big list. I guess only Lindsey and her guy friends would know if they might be in the running to be his father. You know, timing and all that."

"How many guys around town do you think... spent time with her?" Savannah asked.

"List might be shorter if you wrote down who hasn't been with her," he said with complete indifference. He took another bite of his burger.

"So back to him being smart. Avis reads a lot?" she asked, still trying to find a way to buy into the smart Avis angle. She supposed from a news story point of view, it would be an interesting spin.

"Aw, man. He's read everything. And I mean everything. Book after book after book. He's even read a couple of books written in French and other languages."

"He reads French?" she asked, with raised eyebrows.

"Yeah, man. Taught himself. I think he's working on Italian or something now. Not that he'll ever use it for anything other than for reading. Hell, he hardly talks in English, other than to me. Don't see him ever finding the need to speak another language. Avis says most people don't say anything interesting, and they listen even less."

Savannah sat and pondered her next question and tried to figure out where she was going with the Avis Humphrey story. Before she came up with her next question, Leo chimed in again.

"Hey. Do you know where the word, 'no sirree Bob' comes from?"

"No, I do not. Why don't you enlighten me?"

Leo looked at her blankly, and quickly realized she didn't quite understand how the process worked: Leo asked a question and Avis usually answered the question. But right now, Avis wasn't available, and Savannah seemed smart, sort of like Avis. He began to rethink that presumption.

"Hell. I don't know," he answered between bites. "I thought maybe you might be able to tell me. Guess I'll have to ask Avis when we get back to the stream."

He wouldn't ask him though. He and Savannah had to go grocery shopping, and swing by the garage to make the arrangements for someone to pick up and fix her car. Then they had to go by the trailer and pick up some clean clothes and a couple of books for Avis. On the way back out of town they were going to swing by her car and pick up some clothes she had stuffed into a bag in the trunk. Where the word, *no sirree Bob* came from, would be a long-forgotten question by the time they were all sitting around the fire watching trout simmer in the pan. It was likely Avis would have caught a lot more fish without Leo around.

The waitress walked to their table and laid down the check before slipping away to the next customer.

"You buying?" Leo asked, more as a statement than a question. He didn't realize the comment's significance, but Savannah did. It was clear to her she was already becoming the third member of the Avis Humphrey gang. And for some strange reason, beyond anything she could logically justify, she liked hiding out in the woods like Bonnie and Clyde and their sidekick Leo.

"I'll buy if you answer a couple more questions." They both already knew she was going to pay for lunch and he was going to answer just about any question she asked.

"I'm in," Leo said while he watched a couple more reporters come through the door and look around for a non-existent empty table.

"So, Avis doesn't have any brothers or sisters?"

"Nope. He's the one and only."

"Aunts and uncles?" she asked as she jotted notes on her pad.

"Not that I know of. Don't think there's many branches on the Humphrey or Beckham trees."

"So, I guess there's no cousins either," she stated without looking up.

"There a couple of 'em up in Maine somewhere. Wayne something or other and he's got a couple sisters, I think."

"How do you know about them?"

"Wayne came down for a couple days a few years back. I think they still talk to each other now and then. Ain't like Avis has any other relatives to talk to."

"Are they from the Humphrey or Beckham side?"

Leo stopped munching on his burger and gave her a puzzled look again. "Well, since Merle has sworn Avis ain't his kid, I guess there wouldn't be any relatives coming from that side." He shook his head back and forth to make sure he showed her his disappointment in her question.

"Do you know how I could get ahold of Wayne?" she asked, hoping he would be more forthcoming than Avis.

"Goes by *Pellet.* Last I heard he was in the Caribbean working construction or something. Or maybe he's back. I don't know. Avis doesn't talk about him all that much."

"Pellet?" Savannah asked and waited for Leo to provide the missing details. He just shrugged and took another bite of his hamburger.

CHAPTER TWENTY-FOUR

The first steps into the single-wide trailer were a surprise. It was long and narrow and seemed to go on much further inside than it did on the outside, but that paled in comparison to what she was looking at. Standing in the entryway and taking in the appearance of Avis's home was shocking for Savannah, *and* for Leo. It was pristine, immaculate, and spotless. It looked clean. It smelled clean. Everything in the kitchen was neat and tidy and in its place. The kitchen table was polished, as was the dining room floor. The living room was dusted and vacuumed. Windows were shiny and books and pictures on the coffee table were neatly stacked. The TV control sat on the couch, along with six brightly colored and fashionably placed pillows.

"Wow. I didn't picture this," Savannah mumbled.

"Wow is right," Leo added. "I ain't never seen this place so clean. I'm guessing Agnes must be back. Although I've never seen her clean the place like this. I mean, she's a clean freak, but not this clean."

"Agnes?" Savannah asked and looked around as if this small piece of information should have been shared with her before she walked into the trailer. She wondered how many more Avis women she would have to hear about.

Leo started to open his mouth, then stopped and listened for anyone else inside the trailer. "Anyone home?" he called out. No response. "Hey Agnes. You here?" No response again. Leo sighed and looked at Savannah.

"So. Agnes?" Savannah asked again.

"Well, as you've probably figured out by now, Avis is a pretty go-with-the-flow kind of guy. Generally speaking, I think that's a good thing. Agnes is the only thing I've ever questioned him about." He stopped talking and walked down the hallway to the bedroom. "Just making sure," he said as he poked his head into the first open bedroom. Savannah stood just inside the front door and looked at the fresh flowers in an old canning jar sitting in the center of the dining room table. She glanced to her right, into the kitchen. The very clean and sparkling kitchen.

After checking the second bedroom and the bathroom, Leo walked back into the living room. "Anyway, back to Agnes. Avis dated her a couple of times back in high school, but I guess she's what you might call high-maintenance."

"Is she good-looking?" Savannah asked—and then wondered why she would have asked the question or cared one way or the other.

"Yeah. She's pretty hot, but she's crazy. And I don't mean good crazy. I mean just regular old bat-shit crazy. Avis didn't agree with me for a long time, but I swear she's gotta be bipolar, or something along those lines. Avis used to say she was just selfish and self-centered, but not actually crazy. Then one weekend, after one of their blowouts... or I should say, after one of Agnes's blowups, Avis finally said to me, 'Yeah. She's probably crazy.' It wasn't like it was a news flash to me."

"So, what's their story now? I mean, you've been out of school for almost a decade."

"I don't know what the hell their story is. Five or six years ago they hooked up again and started dating. She's never officially moved in, but it wasn't long before all her shit was here and when I asked Avis if she was all moved in, he just shrugged and we, Avis and me, went fishing. Agnes wouldn't ever get herself dragged, kicking and screaming, to go fishing. She's way too prissy and high-maintenance for shit like that."

"So, they live together? He didn't mention it." Again, Savannah thought it strange that she cared one way or the other.

"No. Like I said, Agnes is a crazy woman. After they lived together for a year or so, she got mad about something and one day when we came home from fishing, all her shit was gone."

"What was the fight over?"

"Probably wasn't over nothing. He probably looked at her wrong, or something like that," he said, and glanced around again just in case she came out of a closet or cupboard or appeared out of thin air. "Avis didn't seem to be too upset by it. He just shrugged again and didn't say a word about it. About a year later he came home one day, and all her stuff was back in here. Everything was all in its place and she acted like she had never left. I think she's done it three or four times now. She left about a year ago and Avis said he didn't think she was coming back this time."

"It didn't bother him that she wasn't coming back?"

"No. I think he was actually a little relieved. He told me once that sex with a crazy woman was fantastic, but after the sex you still had to put up with a crazy woman. He hasn't said much about it since she left, but I think despite not getting to have crazy-woman sex, he was glad to see her go the last time."

"So, all the cleaning is, Agnes?"

"Yeah, it's got to be her. She's a bit of a fanatic. Must have watched the news and smelled money."

"If she's a money girl, what did she ever see in Avis? It doesn't sound like there was a bright future on his horizon."

"Who knows. Free rent? A place to hang out? Maybe he's that good in bed. I try to stay away from Agnes conversations. Hell. I try to stay away from Agnes. I'm not getting any crazy-woman sex, so there's no upside to Agnes for me."

Savannah took another few seconds to look around the trailer and tried to imagine what it looked like before the bipolar sex maid sanitized the place.

"Am I safe if she shows up?"

"Yeah. I think so." The *think so* didn't comfort Savannah. "If I say Go! Run to the truck. I'll slow her down," he added.

Those words were not comforting either, but Avis had told her that Leo could give her a tour of his castle and library. The trailer was small and the tour couldn't possibly take that long. She was still questioning whether or not the books actually existed. She also thought, presuming she didn't get killed or maimed, the crazy ex/current girlfriend might be a spicy twist to her story. It would be good to get a couple of pictures of her and find out if she was really as good-looking as Leo had implied. Again, she wondered why she cared.

Leo led the way down the hall and pushed the first door open and said, "The master suite," with a grin on his face as if he were giving her the grand tour of the royal boudoir. The room was already heavy with Agnes's perfume. A slinky nighty was laid on the neatly made bed and a picture of Avis and Agnes standing in the front yard was sitting on the nightstand in a gold frame. Savannah walked over and picked up the photo. "She's pretty good-looking," she said and felt a slight sting of disappointment.

"Well, she's crazier than she is good looking, if that tells you anything," Leo added.

He waved toward the open bathroom door as they walked past. Savannah poked her head inside for a second and then continued down the hall. The hallway dead-ended at a closed door and Leo hesitated and smiled as if she were about to see what was behind door number three. He swung the door open and stepped aside to let her in. There were books everywhere. All four walls were stacked nearly floor to ceiling with books. The center of the room had piles everywhere. Small piles and big piles. There were novels, biographies, children's books, religious books, car manuals, cookbooks and books of every other subject imaginable. On the top of one stack, about chest high, were three thick, heavily worn books. Each of them looked as though they had been read a few hundred times, long before Avis had been born. She looked at the spine of each book and shook her head.

"The Bible, Koran, and Tora. Are you telling me he's read every book in this room?"

"Twice this many. These are just the ones he hasn't gotten rid of yet."

"Really?" she retorted with a tone of skepticism. Her disbelief didn't come from mistrust. It was just an overwhelming amount of reading material and much of it looked to be high-order reading. Avis didn't come across like a high-order thinking or reading kind of guy to her.

"I told you, Avis is a smart guy."

She reached into her shoulder bag and pulled out her phone. "I've got to take a couple of pictures. I don't think Avis will mind."

Leo didn't answer. As far as he was concerned he was just the tour guide. All the details and permission of the tour were between Avis and Savannah.

She snapped a close-up of the holy books and then a shot of Leo standing in front of a pile. She wished Avis were here to have his picture taken, but given the fact that Agnes was back in the picture, maybe it was a good thing he had refused to accompany them.

CHAPTER TWENTY-FIVE

Jake moved to Watermill from Silicon Valley in 2000, just before the dotcom bubble burst. He cashed out his stocks before they went from twenty dollars a share to two cents a share. And while he didn't make enough money to remain in Silicon Valley and never work again, he did make enough to ease into Watermill, New Hampshire and buy a small house on the edge of town. After that, he spent his days writing programs for video games, or playing video games. It was all the same to Jake.

He was originally from Cincinnati, Ohio, so while there was a transition involved in moving to a small town in New England, it wasn't as if he were a California boy trying to fit into a whole different world from what he had been used to. He was not Denny from Miami via LA. He was Jake from Ohio. And as it turned out, gray and dreary looked pretty much the same wherever it took place.

It takes time to assimilate and be accepted into a small town anywhere in the world. Watermill, NH was not the exception to that rule. Given that Jake rarely ventured from his house during his first five years after arriving, other than to buy groceries and do whatever task were required to survive, his acceptance by the locals did not happen on an accelerated pace. But it's an odd phenomenon that happens in a small town: No matter how quirky an outsider may be, if they are given enough time, they are no longer the stranger who wandered into their town and made themselves at home. At some point, they become part of the local fabric.

In 2001 Jake was the new guy whom nobody knew what to think of. And when he occasionally wandered out from behind his computer screen, it was nearly impossible to understand what he was saying. After a decade of spending far more time communicating with computers than interacting with real live humans, he spoke more like he was writing computer programs than actually talking English. He spoke in long, continuous sentences without spaces between words or letters. His sentences—and entire conversations, when he rarely had one—were a slurry of sounds and syllables that could not be understood by those who hadn't learned his language. It didn't help that he was odd and fidgety and constantly moving about, distracting anyone who might be trying to focus on what he was saying. His feet shuffled as if he were always about to walk off, even when he had just arrived. His hands picked things up and then set them back down again just so he didn't have to figure out what to do with them.

By 2003 he was known in town as the peculiar fella who mumbled when he talked. And almost everyone knew he either worked or played on computers, but almost nobody was sure which it was.

By 2010 he was mostly known as the computer nerd who kind of kept to himself. But those who knew him better, like Carmen at the All American and a couple of other local computer nerds, who did not begin to scratch the surface of his level of genius, had learned to understand his computer-program-type English. And while they may not have spoken highly of him, they no longer spoke ill of him. He was just Jake, the fidgety computer genius who lived down on Dean Street.

Then in 2015 it happened. Jake crossed over from being an outsider to being a welcomed citizen of Watermill. And it only took fifteen short years. It happened when he overheard the owner of a local sweatshirt factory rambling on to Carmen about some computer programming problems he was having and how they were causing serious problems at the factory. He went on and on, and pissed and moaned, and then rambled on some more about the tech company he had hired that cost him thousands, and the system was actually operating worse than it had been before. He finally blurted out in exasperation, "I'm telling you Carmen, this thing could put us out of business, and eighty-five people are going to be looking for work."

Jake stood quietly with two 2-liter bottles of Coke in his hands and listened to the entire conversation from behind the potato chip rack. He picked up a small bag of Doritos and then put them back down and then picked up a bigger bag and set that one down, too. He set down the two bottles of Coke he was holding and picked up two more bags of chips and then put all the chips down and picked the soda back up and grabbed three large bags of Salt & Vinegar chips before walking around and giving his input.

"Ifyou'rehavingcomputerprogrammingproblems,I'mcertainIcanfixi t," he said in one long, slurry word that came out of his mouth as fast as his mind processed it; and then he looked at Howard for a response. He set everything on the counter and stepped back and then immediately stepped forward again and moved everything six inches to the left and then stepped back once again.

"If you're having computer programming problems, I'm certain I can fix it," Carmen repeated as if she were a translator for a Japanese tech company.

"You really think you could fix it? I mean you haven't even looked at it yet," Howard responded.

"Idon'tmeantosoundarrogant,butI'mkindofconsideredageniusinmyf ield.Iknow...it'shardtotellfromlookingatme,butI'mdamngoodatwhatIdo," he said, and kind of motioned toward his oversized and worn-out green sweatshirt and ragged and baggy blue jeans with holes in the knees and his green Chuck Taylors that looked to be at least ten years old.

Howard looked at him, and then to Carmen for the translation from English to English.

"He said, 'I don't mean to sound arrogant, but I'm kind of considered a genius in my field. I know... it's hard to tell from looking at me, but I'm damn good at what I do,'" she said with a shrug, to make it clear she was not vouching for him, just translating.

Howard rubbed his chin and listened to Carmen and then looked from her to Jake and then back to Carmen. "Ask him how much this would cost us."

Carmen stood behind the counter with a puzzled look on her face and glanced at both men before saying, "He speaks English, Howard. He knows what you're saying."

"Oh. I'm sorry," Howard said, and nervously laughed at himself and started talking to Jake again. "So, what kind of cost do you think we're talking about?"

"I'llcomebyaroundnoontomorrow.We'lltalkaboutitthen," Jake said. He slid the two liters of Coke and the three bags of chips about six inches back to the right.

"Noon tomorrow," Howard said, proud he was picking up on the language. "I'll be there waiting for you."

As it turned out, Jake spent a week reprogramming the factory. He not only fixed the problem, but when he was done, everything ran more smoothly and glitch-free than it ever had. And to top it all off, he did it for free. That was when Jake was transformed from weird outsider into a full-fledged local of Watermill, New Hampshire. Or at least as close to one as anyone could ever be who wasn't born there.

Avis wasn't the least bit surprised when Jake told him about what he had done at the factory the week after he had dazzled Howard and the gang.

The two of them had met three years earlier when Jake was trying to find a book on mythology in the Watermill Library. While all the information was readily available on the net, Jake said there was something cool about holding a book in his hand with a picture of a three-headed dragon jumping off the page. He liked to flip back and forth between the pictures that caught his attention; he wanted to use them in one of his gamer worlds. The two men struck up a conversation about mythology and Avis enlightened Jake on how many of the creatures of mythology represented aspects of human nature. Avis stopped by the house on Dean Street a week later and found Jake already in the final stages of developing a new video game with a three-headed dragon in a small New England town. From that point on, the visits and the discussions became a weekly occurrence between the scraggly, lanky fisherman and the scraggly, soft, pasty computer nerd, the two most brilliant minds ever to reside in Watermill.

C'

Leo and Savannah
around as if they tho␍
might be lurking in the si␍
harmless, neither Savannah nor ␍
presumed the initial meet and greet wou␍
sort of welcome with a polite, but cold, hug an␍
wasn't forthcoming as to the whereabouts of Avis,
quickly replace cordial Agnes. As he had pointed out to Avis ␍
there was no upside for Leo to be involved with crazy-woman tanu␍

Before they got halfway to the truck, a red Toyota Yaris with
Avis Rental Car license plate on the front bumper pulled into the driveway.
They both froze in their tracks. Leo stopped breathing for a second and waited
to see who was going to step out of the driver's door. He exhaled a deep sigh
once he saw it was a man he had never seen before. Not Agnes.

"Hey. How's it going?" asked a young tanned guy with an oversized
grin on his face. "You're Leo, right?"

Leo looked at Savannah and shrugged. "Who's asking?"

"Denny Wilson." He reached out his hand to shake Leo's hand. Leo
left it hanging, just as Avis had left Savannah's hand hanging when they first
met. "I'm a reporter from Brick House On-line. We're a small news site from
Miami, and I'm here to do a story on your friend Avis."

"Are there brick houses in Miami?" Leo asked as if that was a
logical question to ask. He recalled Avis telling him about Florida homes
being stucco when Leo had asked, "Hey Avis. What kind of siding do you·
like best on houses?" That led to a conversation about what the outside of
houses were covered with in different parts of the world.

"No. I don't think so," Denny answered as he tried to move past the
small talk. "I haven't really seen many brick homes around Miami."

company called Brick House On-line? Is it in a
tinued asking on his single-lane thought path.

m... I don't really know, to be honest. I mean, no.
ing, and I don't know where the name came from."
hy he, the reporter, had already answered three questions
sked even one.

ah had begun adjusting to Leo's thought process over the
s, as much as one could adjust to it, and now it was Savannah
Denny instead of Avis smiling at her, as Leo continued, "So, you
a paper called the Brick House in a place that doesn't have brick
and you don't know why it's called what it's called. Don't you think
would be a good question to pop into a reporter's head?" Leo asked as
looked at Denny. Then he turned to Savannah and asked, "Don't you think
ou'd want to know why your company in Miami was named Brick House
On-line?" Now he had asked four questions to none.

"Yes, I would, Leo. Yes, I would certainly want to know why the
company I worked for was called Brick House when there were no brick
houses," she added with a raised eyebrow to Denny.

Denny raised his hands into the air and said, "I got nothing." The
response was good enough for Leo and he reached out and shook Denny's
hand.

"Yeah. I'm Leo. This is my friend Savannah."

Savannah liked the sound of that. *My friend Savannah.* Once upon
a time she had had a lot of friends, but time and circumstances took them
away one by one. Over the past year or two, everyone in her life seemed more
like associates than real friends. A warm feeling ran through her as she
realized this was probably the happiest she had been in a long time.

"You just get to town?" Leo asked.

"Nah. I've been here for a few days. I got sent on a wild-goose chase
yesterday and spent the entire day walking along some river. Just about
everyone in town has talked to at least ten other reporters, so there's nothing
new to find out there. I keep stopping by here hoping to find Avis home, or
to run into you."

"Well, you can stop coming by because Avis ain't going to be here for a while," Leo said as he started walking toward the truck. "And how'd you hear about me?"

"A woman named Agnes was here when I stopped by yesterday afternoon. She said if I find you, I'd probably find Avis." Denny confirmed what Leo had already assumed. Crazy Agnes was back.

"Well. Avis will talk to you guys when he's ready, and he's not ready today. Probably not going to be ready tomorrow either," he said and stepped closer to the truck. Savannah climbed into the driver's side and Leo motioned for her to slide over. Denny presumed they weren't going anywhere, since he was parked directly behind them. He was surprised when Leo threw the truck into drive and turned hard to the left and drove straight across the muddy walkway, across the lawn and through the small ditch, and headed west.

Denny hopped into his Toyota Yaris and quickly threw it into reverse and started to follow. The thought of going back to Miami empty-handed, or having no update to share with Theresa later that night, made him cringe. And the thought of throwing in the towel and heading back to Los Angeles made him nauseous. All he could do for now was follow Leo and Savannah and hope they would lead him to Avis.

Leo didn't speed or drive recklessly. In fact, Savannah thought he was driving slowly just to let Denny catch up with them. A mile down the road he slowly turned left onto a slightly overgrown dirt road. Denny followed as they eased along at less than twenty miles an hour. For five minutes, they drove straight and then rounded a curve, followed by a small hill. At the bottom of the hill the truck splashed through a stream that was less than twenty feet wide and less than three inches deep.

"Hold on," Leo said to Savannah as the truck eased out of the mud. Denny's rented Yaris had just reached the edge of the water when Leo slammed on the brakes. Denny followed suit and slammed on his brakes and squeezed the steering wheel tight with both hands. The Yaris came to a dead stop in the middle of the stream, less than two feet from the back of the pickup. Leo honked once and waved his hand out the window as the truck pulled away. Denny hit the accelerator to follow, but nothing happened except the tires made a loud whirring sound and spit muddy water up and into the air. He quickly threw the car into reverse with the same results.

"Aw! Son of a…!" He didn't finish what he was saying. He just sat for five minutes and tried to not let his anger end up in the same place it had ended up yesterday. With one final cleansing breath, he swung the car door open and plunged his feet and his Ralph Lauren brown loafers into ankle-deep mud and water.

"Son of a bitch!" he yelled to nobody but himself.

His shoes were almost dry by the time he walked the two miles back to town and into the Rusty Wrench to arrange for a tow truck to pull his car out of the muddy water.

CHAPTER TWENTY-SEVEN

While Denny sloshed his way back toward town, Leo circled around and drove into the parking lot of the All American. He pulled in and parked the truck directly in front of the store and went through the normal process of listening to the engine sputter and cough for ten or twenty seconds after the key was turned off. Carmen heard the sick-sounding truck from behind the counter and glanced out the window. She doubted with everything going on Avis would be stopping by. And she knew Leo wouldn't bring his cheap ass into the All American without Avis to pay for the beer. Savannah sat in the passenger seat and tried to peer through the advertisements and stickers on the window to see the woman who was so stunning, she convinced Avis Humphrey to buy a Powerball ticket he didn't want and to pay more money for beer just, so he could see her.

"You going in or what?" Leo asked. He almost never went in. Carmen just didn't interest him all that much and the beer was too expensive to buy. Not that he was buying.

"Don't rush me. I'm trying to get a look at her before I go in."

Leo watched her as she peered through the dirty windshield for another minute or two. "Man. You and Avis are so much alike it's scary," he said, referring to Savannah and Avis and their nearly identical window peering routines.

Savannah shrugged and kept trying to catch a glimpse.

He caught her by surprise with the next question. "When do you suppose you two are going to stop pretending you don't like each other?"

"Excuse me?" Savannah asked as she kept looking out the window toward the store without showing she was torn between denial and embarrassment.

"You and Avis. When are you going to tell him you like him?"

"Excuse me?" she repeated again and stopped trying to find

131

Carmen.

"I've known Avis my whole life Savannah. He's smarter than me, but I still know him better than he knows himself. You're getting under his skin."

"Well, you don't know me," she said, as she tried to act irritated at the suggestion. But irritation came hard, as she enjoyed the thought of getting under Avis's skin. She presumed that was a good thing.

"Hey. I might not be book-smart like Avis, but I ain't blind. You two are made for each other. Anyone can see that."

Savannah stared back at Leo and tried to formulate an argument in her head, but none came. She thought about denying what Leo had just said, but she didn't. She just looked at him and turned red and finally reached down for the door handle. "I'm going in to meet this Carmen woman and see what all the hoopla is about."

"Want me to come in with you?" Leo asked, hoping she would say No.

"I think I can handle it on my own, Leo," she said, and creaked the door open and stepped out and swung it closed.

Thirty minutes later the door creaked again, and Savannah slid into the truck and blankly stared out the windshield without saying a word. Her face was red and Leo couldn't quite figure out if she was mad or embarrassed.

"Well?" Leo asked, irritated she wasn't saying anything.

"She's hot. There's no doubt about that," Savannah mumbled.

"Hot enough to sell Avis a Powerball ticket, right?" he asked with a grin.

Savannah smiled and shrugged. "Hot enough to sell *me* a Powerball ticket," she answered, holding up a pink ticket in her hand. Leo laughed hard and shook his head as he once again considered how much she and Avis were alike.

"You were in there a long time so I'm guessing she shared a bunch of stuff with you. What's the scoop?" Leo asked. "Any juicy girl-talk about Avis?" He grinned.

"Nope. We didn't really talk about Avis all that much, other than she talked about him coming in and buying the ticket. She really gets a kick out of how goo-goo ga-ga he is over her."

"So, is she ever going to let the boy in or what?" Leo asked. "I'm getting tired of coming here just to buy expensive beer."

Savannah thought it was ironic that Leo's best friend had just won nine hundred and sixty-seven million dollars and he was still concerned about paying a dollar too much for cheap beer. "I'm afraid I have some bad news for poor Avis," she said with a smile of satisfaction.

She knew Leo was right. She had never clicked with anyone as quickly as she had with Avis. By the end of the first day, without even giving it a thought, she knew they were a good fit. It felt like they were meant to be together. After meeting Carmen, she thought it was a good thing they weren't in competition for Avis. Savannah wouldn't have stood a chance.

"Oh. Poor guy. The dream is coming to an end," Leo answered with a bigger grin than Savannah. "He's gonna take it hard."

"Well. There's more," Savannah added. "I've got a much better chance of getting Carmen into the sack than Avis does."

"What's that supposed to mean?" Leo asked with a confused look on his face.

Savannah sat silent for ten seconds and let Leo process the news.

He suddenly sat up straight and looked at Savannah as if his light had just switched on.

Savannah started up again. "Carmen is a lesbian, Leo. She may flirt and play with boys, but she's into women. Completely in," she said with a raised eyebrow toward Leo.

"Get the hell out of here," he blurted out, and then sat silently and pondered what he had just heard. He found himself trying to catch a glimpse of the stunningly hot lesbian behind the window stickers. "Carmen is a lesbian?" he mumbled and squinted his eyes again as he tried harder to see her, as if suddenly she would look different now that a new perspective had been shared. After not catching a glimpse of her through the window, he looked back to Savannah, and looked her up and down as if he were putting things together in his head, and then waited for more.

"And stop thinking about me and Carmen having sex, Leo," she snapped.

"Hey. You just can't blurt out that kind of information and then go all-silent and not expect me to fill in the blanks. I need details."

"Let me just say that I am NOT a lesbian and I still had to think about what she said before politely turning her down. That is one damn sexy woman."

"And you bought a Powerball ticket." Leo laughed hard and started the truck. "Here's a thought for you to ponder," Leo said as he pulled out of the parking lot. "Avis would probably trade his winning ticket for your ticket if you could get Carmen to sleep with him."

"She's a lesbian Leo."

"So. And how come you didn't buy beer? Avis always buys beer."

"I never made it past the cash register," she said and looked down at the Powerball ticket she was holding in her hand.

CHAPTER TWENTY-EIGHT

It was almost lunchtime the following day when Leo and Savannah pulled into the grassy parking spot not far from where Avis was brooding. Leo was nearly as anxious to watch Avis's face and hear his response, when Savannah broke the Carmen-lesbian news, as Savannah was to tell him.

Before either of them got a word out, Avis started in. "Damn. The two of you get here later and later every day. Pretty soon you're just going to stop by to see if I caught any fish for dinner, and then eat and head back home."

Savannah smiled and winked at Leo. "I think he's a bit worked up today Leo. What do you think?"

Leo didn't answer. He just grinned like a little kid on Christmas morning and waited impatiently.

Avis asked, "Did you get lost on the way here? Maybe forgot where I was camped?"

Savannah smiled again and shrugged. "Didn't know you missed me so much. You must be anxious to answer a few more questions."

"Funny you should say that. Being that I had plenty of time to think it over while I've been sitting here all by myself, I've come up with new rules for your questions."

"What happened to 'Catch a fish and you'll answer questions'?" Savannah asked.

"Too easy," he mumbled back.

"So, what are these big new rules, Mr. Humphrey?" she asked as she plopped herself down onto what had become her seat on the log.

"Whatever questions you ask me, you've got to answer, too."

"You mean like if I ask you your favorite color, I'll have to tell you mine?"

"You got it. No more prying into my life without me prying into yours." He was more or less aware he was laying his cards on the table and letting her know he wanted to get to know her better, but more importantly, he was the one calling the shots. He liked being in control.

"Sounds outstanding," she answered. "Let's get started."

Leo opened the tailgate of the truck and took his seat. Avis sat down on his log and readied himself for the, what's your favorite-color question.

"First question of the day," Savannah began. "Do you know any lesbians in Watermill?" She pulled her notepad out and looked at Avis as though she had simply asked him why he didn't keep the money. Or what was the saddest or happiest day of his life. Or even, what is your favorite color?

"Did you actually go to college to learn how to interview people? Have you ever considered asking for a refund?" This time he managed to throw an insult while answering a question with a question.

"Well?"

"Do I know any lesbians?" he echoed with a puzzled look on his face. "What the hell kind of question is that?"

"Just an interview question. Trying to get to know you and the people around you. So, do you? Do you know any lesbians in Watermill, Avis?" And then she added, "By the way, you just answered another question with a question. That's against the rules," she said without looking up at him.

"Hmph," he shrugged at her.

"So? Lesbians?"

"Yeah. I know a couple. Maybe a few... I guess. Not sure where you're going with this, but I'm not discussing anyone's sexual orientation in an interview. Your turn. Do you know any lesbians in Watermill?" he asked with raised eyebrows, as if he were expecting her to announce she preferred women and as luck would have it, she had found one. It also occurred to him that she was doing it again—she was getting under his skin, and he still wasn't sure how he felt about it.

Savannah grinned wide and looked over toward Leo. "Leo, do I know any—"

"From what you told me last night, I presume you do," Leo answered without enough patience to allow her to finish asking him her question.

Avis looked at Leo and then back at Savannah. They both looked directly at him as if to say, "You wanna know who it is?" Avis stared blankly at her and didn't respond until he had had enough of the smug look on her face. "Well?" Avis snapped.

"Carmen Marden," Leo called out.

"Get the hell outta here." Avis blurted out. It was the same response Leo had blurted out the day before.

"Afraid so Avis. She not only does not have the hots for you, she's never *going* to have the hots for you," Savannah said in her most mockingly compassionate voice she could conjure. She was again a little surprised at how relieved she felt knowing Carmen was more or less out of the picture.

"What makes you so sure? I mean, about her being, you know... not into men or me?"

"Well, when I interviewed her she was very friendly. *Very* friendly," she repeated. "After we talked for a while, I was leaning on the counter and she reached out and ran her fingers over my face and said, 'I get off at nine if you want to get a drink or something.' She emphasized the *or something* part."

"And then Savannah bought a Powerball ticket!" Leo cried out and shook his head back and forth. "The two of you are hopeless. Like you were made for each other." Leo shook his head some more.

Savannah smiled at Avis with her head tilted to one side and waited for his response.

He sat in shock. "Maybe she was just playing around with you," Avis said.

"I'm not about to go into full-disclosure mode, but she said a lot more to me than what time she got off work. According to Leo, you guys are good at filling in the blanks, so I'll leave the conversation to your imagination."

"What the hell is happening to my world?" Avis mumbled and shook his head as he looked down at the ground. "I bought a damn ticket I never wanted just to impress a woman who evidently is never going to want me. That's a hell of a thing, don't you think?" It was a rhetorical question.

"Then I tried to go fishing to hide from reporters and one of them climbed into my damn truck and went fishing with me. Damn," he mumbled. He looked up from the ground and saw Savannah smirking in silence, and immediately grasped for something to cushion the onslaught of blows to his ego. "Good news, Leo. I guess we'll be buying beer at the Shop & Save from now on."

"Oh hell no," Leo shot back. "I'm hanging out with Carmen from now on. She finally got interesting. Besides, you pay for the beer anyway."

"And you invited me to go fishing," Savannah reminded him one more time.

Avis shook his head back and forth again in disbelief that his dream, Carmen, had suddenly crashed. "Next question," he mumbled.

He glanced back at Savannah and saw her still sitting with her head tilted and an expression showing mock compassion. Their relationship had just turned a corner or crested a hill or done something that somehow unofficially signaled that they were probably more than just a reporter and a storyline. He wasn't certain, but he thought he liked it better when he believed he was torn between Carmen and Savannah. Carmen was gone now, and he was starting to think Savannah was a bit of a pain in the ass.

She flipped through the pages of notes and slipped into a more serious interviewing mode. "All right. Next question. You told me why you picked Alice Chen to take care of the money for you, but you didn't ever say what you wanted her to do with it."

"I'm going to have to make another rule change," Avis answered. Savannah looked puzzled at his response. "When your question is something *you* can't answer, I get to ask you a question of my own."

"You sure have a lot of rules," Savannah said with a wrinkled forehead.

"Deal or no deal?"

She took a deep sigh. "Fine. Deal. Question for question. But I'm not telling you any lesbian sex stuff. Got it?"

Leo looked disappointed. Avis nodded in agreement. Then, of course, he and Leo both wondered if she had any lesbian sex stuff to share.

"I didn't care what Alice did with the money. I mean... I presumed she would do something good with it, because that's the kind of person she is. She's the kindest person I've ever met. But the truth is, if she had bought herself a small town and named it Aliceville or Chen City, I would have been okay with it."

"Chen City, New Hampshire. What might a place like that be like?"

Avis shrugged. "If Alice was mayor, it would likely be a good place to live. Probably wouldn't be any reporters," he added as an afterthought. "I know one thing for sure, I didn't mean for this all to ruin her life. She's been in hiding for two weeks now. I feel bad that I ever dragged her into this mess."

"Have you heard from her? Do you know what she's decided to do with the money?"

"No on both counts," he said and shook his head back and forth again. "I just feel really bad about what has happened."

"What do you think she'll do with the money?"

Avis looked up at Savannah with a puzzled look on his face. "You do understand the concept of question for question, right? I think you've asked four questions now."

Savannah rolled her eyes. "Fine. What's your question?"

Avis turned his head to one side and looked at her out of the corner of his eye and rubbed his chin, as if he were sizing her up. "You don't really seem like the reporter type to me. I just don't see you going into an office every day, writing stories about the local home show or a car accident on I-95. I can't picture you writing stories about the town council fighting over whether or not to paint the library. So, I guess my question is, What are you doing here? I mean, how did you end up in Watermill, New Hampshire, looking for Avis Humphrey?"

Savannah pondered the question and her answer for at least thirty seconds before speaking. She wasn't a sharing-personal-information kind of girl, but something had changed and sharing with Avis just felt right. Hitting rock bottom and then meeting a guy who actually didn't want to win the lottery just a few days later had somehow changed her outlook on life. Maybe his lack of greed called out to her, although she couldn't really see how. She had always liked having nice stuff and never imagined she could ever have too much money. At least she had always felt that way up until a few months ago. Then her life went to hell and she began to question everything. Rock bottom arrived when she came up with no answers to her questions.

Savannah took a deep breath and began talking. She told him about her perfect, yet emotionally empty life of being a reporter. Then she told him about her engagement to a man who checked off all the squares on the "wonderful husband requirement" list. Last but not least, she shared details about her fairytale upper-middle-class white girl upbringing in suburban southern Maine. Once she had painted a clear picture of her absurdly quintessential life, she told him about the crash of it all. Time slipped away from her. After she had talked, non-stop, for over a half-hour, and after both Avis and Leo were bored to the point of nearly falling asleep, she described in detail, about deciding to kill herself a week or so ago.

They both perked up a bit at that part of the story. When she finished talking, she looked at Avis and waited for his response.

Avis leaned forward with his elbows on his knees and considered everything she had shared. He shook his head back and forth in disbelief. She could almost hear the wheels turning in his head while she and Leo both waited for a response. Then a smile broke out on Avis's face. "So, I saved your life."

"What?" she asked with a puzzled look on her face. Her forehead was wrinkled, and her eyes squinted as if perhaps she hadn't heard him correctly, or she simply couldn't understand what he had just said. "You saved my life?"

"Hey. If not for me, you probably would have killed yourself. So, I saved your life. I mean, if not for Avis Humphrey your life was so meaningless you were going to do yourself in, but then I entered the picture and…. Shazam! Here you are, alive and well."

"Oh… my… god. I shared the most intimate details of my life with you and all you can do is cling to your vain opinion of yourself and take credit for me being alive today. Maybe I should have just stayed in Biddeford and finished what I was doing."

"No! I want lesbian sex details," Leo called out from his seat on the tailgate.

"There are not going to be any details, Leo. I'm straight. And as for you," she looked back at Avis, "You're an ass." She closed her tablet and slammed it down on the log. "I'm going fishing."

"No more questions?" Avis asked with a raised eyebrow, a shrug, and a wide grin on his face.

"Later," she snapped as she grabbed her pole and the can of worms and headed for the stream.

It took Leo less than fifteen minutes to get his hook hung up on a branch that was hanging down in the water. He stood in knee-deep water and reached down to get his hook untangled and a thought jumped into his head.

"Hey Avis."

"Yeah, Leo."

"This whole world-wide water shortage thing I've heard them talking about on TV: How can I be standing in all this water while they're saying our planet is running out of water?" He tugged hard on his line and it snapped. He would have been just as well off standing on the shore and breaking it from the comfort of dry land.

"Well. It's not that we're actually running out of water, Leo. It's more like the water is in the wrong places."

Leo stood up straight in the knee-deep water holding his hook less line in his hand and gave Avis a puzzled look. "Isn't water just where it is?"

"One would think so, Leo. But humans are strange creatures. Most animals would go to the water if they were thirsty. If they needed lots of water, they would live near lots of water. But we humans have decided we should live where we want to live and bring everything to us." He jerked up on his pole and set his hook in a fish's mouth and began to reel in a trout while he kept talking. "So, we build cities in the desert and pipe the water a thousand miles, so our toilets can flush, and our grass can be watered, and our golf courses can be green in places where grass is clearly not meant to grow."

"Like Vegas?"

"Yeah, but it's happening all over the world. China has more water in the north, but more people in the south. They got big water problems there."

"Why don't they just move closer to the water?"

"Because people don't do what they should do, Leo. People do what they want to do. Haven't you heard? It's all the rage," he said as he lifted a nine-inch trout from the water.

Leo climbed out of the water and sat down to tie a new hook onto his line. His thoughts had moved on to something else. Savannah fished in silence and tried unsuccessfully to reason her Avis Humphrey emotions out of her head. Avis put the trout in a bucket and placed a new worm onto his hook and fished in silence. He wasn't even trying to get his Savannah Gardiner emotions under control.

A few hours later Avis was cooking a half-dozen trout in the frying pan, four he had caught, and two Savannah had caught. And as usual, Leo continued his never-ending stretch of bad luck and didn't catch a thing. Savannah reached down with her fork to pluck a piece of fish from the pan and Avis slapped her hand.

"Did you just slap my hand?" she chided.

"Patience is a virtue, young lady," he answered while still focusing on the pan sitting over the fire. "Don't you have more questions, or are you all done?"

Savannah's mouth was watering as the fish sizzled in the pan, but she decided she'd better ask questions while Avis was willing to answer them. "Why didn't you just give the ticket away yourself? If you didn't want to keep it, then you could have given it to a thousand charities. Problem solved."

Avis continued to look down at the pan and push the trout around with his fork. "I tried to give it away. Remember? I was giving it to Alice Chen."

"Yes. I know you gave it to Alice, but why drag her into the mix? It was your ticket, so why not just give it to the United Way or the Salvation Army or some organization like that?"

He picked up the pan and slid two fish onto each of the three paper plates and handed one to Savannah. "Didn't want to be bothered with it. You gotta remember, I wasn't supposed to be found out. My name was staying out of it. Alice was going to a lawyer to work out the details and then give it to whomever she wanted." He opened a beer and handed it to her and then passed her a bag of chips. "Then some loudmouth in the lawyer's office spread the news and here we are, eating fish and chips and drinking beer on a riverbank in New Hampshire."

"Here we are," Savannah said with a smile and raised her beer to him. He raised his in return.

"My turn," he said after taking a sip. "Tell me something you've done to make the world a better place."

"Oh. That's easy. I did a year in the Peace Corps right after college. Spent a year in Africa."

From the look on his face, Avis appeared to be less than impressed by the grand sacrifice she had made. "Hanging out in Africa for a year doesn't necessarily mean you made the world any better." He mumbled and took a bite of fish. "That was the question. What did you do to make the world a better place?"

"So, what great humanitarian thing have you done?" she snapped at him and pushed some chips into her mouth. "I mean, other than giving away hundreds of millions of dollars... and ruining Alice's life."

"I adopted Leo," he blurted back.

Savannah started to respond to his claim, but then thought about Leo's never-ending questions and his inability to catch fish and decided Avis might be a bigger humanitarian than herself after all. "Okay. My turn again."

"Tomorrow," he said without looking up.

"Why tomorrow?"

"Because I'm done answering tonight and Leo's going to take you home in a few minutes." Avis was calling the shots for now. Questions were done for the day.

"You should have Leo introduce you to George tomorrow. You'll like him. Maybe come out here later in the day... since you two seem to be getting later and later every day anyway."

CHAPTER TWENTY-NINE

There was a lot of suspicion and a bunch of hot rumors floating around town, and Harvey Sullivan thought he was the only individual who knew for certain how many different men were getting a DNA test. He not only thought he knew how many, he also thought he knew exactly who they were. Being the town mailman, he had delivered six test kits to six different addresses where men who would have been the right age to be Avis's father lived. The right age, of course, would have ranged from about eighteen to thirty-five back in Lindsey's heyday, which meant the kits were being delivered to men who now ranged from their mid-forties to their mid-sixties. Harvey was man number seven. Ironically, the 'mail order seven' were not the only men in town who did not buy DNA kits at the local drugstore. An additional five more kits had been delivered within the last couple of days under Harvey's radar. Of course with confidentiality not being a realistic goal in Watermill, the DNA testing was now the talk of the coffee shop, and the hungry reporters finally had something else, other than the Pirate, to talk about.

Getting their hands on a kit and taking a swab from the inside of their mouth was the easy part. The hard part would be getting a swab from Avis. After twenty-six years of neglect and denial of all fatherly obligations from every man in town, Avis wasn't likely to be interested in finding out which one of the backseat boys, if any, were his deadbeat dad.

One of the latest rumors to be floating around was that Ed Fitzgerald, the attorney whose law office bungled the whole Powerball process with Alice Chen in the first place, was filing stacks of paperwork on behalf of several individuals who wanted to ask the court to compel Avis to provide a DNA sample. The reasoning was a bunch of legal-eagle gobbledygook that only made sense to Ed. His hourly billing rate tended to clear up a lot of things in his mind.

Merle was the first to come forward and ask for Ed's legal opinion on the DNA test. He also asked about filing for a competency hearing for Avis. It was Merle's overtly greedy opinion that anyone of sound mind would not give that kind, or any kind, of money away. He thought if everything played out in his favor, maybe he could look after the estate for his long ignored, and troubled, possible son. After three hours of billable discussion, Ed finally convinced him the mental fitness angle was probably a no-go, at least for the time being, but the DNA request more than likely had at least a long shot of getting a favorable decision from the local judge. At the very least there would be more billable office hours and then a billable court hearing. By the end of the week, with a half-dozen donors paying him $350 an hour, Ed was certain it was all worth pursuing. Even if nobody else succeeded in making money off Avis's good fortune, Ed was going to cash in on some of the Powerball revenue.

"So... I hear about half the town is trying to get a judge to make Avis take a DNA test," Ernie said to Savannah, who was sipping her morning coffee while sitting at the counter.

"Who did you hear that from?" Savannah asked, although in the short time she had been in Watermill she had already come to understand the only difference between public knowledge and private information was the private stuff was prefaced with a quiet, "I'm not supposed to say anything, but..." or something along those lines. Most of the good stuff was private stuff.

"Oh, you know. It all starts out with someone who is supposed to know, who is sharing it with someone who should maybe sort of know, and then onto somebody that just doesn't need to know. Eventually it always ends up here. By then of course, everyone knows," he said with a shrug and poured more coffee into her cup.

"Who's the lawyer?"

"Fitzgerald. He's the only game in town. Although, I'd be surprised if outsiders didn't jump on the boat soon, know what I mean? A lot of money on the table. Money draws lawyers like blood draws sharks."

"I suppose so, Ernie," she said as if they were old friends.

Thanks to Leo, word had already spread around the region that she and Avis were an item of sorts and half the town had already started to welcome her as one of their own, while the other half had decided she was just a moneygrubbing whore trying to cut into their stash. It was a small-town thing that gave them the feeling they should worry about Avis's money as if it were their own. It wasn't like they were expecting to get their hands on any of it, they just didn't think an outsider should get it either. Reporters began looking at Savannah more like an interview subject, as opposed to being the competition, but they got nothing from her. "Lot of money on the table," she echoed back at Ernie.

"Guess maybe Avis understood what was going to happen right from the start, huh?" Ernie asked, not expecting an answer. She smiled but said nothing. She didn't answer questions about anything since she had become part of the story.

"Hell of a thing," Ernie mumbled and wiped the counter.

"Hell of a thing, Ernie," she echoed, staring into her coffee. "Hell of a thing," she repeated just as a gray-haired, fat-faced, pot-bellied guy with yellow teeth and bad breath slid onto the stool next to her.

"Hey, Savannah. Long time no see." Charlie Libby was an old-time newspaper hack from Portland who was about as likeable as he was skinny. He'd steal a scoop from his own mother, and blame her for being careless with the information, if it got him a story.

"Fuck you, Charlie," was all she said before she stood up and winked at Ernie and walked out the door.

Charlie got up to follow her, and saw a guy sitting in the corner with an eye patch on. He turned to Ernie and asked, "Who's the pirate?"

Before the end of the week, Charlie's story about all the possible Avis fathers was written and printed. It seemed the confidentiality of the Fitzgerald Law Office had not improved. After the good townsfolk read his story, things in Watermill started to turn in a new direction. The human-interest story about the compassionate young man who generously gave away almost a billion dollars started taking shape as just another sex-laden, money-grubbing, lawyer-tainted, family-dirty-laundry-airing small-town-America saga that was likely going to have a couple of divorces to add some spice to it before it was all said and done.

Avis just stayed in the woods and received the bits and pieces from

Savannah and Leo. The little he heard didn't surprise him all that much, human nature being what it is.

And, of course, Charlie wrote a bit about the emu farmer pirate who lost his eye in some sort of industrial accident about fifteen years ago. The pirate was vague on the details other than he was a close cousin to Avis Humphrey and he had an emu farm on the outskirts of Watermill.

With all the DNA kits being one donor short on a sample, Merle, who was always on top of the money game, tried to pay Agnes for a sample from Avis's trailer, but he was too late. In her zest to make everything clean and sparkly and like new for when Avis returned home to have unforgettable sex with her, she had scrubbed and bleached away any and all useable DNA samples. Her potentially profitable partnership with Merle was short-lived.

Merle was aware he was the best candidate for fatherhood—other than Jazzman of course, but nobody knew who or where he was. All the other backseat boys were long shots, at best.

Agnes had initially liked the idea of partnering up with Merle. He was tenacious, and if any of the potential dads could extract money from Avis, it would likely be Merle. In retrospect, she was relieved when their partnership went bust. The morning after Merle had come to the trailer with the package full of swabs and had unsuccessfully tried to find an Avis DNA sample, Agnes stepped out of the shower and began to towel herself off. She glanced up and saw her naked reflection in the full-length mirror hanging on the bathroom wall and stood and admired what she was looking at. It was then that it dawned on her that the proper tools to get to Avis's money, were not likely cotton swabs.

CHAPTER THIRTY

"My father was a hard man. Nerves of steel. Eyes of steel. Face of steel." George spoke slowly and methodically, in a quiet weathered voice, as Savannah sat and listened to his story. "If he was in one of his moods and glared at me, it was like he was looking right through me. Yeah, man. Nerves of steel, eyes of steel, and when he was inclined to let loose, he had fists of steel, too. It's been over sixty years, but I can still feel some of them ass-whooping's like they just happened yesterday." He looked out toward the flower garden in the middle of the park and sat motionless on the bench, except he gently shook his head back and forth and drew in a deep sigh. "Just like yesterday," he quietly repeated.

"I presume you're not from around here?" Savannah asked. It wasn't a real question. She was just fishing for information and making small talk. It wasn't likely this gentle old black man who spoke with a slight southern twang was originally from Watermill, New Hampshire. It wasn't even likely that a young black man with a New England accent would have been from Watermill. It wasn't that it was segregated, it was just a small New England town. It was a place that never had anyone to integrate. At least, not before George arrived.

"No, ma'am. Originally from the other side of the tracks of Elmore, Alabama."

"Which side of the tracks might that have been?" she responded with more than a good idea of which side it was. Given his age, and the time frame when he was raised down in Alabama, the wrong side of the tracks was a safe bet. Governors Patterson and then Wallace would have been running things in the good ole boy kingdom back then and the KKK was in its heyday. There weren't many "right side of the track" neighborhoods for Bama Blacks back in the fifties and sixties. Savannah was trying to understand how the universe had spun a plan where an old southern black gentleman ended up being a friend, and a kind of father figure, to a six-year-old New England white boy.

"Weren't no good side of the tracks in Elmore back then, but I was from the worst side. Mostly shacks. Everyone was poor. Nobody had too much... or even enough, for that matter. No money, no stuff, no future." He looked down at the ground as if he might have been watching an old rerun on TV. A tragic old rerun of his younger life.

"But you're here now. How'd that come about? How did a man from Elmore, Alabama end up in a cozy little town in New Hampshire?" She knew the question sounded bad, but she wasn't being judgmental. Savannah thought the goodness of the real world was often overstated and fairy tale endings were not always what they seemed to be. She hadn't completely shaken her post-almost-suicidal attitude. Anyway, there wasn't a tender way to ask, "How did a poor black man from Alabama end up living a decent life in the all-white world of Watermill, New Hampshire?" without it sounding exactly like it was. Unlikely. Unfair. Perhaps bigoted. But honest.

"Blessed. Yes ma'am. I've been blessed my whole life. At least I've been blessed for *most* of my life. Always have been and I suspect, God willing, always will be. Things have always had a way of working out for me." She doubted that *blessed* was the answer she would have given if she had been raised in George's shoes.

When George stopped talking, she listened to the Red Sox game he had tuned in on his small green battery-powered transistor radio. Whoever was batting fouled off a couple of pitches while George drifted back to memories that sometimes still haunted him and occasionally made him smile. He shuddered when he recalled his father coming home drunk and kicking the hell out of him on his twelfth birthday. George had foolishly thought there might be a birthday present. The beating was to remind him there were worse things in life than not getting things for free. Sixty years later that birthday gift still stayed with him. He didn't share that story with Savannah. Couldn't see any good could come from telling a story that would only get pity showered on him. He wasn't a fan of pity.

"Anyway" he started up again, breaking the silence and the memory. "When I was 'bout eighteen, I was working at a junkyard when this guy came in to buy a bunch of beat-up old cars. Seemed like something fishy was going on 'because there wasn't no good reason to buy a bunch of old junk cars in Alabama and truck them all the way up to New England. Least not as far as I could tell. But I was getting paid two and a half dollars an hour, straight cash, and it wasn't my place to question. Weren't none of my business. I helped load the truck and took the cash. Them were my only jobs and that's what I did."

"Hard work?" Savannah asked and scribbled a note in her pad.

"Nah. Not really. The heavy lifting was all done by a big forklift. Once it was set in place everything had to be tied down with chains and straps. That's what I did mostly. I was young and strong and climbed around the cars and tossed chains and latched them here and there. You know how it is when you're young. Never get tired and ain't nothing you can't do."

"So, how did you end up here? Long way from Elmore to Watermill."

"The guy who was driving the truck was a little worried he might have to fix the chains and such while trucking up from Bama. He was a big fat guy who chain-smoked cigarettes and stuffed himself with Twinkies and coffee when he wasn't smoking. He told me he'd pay me two hundred bucks and give me a bus ticket back home if I rode along with him. Hell, man. I'd never been out of Elmore County and never had two hundred dollars all at one time. The man was asking me if I wanted to see what the rest of the world was like. Can you imagine that? A poor black kid who didn't finish school was being asked, "Son, do you want to escape from prison or would you like to stay here?" And he was going to pay me to escape and give me a ride. I hopped in the cab of his truck and never went back."

"You never went back to see your family?" Savannah asked somewhat shocked. "Surely, you've gone back at least once or twice to visit."

"Nope. Never looked back all that much, and never went back at all. You saw me shudder a few minutes ago. That's what I do when I think back to where I came from and when I consider what my life would have been like if I had stayed. I don't let that ole dog sneak up and bite me too often. Just not worth looking back. Not worth pondering."

"Did you go to work for the truck driver when you got up here?"

"Nah. He was from Maine. Name was Randy something or other. We stopped, and he got us something to eat in Manchester and I asked if he needed me to go the rest of the way or was he all good. He said he'd make it the rest of the way all right and paid me two hundred and fifty dollars, since he didn't need to buy me a ticket back home. Thought that was pretty good of him. Like I said, I was getting two and a half dollars an hour back in Elmore. Never seen him again."

"So, what did you do then? You had two hundred and fifty dollars in your pocket. You didn't know anyone. You didn't have a place to live. And you had never been away from Elmore, Alabama. Seems to me most people would have been a little scared."

"I think I was so excited that I plum forgot to notice how scared I probably was, or how scared I should have been. Found myself a warehouse job and a cheap place to live and I started life all over again. Started fresh. No steel looks. No steel fists. No more two and a half bucks an hour. No bad side of the tracks. Least not as bad as they were back where I came from. No more going to bed hungry. Time and life took me through a couple jobs and a couple of towns and more than a few bumps in the road. Ended up in Watermill twenty years ago when the company I worked for opened the new J. Peavey Hardware store on Main Street. This place... man, this place is like heaven's door compared to where I came from. No ma'am. I never went back and ain't never going back."

They sat and listened to a few more pitches on the radio. A couple of strikes. A base hit and then a strikeout, and the inning was over.

"Have you ever heard from your family or any old friends?"

"Didn't ever tell em where I went. Just went to work at 6:30 one morning and never went back to the shack."

"So, they don't even know what happened to you or if you're okay? Or even alive?" Savannah asked, unable to comprehend what it would be like to slip away and never look back.

"My world wasn't like the world you come from, ma'am. Don't suspect they realized I was gone, for quite some time. Don't suspect they much cared once they realized."

"And you don't know what happened to them?"

"Hope God had mercy on them. Hope He spared them from the hell I was living in back then. Hope He saved some of them. Hope He forgave some of 'em." George hung his head and stared at the ground again. "Hope He forgave him," he whispered.

The game came back on and George listened to the announcer do the play-by-play while Savannah pondered a life she could only imagine. She was an upper-middle-class white girl who not long ago considered killing herself because her life seemed pointless. Not hopeless, just pointless. She was not beaten or poor or full of dark despair. At least not *real* despair. If she was completely honest, she was, at worst, temporarily bored and lost. There had been a few bumps on the road of her life, but nothing she could have even stretched into a tragedy. Certainly nothing that could have justified her doing something as selfish as the Big Quit. No looks or fists of steel. No dead-end job at two and a half dollars an hour. No lack of education. No poverty. No social injustices. Or at least no social injustices she was on the wrong end of.

George, on the other hand, loved life because he was spared from the eternal poverty and beatings of his childhood days. He had survived living on the poorer side of a poor town and lived to see the better side of a different set of tracks. He had endured being raised in a place and time and with a mindset where odds were he was going to die nearly as poor, or poorer, than as he was when born. For the first couple of decades of his life his salvation had likely been that he didn't fully grasp how hopeless his future was likely going to be. As they sat side by side on the bench near the stonewall at the edge of the park, she had endless opportunities in front of her; and he was, at best, a middle-class old man who lived in a town where there were no other blacks. But George was grateful and humble and somehow at peace in a way she didn't quite understand.

"How old are you, George?"

"All I know is I ain't dead yet," he said with a grin. "And God is still being good to this old man." He smiled a wide smile of contentment and gratitude. "And me and Avis still go fishing now and then. It don't get a lot better than that."

"Oh yeah. Fishing with Avis," she said with a tone of sarcasm.

"Don't get a lot better than that."

"You been fishing with him?" George asked with a surprised look on his face.

"Yes I have. With him and Leo, for a couple of days now."

George laughed out loud and reached out and patted her on the shoulder. "Good Lord. Fishing with Leo is like going to the dentist. He's a good kid," he said, describing Leo as if he were still the twelve-year-old chatterbox who followed him and Avis around. "But good God almighty, the boy cannot stop talking. Fish hear him coming from a hundred yards away." They both laughed at the vision of Leo asking questions. "Hey Avis, this and hey Avis that," George continued. "There's no end to his questions."

"How about you? Does he ask you questions?"

"Aw. Once in a while, but he likes getting answers, so mostly I shrug like I don't know, and he goes off and wears Avis out," he said, shaking his head back and forth. "You know, one time I was right in the middle of reeling in a big trout. Pretty one, probably a foot long. Just about the time I was reaching down to grab it, Leo says, 'Hey George, do you think God minds that you eat trout, being that you're a church guy and all?' Can you imagine that? A ten-year-old kid trying to ruin my big catch like that?" George laughed and shook his head back and forth again.

"So... do you?"

"Heck no! Even Jesus ate fish. I told that boy if his conscience bothered him then *he* should eat crackers while we ate our fish."

"So, what did Leo eat when you cooked the fish?" Savannah asked, scribbling in her notepad again.

"Oh, he ate the fish. Forgot all about his silly question and ate like he was starving. I guess he was just asking like he always asks. Don't know where that boy comes up with all his questions." He glanced up at the puffy clouds in the blue sky and took a deep breath. "But he never runs out of them," he added and took another deep breath and looked around for a few more seconds and listened to the leaves rustling in the breeze. "How you liking fishing, ma'am? I mean, when Leo quiets down. Enjoying yourself?"

"Well, first of all, please call me Savannah. I'm sure I'm not old enough to be called *ma'am* yet."

"All right. How do you like fishing, Savannah?" He liked her. He liked the sound of her name and her smile. She was pretty, and she was friends with Avis. That was enough for him, but *fishing* with Avis put her over the top, on George's list.

"It's growing on me," she answered as if she were trying to convince him that she didn't enjoy it all that much. They both knew better.

"Fishing is good for the soul, Savannah. I've done a bunch of good thinking when I was fishing," he said, as if she needed convincing. "Tougher to think when Leo's with us," he added, as if it were the first time he had ever pondered that point.

Savannah looked at George and smiled. It struck her that if she stayed in Watermill for a while she would probably be friends with George too. She hadn't made a new friend, or at least a real one in such a long time, she had forgotten what it felt like. In the past week, she had become a part of the Avis Humphrey gang. George was just the newest member to welcome her. Now that they had met and chatted for a while, she thought it was time to start asking about Avis, but she didn't feel like going there yet.

"You're pretty happy here, George? Pretty okay with life then?" She wasn't even sure why she asked the question. It just wasn't all that often she met someone who came across as perfectly content.

"I am." He spoke slowly and softly. "I am," he said quietly again as if he were reminding himself of how blessed his life was. "Thankful for the air I breathe."

What could she say in response to that statement? No questioning or probing or pondering would solve the mystery of the irrefutable. There was no reasoning that would adequately explain how someone as blessed as Savannah could be less contented than George. They sat without talking as three Red Sox in a row struck out and the game on the radio broke for more advertisements.

"So, Leo told me you and Avis are pretty close. Do you mind if I ask you about that?"

"Oh. Maybe next time. Getting a bit tired today, but I'll probably be back here about the same time tomorrow if you would care to come and sit with me again. No game on the radio tomorrow. Sox are heading to New

York day after tomorrow, but nothing but talk shows tomorrow. Don't listen to them much. If not tomorrow, I'm out here just about every day until winter comes back. Never liked the cold all that much."

He stood up with his little green radio in his left hand and shook Savannah's hand with his right. She watched as George hobbled across the lawn toward town and barely heard him whisper, "Thankful for the air I breathe. Amen."

It caught her off guard when she realized she was *not* thankful for the air that she breathed. Or for much of anything else for that matter. She looked up at the sky and clouds, just as George had done, and took a deep long breath. She liked how it felt fresh and clean and good and she smiled at her new friend who continued to walk away across the park.

CHAPTER THIRTY-ONE

Avis was mildly surprised, and a bit irritated with himself, that he had missed seeing Savannah over the past two days. He had almost given up on her coming out for a visit when her car pulled in and she swung the door open and stepped out into the moonlit grass. Leo had come and gone for the day, but Savannah had stayed back in town and tried to get the pulse of what everyone else was doing and saying. As it turned out, most of the town wasn't saying much other than Alice Chen was still in hiding and Avis was still fishing somewhere out in the vast New Hampshire forest. The second biggest story, other than Avis himself, was half the men in town were now hoping to be his dear ole long-lost dad. But the new and bigger story rolling through the town with some serious steam was the woman reporter from Maine who had hooked up with Avis. Nobody had confirmed it yet, but it was still the hot rumor of the day. Everyone at the diner, the post office, and the All American were talking about it. Of course, it started out just like every other small-town rumor started. Someone, in this case Leo, told someone who told someone who told everyone, and that was that. All the townspeople needed now was a sighting, confirmed or unconfirmed, of the two of them actually together, and the gossip mill would explode.

As she stood beneath the stars with no streetlights within ten miles, the stars looked almost within reach of her long slender fingers. The hood of the car was warm from the engine she had just shut off, and the outside air was fresh, almost brisk. Savannah leaned on the hood and breathed in everything. She smiled and rested back on her elbows as she looked up toward the heavens. The moon was full and lit the camp like daylight as Avis watched her. He stood by the fire for a long time and just looked at this new woman who had slipped into his life without his permission. She had snuck up on him, and that was something that didn't happen often to Avis Humphrey. He was rarely caught off guard. Savannah had been a complete surprise. At first, he thought she was an irritating surprise, but a surprise nonetheless. She was just another reporter looking for a story. The only differences had been that he was lucky enough to stumble upon her, and she was somewhat attractive.

There was a faint voice whispering something in the back of his head, and the message was getting clearer. He gazed for a minute toward the same stars she was watching, and then he began walking toward her. As he got closer, he was again taken by surprise. He'd known Savannah was attractive, but until now, he had not appreciated how truly beautiful she was standing beneath the brilliant night sky. She was long, lean, and mysterious, and undeniably sexy. This woman, who had been hanging with him and baiting hooks and throwing fish up and into trees and asking irritating questions, looked breathtakingly beautiful in her white V neck cotton T-shirt, faded blue jeans and flip-flops.

"Excitement get to be too much for you in Watermill?" he asked, looking up at the stars.

"No. I just thought you might like some company. I brought a bottle of wine. I'm getting a little tired of drinking Pabst Blue Ribbon." She reached into her shoulder bag lying on the hood and pulled out the bottle and a paper bag with bread and cheese inside. "You can do the honors," she said, and handed him the bottle as she tore off a small piece of bread and stuck it into her mouth.

"Cups?"

"In the bag," she said as she waved toward the bag while wandering toward the fire. She sat down on her log and waited for her genius fisherman to join her.

Avis followed and poured wine into the paper cups and handed one to her and turned to walk to his log.

"You can sit by me, you know," she said.

He smiled and sat down beside her. They watched the fire and sipped wine and said nothing for nearly ten minutes. The wood crackled in the flames and the water trickled over the rocks near the riverbank. Crickets chirped off in the distance and Savannah's hand lifted up as she pointed at a shooting star.

"Have you ever seen the Aurora Borealis?" Avis asked as they continued to look up into the night sky.

"No. I mean, I've seen them on the Internet and on TV, but not while I was actually looking up into the sky. Have you?"

"Oh yeah. Just about the most beautiful thing I've ever seen. I swear, when they're really good, the sky looks like there's a multicolored sheet of stardust being gently waved in the breeze. It's the closest thing to supernatural I've ever experienced."

"Sounds amazing," she whispered and took a sip of her wine.

"You'll have to watch for them in the fall," he added, still looking up.

She reached over and put her hand onto the back of his and gently squeezed it as she laid her head onto his shoulder. She couldn't recall ever feeling this comfortable with anyone else, and she was a woman who was comfortable with nearly everyone. But Avis was different. He was simple, but intelligent. According to Leo, he was not only intelligent, he was a genius. And she was starting to wonder if he wasn't correct. Avis was strong, but gentle. He was independent, almost a loner, but he was comfortable to talk with. She presumed his independence was a survival instinct he had honed as each member of his family had abandoned him, one by one. Avis Humphrey was an anomaly. He was a kind, good-looking man who had just won nine hundred million dollars, and his biggest concern was how to get rid of it without affecting his fishing schedule.

"I guess it's my turn for a question," Savannah said without lifting her head up off from his shoulder.

"What makes you say that?"

"You asked me if I had ever seen the Aurora Borealis. Now it's my turn."

"Mmmm. So I did." He took a deep sigh and savored the last moments of peace and silence. "Ask away."

"Do you want to kiss me?" She lifted her head up off his shoulder and watched him as he pondered the question for a moment, as if it were a difficult one to answer.

"Is this something you really have to think about?" she asked with an irritated look on her face.

The truth was, it *was* something he did have to think about. Agnes and the others were easy. They were sex partners. They were fun. They were almost meaningless relationships. Savannah already felt different to him, so when she asked, "Do you want to kiss me?" he took time to savor the moment. For reasons that he had only read about in books, he presumed this was going to be a life-changing moment.

"I've been thinking about kissing you for the last two days. In fact, I've been thinking about it ever since I found out I saved your life," he added to keep the moment light.

Savannah didn't smile at his joke. She closed her eyes and leaned forward. They kissed a long soft kiss and then he put his arms around her and they kissed until the rest of the world disappeared.

"So, I guess we're even now," she said with their lips still almost touching.

"What's that supposed to mean?"

"Now I'm saving your life." She leaned in and kissed him again and the questioning was finished for the night.

CHAPTER THIRTY-TWO

Leo pulled into the campsite at 8:15 in the morning. It was a record-early arrival for him and most certainly the earliest he had ever made it to a fishing hole without being dragged there by Avis. An hour earlier, he had rolled out of bed and stumbled half-asleep toward the bathroom. The door to the bedroom where Savannah was supposed to have slept was wide open, and by all appearances the bed hadn't been used. He stopped and looked at the neatly made bed and waited for the fog to lift and for his brain to engage. His eyes popped wide open and he stood up straight. He was suddenly wide awake and putting the pieces together. Fifteen minutes later he was out the front door and, on the way, to confirm what he presumed to be true.

"Well, well, well. What have we here?" he said with a raised eyebrow as he climbed out of the truck and wandered toward the smoldering fire that was puffing smoke up and around Avis and Savannah.

"Good morning, Leo," Savannah answered. She got up from her log and kissed him on the cheek.

"Where's the coffee?" Avis barked at the empty-handed Leo.

"Didn't have time to get any. I was worried about Savannah and all. She didn't come home last night, and I thought something might have happened to her."

"How saintly of you," Avis mumbled.

Savannah just rolled her eyes. "Damn it, Leo. Now I have to drive all the way back to town to get coffee?" She shook her head back and forth at Leo. He looked at her with a clueless grin on his face. "You're right," she said glancing at Avis. "Your humanitarian load is probably heavier than my year with the Peace Corps."

"At least yours was temporary," Avis mumbled and kicked dirt onto the smoldering fire.

She walked back to her log, picked up her bag, and stepped toward

Avis and gave him a soft kiss. "I'll be back in an hour or so. Need anything else while I'm in town?"

He tugged at her hand and leaned in and gave her another kiss. His life had never felt so right.

"Carmen's not going to be happy," Leo said to her as she walked past.

"Who knows, maybe Avis will have both of us," she answered with a wink. Leo smiled at her, ninety-nine percent certain she was teasing him.

The two men stood in silence and watched her drive off with their minds in different places. Avis was recalling last night and absorbing how everything seemed peaceful and good for the first time in a long, long time. The dark clouds of his past were being purged away by a new light, and it was a cleansing feeling. He felt new. Leo was pondering Savannah's 'Carmen' comment.

"Let's fish," Avis said as he turned and picked up his rod.

"Nah. Let's drink some coffee." Leo headed back to the truck to get the cups of coffee he had picked up from Ernie's.

"Thought you didn't stop and get any. You know, with all your concern for her safety and everything."

"Just messing with her. Besides, I thought we'd shoot the shit for a bit. Kind of a big deal, right? I mean... she's no Agnes."

"You got that right, Leo. She's no Agnes. I suppose she is what you might call the real deal."

"The real deal. I like that. And she fishes, too. Gotta like that."

Avis sat down on her log. Leo sat on Avis's log. They drank coffee and talked and laughed for the first time since the ticket news broke. Leo told Avis about all the happenings around town, including a couple of potential new father additions coming out of the woodwork.

"You know what I heard? I heard Tim Laudenberg got thrown out of his house when the news got around he had been to see Fitzgerald and tried to climb onto the DNA train. I gotta tell you, Avis, Lindsey banged a bunch of guys around town. I mean, the number just keeps growing."

Avis shrugged and fiddled with a stick he'd picked up off the ground. The rumors of the finely-honed skills of Lindsey Beckham were legendary around Watermill, and Avis had heard as many stories as everyone else had over the years. Whatever pain or discomfort the news had brought to teenage Avis was long gone. He had no ill feelings toward her any longer. In fact, he had no feelings about her at all. While it would have been an overstatement to say she was dead to him, the truth was he didn't care about her one way or another. She drove away and never came back. That was all he needed to know.

"Oh, and by the way, I'm pretty sure Merle has always loved you and wants to be the best father he can be to you now. At least that's what he said in his TV interview, and you won't guess who he was sitting with when the cameras were on him."

Avis thought for a moment and almost said who he was almost certain was by Merle's side, but he decided to let Leo have his moment.

"Lindsey," Leo blurted out. "She sat there looking like... hell, I don't know what she looked like. Guess she looked like she aged pretty good, and she smelled money in Watermill all the way from Montana. That's what she looked like to me, anyway."

"I figured she'd be coming back when she got the news," Avis said without looking up. "In fact, I thought she would have been back the day after the news broke," he added.

"She must not watch the news much. I heard she got back the day before yesterday. That's what Carmen told me," he said.

Avis shrugged again and thought about Savannah's soft, sweet kisses. The smell of her hair lingered in his mind and her voice drifted around in his head. "I think I love her, Leo."

Leo froze and stared at him. He'd known Avis nearly his entire life. Other than his infatuation with Carmen, he had never seen him emotionally attached to a particular girl or woman. In less than a week Savannah had slipped into his life and turned him inside out.

"The real deal. Isn't that what you called her?" Leo asked and kicked a stick lying on the ground.

"Yup."

"Does that mean I can have Carmen?"

"What the hell. Why not? Can't do any worse with her than I did."

"So now what?" Leo asked, not joking around any longer.

"Fishing, I guess."

"No. I mean, with you guys? She's from Maine and you're living in New Hampshire. You got like a billion dollars you gotta do something with. Alice is in hiding. And of course, you adopted me. That's what you told Savannah." He smiled, but he was still in a serious mode. "Everything's changing, man. So, now what?"

"Fishing. That's the only answer I've got for now, Leo," he said as he picked up his pole and headed toward the stream.

* * *

It was after lunch before Savannah returned to Leo and Avis. When she had walked into Ernie's to get coffee a few hours earlier he mentioned that Leo had already picked up three cups and doughnuts to boot.

"That little..." Her words trailed off and she smiled and momentarily closed her eyes. She tried to decide whether Leo was prying at Avis for intimate details or just wanted to hang out alone with his best friend. Either way, coffee for one was all she needed. On her way out of the door of Ernie's, she stopped and looked over at the creepy one-eyed guy sitting in the corner. He was fidgeting with his eye patch again, oblivious to the world around him. She stood with her hand on the brass doorknob and almost let go of it and walked over to confront this fraud, whomever he was. An instant before she could make up her mind what to do, the knob turned from the outside and the door opened and banged against her foot. Savannah jumped back, and Denny Wilson gave her an irritated look as he brushed past her and headed to one of the stools.

"Coffee," he mumbled without making eye contact with Ernie. Ernie, who was indifferent to it all, poured the coffee. Savannah was torn between her irritation with One Eye and almost being run over by the horse's ass who appeared to be having a bad day or week or life. She glanced first at one and then the other, and then gave up on both of them. She sipped her coffee and stepped out of the door and took a deep breath of fresh air and headed toward her car without noticing the Jeep that pulled up directly next to her, or the woman who was driving it.

CHAPTER THIRTY-THREE

"So, question time," Savannah said, holding her hotdog on a wooden stick over the campfire.

While she was back in Watermill she had shot a quick text to Steve that read, "Story coming soon," and nothing more.

Steve sat at his desk and read it three times and wondered what the hell it was supposed to mean. "Soon? Tomorrow? Next week? Next year? What the hell kind of woman do you live with anyways?" he asked out loud. Bruce looked over at him as if he wondered if Steve expected a cat to respond. He stood up, stretched, turned his back to Steve, and laid back down.

Steve tossed his phone back onto his desk and finished reading yet one more online story about the Watermill Pirate. It was a story not written by his reporter.

* * *

"Leo says you're a smart guy," Savannah said, "Do you really speak French?"

"Oui."

"Seriously, do you really speak French, and did you teach yourself from books and not from CD's or a Rosetta Stone program or something like that?"

Avis looked down at the stick he was holding in his hand. He didn't like talking about himself. The truth was Leo, Alice, and probably George, were the only three people who knew he was really brilliant. "Yeah. I speak French. Taught myself," he mumbled without looking up.

"Any other languages? Foreign, I mean," knowing he was probably going to say English just to be a smartass.

"Oh. A couple, I guess. Spanish. A little Russian. German. A little

Mandarin and Portuguese. Some Aramaic and a bit of Hebrew. But the truth is, I don't really speak as much as I read them. A lot of the books I read aren't in English. Or if they are in English, I don't have them. Besides, it's cool reading in the language they were originally written in."

Savannah sat with her mouth hanging open. Leo had been right. Avis was a genius who liked to fish for trout and work on car engines in a little hick town in New Hampshire. He fiddled with the stick again and drew little scribbles in the dirt, trying to hide his discomfort at talking about himself. She was at a loss for words and searched for a follow-up question when Avis interrupted her thought process. "My turn."

"Oh. Okay. What's your question?"

"How would your parents have taken it if you had killed yourself a couple weeks ago?" He lifted his head and looked her straight in the eyes. He wasn't looking for some vague dance-around response. He wanted her to say the truth out loud.

"It would have destroyed them," she said without hesitation. She waited for a follow-up question or a lecture or a look of judgment, but he said and did nothing other than look back down and continue to scribble in the dirt with his stick.

"I got a question," Leo blurted out. "Why do you suppose someone got up one day and said, 'I think I'll put fizzy stuff in water'? What would make someone do that?"

Savannah tilted her head at him for about the twentieth time and wondered where his questions came from, but she had no good answer for her question—or for Leo's question.

Avis barely moved or looked up. He just rambled on that sometime in the late 1700s the Schweppe family created carbonated water in an effort to mimic spring-fed mineral water, which was all the rage at the time. Savannah turned from Leo to Avis and wondered why he would have that information readily available in his head. Leo had already listened, processed, and accepted the information and moved on to thinking about something else.

"Guess you're not going to eat that hotdog," Avis said, motioning to her charred black dog.

"Damn it." She pushed the burnt dog off the stick and into the fire and stabbed another raw one.

"My turn," she started again.

"You wanna see something?" Avis interrupted her with a grin.

"Excuse me?"

He slowly hyper-annunciated as he repeated his words. "Do you want to see something?"

Savannah sat on the other side of the fire and pondered the question. It sounded like one of those "pull my finger" things her uncle used to say to her when she was a little girl.

"I don't know. Is it something I might actually want to see?" she asked.

Avis smiled from ear to ear, anticipating her reaction to what he was going to show her. "Yeah. You're going to want to see this."

"Okay then. Impress me."

He drank the last swallow of his Pabst Blue Ribbon and tossed the can into the fire. He turned and grinned at Leo. Leo watched for a moment and then looked at Savannah and shrugged. "Got me. I don't have any idea."

"Ladies and gentlemen," Avis said, "For those of you who have never seen one before, this is what a nine-hundred-sixty-seven-million-dollar Powerball ticket looks like." He slipped two fingers into his T-shirt pocket and pulled out a wrinkled ticket.

"You have got to be kidding me!" Savannah whispered, already on her feet and moving to the other side of the fire.

"I thought you gave it to Alice," Leo said.

"I never said I won the Powerball or that I gave the ticket to Alice. That's just the news that was spread around the world by everyone except Avis Humphrey."

"You did win, though, right?" Savannah asked. She momentarily wondered if the entire Avis story had been a complete hoax.

"Look for yourself," he said and handed her the ticket as she sat down beside him.

"So where did the Alice story come from?" Leo asked.

"Well, a week or two after the damn numbers came up and I had lost a sufficient amount of sleep, I went to talk to Alice about giving her the ticket. I figured she would do something good with it." He spoke slowly as if the story was unimportant and nobody particularly wanted to hear it.

"And?" Savannah asked, urging him to continue.

"Well, Alice was pretty blown away, too. After I showed her the ticket and after she composed herself, she said nine hundred and sixty-seven million dollars was too much money to just be giving it away. But I told her one way or another it was going to go. Then she said she would need to talk to a lawyer first and I should put the ticket someplace safe." He patted his pocket as he said, "someplace safe," as if to signify his pocket was an ironclad vault.

"And then what happened?" Savannah asked.

"She went and saw Ed Fitzgerald. You've probably heard he's the local attorney. She was asking him for advice and I suppose someone in his office must have overheard the conversation and then told someone who told someone who told someone, until everyone in Watermill and beyond had been told. That's when people like you started showing up." He nodded toward Savannah to make sure she knew he was referring to her. "Pretty soon you guys had told the whole damned world some country bumpkin gave away nine-hundred and sixty-seven million dollars."

"Technically I haven't told anyone yet," Savannah answered in her own defense. "In fact, if I don't submit a story soon, I'm going to be unemployed and I won't ever be telling anyone."

"Here's something funny," Leo chimed in. "There's about a thousand reporters in town and the only one who hasn't written a story about you is the one who has actually met you. Funny, huh?"

"Oh, just a hoot," Savannah answered. Avis stuffed the ticket back into his pocket and wrinkled it a little more.

"So, you think your T-shirt pocket is a good place to keep something so valuable?" Savannah asked.

"Not all that valuable to me. Don't forget, I don't even want it. Thought about throwing it into the fire a couple of times. Problem solved."

"You wouldn't?" Savannah said, half as a statement and half as a question.

"Oh, hell yeah he would. If Avis says it don't mean anything to him, then it don't mean anything to him," Leo chimed in, continuing his role as the Avis Humphrey Historian & Authority.

Whether Savannah admired Avis or thought he was just in over his head, one thing was for sure: This guy, this millennial, technically speaking, was not your run-of-the-mill guy. Hundreds of millions of dollars were at his disposal and his biggest dilemma was how to get rid of it without disrupting his simple small-town life. Keeping the money had never entered his mind.

"If you don't want the money, why wouldn't you just give it to Leo? He's your best friend, right?"

"Yeah Avis. Why wouldn't you just give it to your best friend Leo?" Leo added, acting as if he might want the money.

Avis reached into his pocket and pulled out the ticket and handed it to Leo. "Here you go."

"What the hell am I supposed to do with that kind of money?" Leo asked, ignoring Avis's outstretched hand as he dug into the Styrofoam cooler for another beer.

"You want me to give you the ticket, and I still have to figure out what to do with it? Now what kind of sense does that make?" Avis asked as he stuffed the ticket back into his pocket one more time. More wrinkles.

"What the hell is wrong with the two of you?" asked Savannah. "Jesus Christ! I bet you couldn't find another two friends in the world who would fight about which one is going to get stuck with nine hundred and sixty-seven million dollars. Seriously."

Leo looked at her with a puzzled look on his face, as if she were missing the obvious dilemma. "I think she's a little upset, Avis. What do you think we should do?" he asked as if she couldn't hear him.

"I don't know, Leo. Maybe I should give her the ticket. What do you think?"

Savannah laughed at the absurdity of his smart-ass comment until she realized he was actually pondering giving her the ticket.

"I don't think so," Leo answered. "She seems to be stressed all out just talking about it. Can't imagine things would lighten up if she had to deal with owning it."

"Are you serious, Leo?" she snapped. "He just tried to hand you the ticket and you actually didn't want it?"

"You gotta lighten up, Savannah. Hey! Do you ever smoke pot?"

She rolled her eyes at the absurdity of the whole conversation. "Once in a while, Leo."

"You got any with you?" he asked, keeping in tune with the typical Leo mode of liking drinking and smoking, but rarely paying for either.

"No, Leo. I don't have any with me," she snapped. "I swear there is something wrong with the both of you?"

Leo shrugged and reached into his pocket and pulled out a joint and lit it up. Avis waved him off and he handed it to Savannah. She inhaled the smoke and looked around and wondered if she was on a reality TV show.

CHAPTER THIRTY-FOUR

Denny sat with his head hung low, and mindlessly stared at the countertop after almost running Savannah over when he pushed his way through the front door. He ran his index finger nervously along a deep scratch and went out of his way to ignore Tom who, as usual, sat at his corner table fidgeting with his eye patch. Denny's mouth opened as if he had something to say, but he said nothing and continued to stare down at the counter. In the past few days he had been exiled from sunny Miami to dreary New Hampshire on a quest to find the urban legend, Avis Humphrey. After two days of staking out Avis's nearly abandoned trailer, he walked god knows how many miles along a deserted stream without seeing so much as another human being. The next day he walked a few more miles in his soaking wet, mud-covered, expensive loafers after being intentionally bogged down in the middle of a muddy creek by Avis's best friend. So far all he had to show for his efforts was a strange interview with a one-eyed guy who may or may not have intentionally sent him on a wild-goose chase into the New Hampshire woods. Then he met an extremely attractive woman at Avis's trailer who claimed to be his long-time live-in girlfriend but seemed to be moving in as she was telling him her story. After she flirted with him for a bit, Denny somehow found himself carrying three heavy boxes from her car into the trailer. As soon as they were dropped in the middle of the living room floor, the flirting stopped, and he was asked to leave. As he backed out of the dirt driveway he wondered if he had just become an accomplice to breaking into Avis Humphrey's home.

"Now there's someone you don't see every day," Ernie said as he set a cup of black coffee onto the counter in front of Denny and nodded toward the front window.

"Who's that?" Denny asked without looking up or feigning the least bit of interest.

"Lindsey Beckham."

"And who might that be?" Denny followed up with as he took a sip of his coffee.

"That, my friend, is Avis Humphrey's mother. She hasn't set foot in this town since she left for Montana twenty-something years ago."

Denny jumped up and off his barstool and scooted across the room and out the front door before Ernie even finished what he was saying. He hoped he would get to her before anyone else even saw her. Thoughts were racing around in his head about the best way to approach her. Polite? Professional? Cordial? Charming? Aggressive? "Gotta get out of this place. Gotta get out of this place. Gotta get out of this place," he kept repeating to himself as he closed the gap between the two of them. If he could just get one good interview, he would be able to climb on a plane and head back to bask in the Florida sunshine before tomorrow night. New Hampshire would be behind him for good. Black flies, gray skies, rain, small-town hicks; they would all be the colorful details he would embellish in the stories he told and retold to good-looking Cuban women back in Miami. He was confident if he could spin the interviews from the resident Pirate and the hot girlfriend into being part of a story that was an exclusive, with *Avis Humphrey's Mother,* he would be miles ahead of every other reporter in town. "So, this is what it feels like to break a big story," he prematurely thought as he jogged down the steps of the diner toward the woman standing by her car.

Lindsey had barely closed her car door and lit a cigarette when Denny reached out his hand to give her a warm handshake. She lifted her hand but didn't reach out. It was one of the many skills she had honed over the years. She knew if she kept her hand drawn close, Denny would either have to reach a long way or step closer to her. Experience had showed her that men typically moved closer.

"Hi, Lindsey. I'm Denny Wilson. How are you?" He discarded any professionalism and went straight into the mode of trying to pick up a good-looking woman in an LA or Miami bar. They were typically younger than Lindsey, but the process was all the same. Smile, charm, compliment, listen, show concern, and move in for the kill. He was good at the game and presumed he had the upper hand. She was attractive for a woman one side or the other of fifty, but she was New Hampshire and Montana good-looking.

She was not LA or Miami hot, where fifty-year-olds were often better looking and younger looking than a lot of thirty-year olds.

Lindsey smiled and smoked and stared at him as he was talking and acted as if she had no idea that almost all the reporters who had overrun the town were all hanging out in the only place there was to hang out at, at 9:30 in the morning in Watermill.

Denny leaned in close enough that their bodies nearly made contact, and he flashed his perfect smile. He had a nice smile, she thought, but in the end, a smile was just a smile. She wasn't impressed by the aroma of his Dolce & Gabbana cologne, his Paul Stuart shirt, his Ralph Lauren Polo pants, or the absurdly expensive gold bracelet hanging on his wrist. But she was impressed that he was six feet four inches tall, well built; solid; perhaps a little over two hundred pounds; olive-skinned with shiny black hair; and, best of all, young. When Lindsey was in her teens, she had liked men in their early to mid-twenties, and that was one thing that had never changed. She still liked men in their early to mid-twenties.

"I was hoping we could talk for a bit. You know, about Avis and everything that's going on," Denny said, still holding on to her hand.

"Denny, sweetie," she answered, flashing her own perfect smile back at him, "I was hoping to get some coffee and settle in for a bit before I dove into all that. I'd already planned my trip home long before any of this came about, so as you can guess, I'm a little overwhelmed." Much like Merle, Lindsey justified much of what she said by inserting threads of truth into her fabric of sort-of truths and complete falsehoods. And the truth was, she had planned a trip home for the better part of the last twenty years. She simply never followed through on any of those plans. She thought about coming home to be a good mother and to raise her son many times over the past two decades. She had pondered about being a decent person and flying in to grab Avis and drag him back to the Big Sky Country where he could live with her and one of the cowboy friends she had made out there, but there never seemed to be enough incentive to get her over the hump. As it turned out, nine hundred and sixty-seven million dollars was just the nudge she needed to get her to take that final step.

"I'll tell you what, Lindsey," Denny said as if they were old acquaintances. "If you want, I'll go get you a cup of coffee and a Danish sweet roll and we can go sit somewhere quiet. Someplace without any distractions," he said, and nodded toward the reporters inside.

Lindsey leaned in until their bodies brushed against each other, and she rested her left hand on his shoulder and gave it a light squeeze. Denny naively thought he was leading the conversation and controlling where the day was headed.

"I suppose I could chat with you for a while. Why don't you meet me over there?" She motioned toward the small parking lot on the edge of the park a block away.

"Cool. That would be great," he blurted out with too much enthusiasm. He squeezed her hand and awkwardly realized he had never let go of it. He flashed another smile and tried to regain his LA/Miami pick-up mode composure and hurried back to the diner before they could be discovered by any of the other reporters inside.

Lindsey stood by the door of her car and watched him walk back to the diner and calculated what the rest of the day might be like. She blew a long, cool stream of smoke up into the air. Denny had a plan, more or less, of how the day would go and what he wanted to achieve. But Lindsey, as always, was a detail-oriented woman. In her mind, the day was instantly planned right down to how long they would talk and how the day would progress, after they stopped talking.

Denny walked straight up to Ernie and said, "Two coffees and a couple of Danish to go and keep the change." He threw a twenty on the counter and leaned forward, so he could whisper something to him. "And I trust you'll not say anything to anyone else."

"Lips are sealed," Ernie said and picked up the money. The truth was he probably wouldn't have said anything anyway. None of the Avis story interested him all that much, other than business had picked up a lot. Even that was starting to wear on his nerves. Same questions every day. Same insincere concern feigned for the community. Same reporters sniffing around for news that might potentially ruin someone's life, but would at the same time, grab someone's attention and make a good headline. As far as Ernie was concerned, all these people could drift back home and let the good folks of Watermill get back to their normal, quiet lives.

A minute later, Denny pulled into the parking lot, which was just big enough for three cars. The crushed rocks crunched under his tires as he pulled the Toyota Yaris in and came to a stop next to Lindsey's rental. She was driving a Jeep SUV. It was nearly twice as big as his little car and it had a spacious backseat covered in soft tan leather.

CHAPTER THIRTY-FIVE

For the first couple of hours, Lindsey and Denny sat on a park bench and shared life stories while they sipped coffee and nibbled their pastries. In the same way Avis had done with Savannah, Lindsey seemed to ask more questions than were being asked of her.

"So, tell me about yourself, Denny," she said, starting things off as she pulled a pack of cigarettes from her purse.

"I think I'm supposed to be asking you the questions. I mean, I'm a little new at this, but that's the way it works, right?" He flashed his boyish smile again.

"We'll get to everything in time. I just like to know who I'm talking to. That's fair, isn't it?" She blew a stream of smoke into the air.

He nodded and shrugged and continued to underestimate the small-town woman he was about to open up his personal life to. "I'm originally from LA, but I live in Miami now. I work for an e-zine called The Brick House On-line."

"LA, Miami, e-zine. It all sounds so exotic. Hanging out in Watermill must feel a bit mundane to you. I mean... no excitement, no entertainment."

"Things are picking up," he flirted back and touched her knee. He really needed the story and he was going to get it today, one way or the other.

"So how did you end up in Miami?" she continued with her line of questions. Denny played along and told his story. Lindsey played along and listened as if she cared. His plan was to tell just enough to get the ball rolling, but over an hour later he had spilled just about everything. She knew about the rich father and the factories. She knew he wanted to be a reporter. She knew about Theresa antagonizing him. And most importantly, she knew they were going to be in the backseat before the day was over. It hadn't yet dawned Denny that up until now, the only thing he knew about her was that she was Avis's mother, and this was the first time she had been back to Watermill in over two decades. And even that little information had come from Ernie. Lindsey had yet to share one ounce of information.

Two hours after they had sat down, the coffee was gone, and the blackflies were starting to swarm.

"Let's go sit in the Jeep and get out of these bugs," she said as she swatted at the insects. She stood up and headed for the car before he had a chance to respond. Not that he would have said No. He was on a quest for an interview. Once they were inside the Jeep, Denny finally began to ask questions and get answers.

"How long ago did you leave?"

"Oh. I think it's been nineteen years now. Maybe twenty. It's been a long time."

"And are you married?"

"Divorced," she answered with a shrug. "Twice," she added with a tone of indifference.

"And how long were you married?"

"The first time, I was married about ten years. Seemed a lot longer. It was good for a while, but in the end, it just didn't work out." She left out the part about the twenty-something-year-old boys she played around with during her ten-year marriage. "The second time was a lot shorter than the first." She didn't mention the second one had been more profitable. The poor banker never had a chance from Day One.

"And you never came back to Watermill? To Avis?" The questions were getting a bit harder, more to the core of the story, but Lindsey wasn't fazed.

"To be honest, I always loved Avis, but there came a point in time when it just didn't seem right to come back home to an almost-grown boy and say, 'Mama's home.' Since he was the only reason for me to come back, I just stayed away."

"And your parents; I understand they moved to Florida. Are they still alive?" he asked. Then added, "Sorry to be so blunt. I'm a little new at this."

"You're doing great, Denny," she said and patted him on the thigh

"And my parents are pretty old now, but they're good. They live in a retirement community down in Ocala. They play mahjongg and hang out with friends at the community center."

Denny nodded and scribbled notes on his small pad and flipped the page. Lindsey reached into her purse and pulled out the keys and started the Jeep.

"We going somewhere?" Denny asked, as he looked up a little surprised at the sound of the engine.

"You just keep asking questions, Denny. I thought it might be better to get out of the center of town where people can see us. I think a couple of cars have already slowed down and have looked our way to see what they could see, and I'd rather not get too much attention, if you know what I mean." It was another Merle-like semi-truth moment. Cars had slowed down because they were coming into town, not because people were looking at them. And as for attention, Lindsey always wanted more, never less.

* * *

Another three hours passed, and the sun was just starting to go down by the time Denny popped the trunk on his Toyota Yaris and pulled out his laptop. He sat in the passenger seat and transcribed his notes from his pad to his laptop in less than a half-hour. He couldn't believe how forthcoming Lindsey had been with information. His biggest challenge now was how much information to share. He certainly couldn't say what he had to do to get the story. Once the notes were in his laptop he began organizing and writing. He played around with a few opening lines before he settled on how to begin.

"Avis Humphrey is nowhere to be found, but friends and family are sharing his story."

He sat back and looked at it for a minute and decided he could always change the beginning if necessary, and then he began typing his rough draft. The more he typed, the better he felt. The better he felt, the faster he typed. A couple hours later he sat back, reread what he typed, took a deep sigh, and hit Save one last time before closing up his laptop. He leaned back in the passenger seat, closed his eyes, and took a deep breath with a smile on his face.

And that's when it hit him. That's when his smile dropped like a brick.

Denny Wilson had whored himself out to get his first real news story. He was raised in a good family by good and decent parents. He'd attended Catholic schools growing up. He always had moral courage and stood by his principles and followed his dreams. Instead of taking the big money to go and work for his father, he stayed strong, composed and stuck with his core values. When Theresa humiliated and dumped on him and sent him to New Hampshire just to harass him, he hadn't complained or showed her his true feelings.

Then he whored himself out and had sex with a woman his mother's age to get the big scoop. He couldn't fully wrap his head around the overwhelming guilt that washed over him. He had slept with plenty of women over the past few years. A couple of them had maybe even been in their early forties. He hadn't slept with any of them for any other reason except both parties wanted to have a good time; but today he had sex with a woman for no other reason than if he didn't do it, he would not get the story. And she was Avis Humphrey's mother. He was three years older than Denny. Hours earlier he had thought he would charm an exclusive out of her, but Lindsey was out of his league. She knew she would charm the pants off Denny, literally, before she would give Denny what he wanted.

At 8:30 that evening he walked into the All American and strolled past Carmen as if she were some eighty-year-old Walmart greeter. He opened the cooler and picked up a six-pack of beer without even paying attention to what brand it was. He set it back down and picked up a twelve-pack. On the way to the counter he grabbed a bag of chips for dinner. He guzzled down the first can of Schlitz before he even left the parking lot. After that, he just drove around the outskirts of Watermill, New Hampshire and threw empty beer cans into the ditches of the deserted country roads. He felt as though he had a self-imposed Scarlet Letter branded on his chest. Even if nobody else ever saw it, he would always know it was there.

CHAPTER THIRTY-SIX

Savannah pulled Avis's truck off the side of the road and into what had become the grassy campsite's parking lot. She reached down and turned off the engine. It sputtered and coughed without her noticing or caring. Avis looked up at her and smiled, happy she had showed up driving his truck and without Leo. At first, she sat and didn't move. Eventually her left hand reached down and fumbled for the door handle. It took her three attempts before she finally made the hinge squawk as the door opened. Her feet swung out but refused to touch the ground. She wanted to get out. She needed to get out. She had to get out. But she froze in place with her feet dangling in the air and her flip-flops almost falling off of her feet. When she finally glanced over her shoulder and looked at Avis, it felt as if someone had just driven a sledgehammer into her chest. She slowly slid off the seat and stood beside the truck, her back facing him. For the first time since leaving Biddeford, she wished she had never come to Watermill. She wished Steve had never called and that Leo and Avis hadn't stopped on the side of the road to pick her up. She wished Avis had never won the Powerball or tried to give it away. Last night she prayed that when she woke up in the morning, it would all be a bad dream. In the end, she never went to sleep. And it was not a dream.

He was squatted next to the smoldering campfire, poking it with a stick when she pulled in. A swirl of gray smoke puffed up from the fire and stung his eyes. He stood up and stepped away from the smoke and watched Savannah through his watery eyes. He watched her as she sat motionless, with her hands on the steering wheel, staring at him. He couldn't know she was at a complete loss as to what to say. When she finally opened the door and climbed out, she just stood by the truck. At first, he wasn't certain what she was doing, but when she walked around to the front of the truck and continued to look over at him with her hands hanging at her side, she almost took his breath away.

Avis strolled toward her looking forward to a good-morning kiss and a cup of coffee. When he got a few feet from her, he saw her eyes were red and puffy. Her hair was a mess and she was still wearing the same white T-shirt and blue jeans she had been wearing when she left the camp the night before. In true Avis form, always thinking, always analyzing, always one step ahead, he stood in front of her and considered what might be going on before he opened his mouth to say a word.

"Avis," she said, and then stopped. Just opening her mouth and saying one word, "Avis," was a monumental task. Her throat constricted, and his name came out garbled, barely more than a whisper. Tears filled her eyes and streamed down her cheeks. Until last night she had no idea a person could cry so much or could produce so many tears. She cried the entire night after the message was delivered. When she finally stopped crying, around four in the morning, it was out of sheer exhaustion. The well of tears had run dry. For the next hour she had sat in numb silence in a chair in the corner and watched Tina Schnell and Leo's brothers and sisters sit and talk and comfort each other. Around midnight Savannah had told them she was going to get a hotel, but they wouldn't hear of it. As far as they were concerned, she was practically family. Leo had told them Avis was falling in love with her, and they were happy. Avis in love was welcome news, especially to Tina. Just after sunrise, Savannah stood up and walked out the door and climbed into Avis's truck. Nobody said a word. They knew where she was going.

"What's the matter?" Avis asked as he reached out to take her hand.

Savannah lurched back away from him. They had fallen in love so fast, and she couldn't imagine breaking this kind of news to him. She could not imagine being the person who was going to inflict this kind of pain onto him.

It hit Avis that something was horribly wrong, and he looked around and wondered what was going on. Avis, always thinking, always paying attention, always putting two and two together. "Where's Leo?" he asked and glanced around as if he half expected to see Leo appear out of thin air.

Savannah began to sob uncontrollably and covered her mouth with both hands and struggled, unable to speak any words that could be understood.

"Savannah. Where's Leo?" he snapped at her.

"God. Avis, I am so sorry."

"Savannah. Where is Leo?" It was one of those moments in life where the answer to his question was obvious, but it had to be said out loud. It had to be confirmed. Knowing was not the same as hearing. He had to hear it. She had to say it.

"There was an accident last night, Avis. After he dropped me off at the house. There was an accident."

Avis froze in place without saying another word. He watched her sob and heard bits and pieces of what she was saying, but everything was a blur. Her voice, the stream, the breeze, his thoughts all became a single buzzing sound that held no meaning. Leo was not a dust swirl. That's all Avis knew. Leo was not one of his fucking dust swirls.

"Leo was going to pick up a pizza..." There was some more talking that slipped past Avis. Just more buzzing sounds, with a phrase here and there making only the least bit of sense to him. "He dropped off the truck and drove the Mustang and..." More impulses flashed in Avis's head faster than he could begin to piece them together. "A drunk reporter from Miami ran a stop sign..." Then there were more sounds that escaped him. "Leo didn't have a seat belt on... they said he died instantly... I'm so sorry, Avis."

Finally. A phrase that rang in his head as clear as a church bell. "They said he died instantly."

Avis went down as if he had been shot. Savannah sobbed uncontrollably. More tears flowed from the well she thought had run dry.

He dropped to his knees and lost his breath. After a lifetime of losing people he loved without showing a bit of emotion, his entire world crashed down upon him. He slouched down on his knees in the dirt, not far from the stream he and Leo had fished in hundreds of times. The same stream they had fished in only yesterday.

"Hey, Avis. Who do you suppose boiled the first egg?" Leo had asked. It was his last question. Avis smiled and didn't answer him. Not all Leo's questions were meant to be answered.

Savannah stood above him, still covering her face as her endless tears flowed and began to drip onto Avis's shoulders and back.

At twenty-six years old, Avis Humphrey couldn't rationalize it any longer. He didn't know how long he had been kneeling on the ground without breathing, but he suddenly gasped for air. Everything began to spin as if he himself were in one of the dust swirls that had haunted him since he was a young boy. And then it happened. He began to cry.

For the first time in his life, Avis Humphrey cried. And his cries grew into painful sobs. Never in his life had his spirit been so wounded. When Merle left, he watched him go down the road and out of sight, but never fully grasped that he was not coming back. When Lindsey leaned out the window and waved and told him to mow the lawn, he watched and wondered when she would be coming back. And when her parents left him, he watched and wondered why everyone he loved always drove away and didn't take him with them. When they came and left for a second time he almost cried, but Tina Schnell had hugged his pain far enough away to make it bearable.

But this was Leo. This was his best friend. This was his brother. This was the one person in the entire world he knew would never leave him behind. While everyone else had been dust swirls that blew in and out of Avis's life, Leo had been like a slow-moving river. He was always steady. Always more or less the same. Sometimes high, sometimes low, but always there. Leo had been a safe, innocent, and steady place for Avis to go to. Almost every good memory in his life was a memory that included Leo. And now Leo was dead, and Avis was in a tornado. *Leo was dead.* If Savannah had driven a knife into his chest it couldn't have hurt more than the message she had delivered. Leo was gone. A dust swirl had finally defeated him.

The Powerball ticket didn't matter anymore. Lindsey and Merle and all the others who hoped to be his father didn't matter anymore. Agnes hanging out in his trailer was irrelevant. The reporters, the rumors, and what anyone thought about anything were all insignificant. Leo was gone. For one brief moment, in an act of desperation, Avis stopped crying and waited for Leo to say, "Hey Avis," but all he heard was Savannah standing in front of him crying and saying how sorry she was. Avis collapsed onto the ground and sobbed with his tears falling into the dirt. Savannah stood frozen above him and cried with him. They were in love, and they shared each other's pain, yet the pain was unbearable.

The day was half-gone when he finally began to calm down enough to realize where he was and what had happened. When he lifted his head, he wasn't lying in the dirt any longer. He was lying in a soft patch of grass with his head resting on Savannah's tear-covered chest. Her arms cradled his head and her hand gently rubbed his back. He took a deep breath and lifted his head and looked at her tear and dirt-smudged face.

"This is... I mean... how...?" was all he could mutter.

"I don't know, Avis. All I know is I love you..." She wanted to add "And I can't believe Leo is gone," but she couldn't say the words again. She didn't ever want to say them again. She wanted to wake up from this nightmare. She wanted Avis and Leo to be standing on the shore fishing. She wanted to hear one of Leo's stupid questions she didn't understand. She wanted to hear Avis answer him with the patience of Job and the wisdom of Solomon. She wanted to play the interview game with Avis and listen to Leo add his color to the conversation. She wanted to do anything other than console Avis because his best friend was dead.

Avis cried again.

CHAPTER THIRTY-SEVEN

The sun was hanging low above the trees, almost ready to hide behind them before disappearing into the dark night. Avis sat next to Savannah on her log and watched the last bit of smoke smolder up from the fire. Their faces were red, pudgy, and dry. They had cried until there were no more tears. Then they had cried some more. Their clothes were dirty and wrinkled. Their hair tangled and matted. Their minds had gone numb.

"You coming back to town now?" she asked. She was well aware reporters were not high on decency, and in all likelihood efforts to pry into his life would intensify now that more drama had been added to the story. Some of them would understand what he was going through and might be respectful enough to leave him alone; the worst of them however, the pariahs of the journalistic world, would ratchet up their efforts to intrude into a life they had already destroyed in order to, "get the story." Avis knew it, too.

"No. Tell Tina I'll be in touch soon. I'm going to need some time. Can't really wrap my head around all of this." As the words slipped from his mouth, his eyes wandered to the grass where Leo's fishing pole lay. A surge of black energy exploded in his chest and he struggled to breathe again.

Savannah reached into the front pocket of her jeans and pulled out a key ring that held a single key. "Ernie stopped by last night and spent some time with Leo's family. Before he left, he gave me this key and said you should go to his camp for a while." She handed Avis the key and watched his eyes begin to water up once again. "He's a nice guy," she added, referring to Ernie.

"Damn. I just can't believe it," he whispered and stared at the key.

She put her arms around him and kissed him on his forehead without saying a word.

Avis spoke. "Tell Ernie I said Thanks. I'll head to the camp when we leave, but you need to make sure nobody else knows. Not even Tina."

After a week in Watermill, Savannah understood the importance of his instructions. While Ernie would likely keep the secret, the chance of a leak doubled with each person who held any information. "Okay," she said, and then paused. "I'll let you know about the funeral arrangements," she added. Her voice cracked, and she squeezed Avis hard and they began to cry again.

They both cried and they both waited for Leo to chime in and say, "Hey Avis. What makes tears come out?" But he didn't chime in. Avis would have had to answer, "You, Leo. You make tears come out."

The leaves rustled, and the birds sang despite the pain in the air. The water continued to flow and trickle over the rocks. The world continued to spin. But Leo's pole sat on the ground next to Avis's log and he did not ask any questions. Ten minutes later Avis stood up and walked to the edge of the water with Savannah by his side.

"You got your cell phone with you?" he asked.

She nodded and pulled it from her pocket.

"Put my number in it. You'll be able to call me at Ernie's camp. Pretty good reception out there."

She gave him a puzzled look and hesitated a moment before saying anything. "I thought you didn't have a cell phone. That's what you and Leo said."

He cracked a slight smile at the thought of Leo going along with his lie. "It's 2018, Savannah. Everyone has a cell phone."

She leaned her forehead onto his chest and mumbled, "God. You guys are such asses."

"I know," he said and put his arms around her, well aware that "you guys" would forever be a conversation about the past. There would be no more new Avis and Leo stories. From here on, it would be reminiscing and recalling, but no more creating. Not for Avis and Leo.

They stood on the shore with arms wrapped around each other for a long time. After the sun went down, they loaded the poles and the few things Avis had scattered around the campsite into the back of his truck. He drove along the back roads toward the Schnell's home and dropped Savannah off about a half mile away from the house. Neither of them spoke a word until she swung the creaky door open.

"I'll see you tomorrow, huh," he said.

"Yes. Do you want me to bring you anything?"

He shook his head no and looked out the windshield.

She leaned over and kissed him on the cheek. "I love you, Avis."

He didn't answer. He sat with his head hung low and thought this was not how it was supposed to be. This is not how they were supposed to remember their first days together. Avis had always been a package deal. If you wanted to be with Avis, then you got Leo, too. It was just the way it had always been. There was never a reason to believe it wasn't going to be that way for the foreseeable future. At least not before last night. He looked at her with the words on the tip of his tongue, but they didn't come out. This was not going to be how he said those three words for the first time in his life.

"I'll see you in the morning, okay?" he answered with a sad smile on his face.

Savannah understood. She slid across the seat and climbed out of the truck and swung the door closed and hung her head as she wandered back toward the house. Avis drove away in silence, too numb to feel anything.

CHAPTER THIRTY-EIGHT

Merle and Lindsey walked into the church and confirmed for anyone who cared, and for anyone who didn't, that the rumor they had rekindled their long-lost romance, was true. Merle was dressed in his reasonably priced suit, which he more than likely bought from JCPenney a decade or so ago, with old but newly polished dark-brown shoes that didn't match the navy-blue suit. Lindsey was predictably wearing a tight-fitting black dress. The back was open and showed too much skin. The front was low-cut and showed too much cleavage. A string of pearls accented what there was to see. Last but not least, her spiked high heels made her already long legs seem as if they went on forever. Nearly the complete menagerie of Avis's potential fathers watched her, as she sashayed down the aisle, and fought the urge to smile at the memory of their backseat adventures with her. The Jazzman was the only one missing.

If Denny had been upset and repulsed with himself for hooking up with Lindsey to get his big story, his repulsion would have been amplified if he had found out she and Merle had entertained themselves on the same backseat at the same lakefront spot only twelve hours earlier. After two and a half decades, Merle Humphrey finally made it to the *Lindsey Beckham Backseat Experience*. He was ecstatic. Lindsey had had better. Certainly, the Jazzman was still the standard that all men, including Merle, were trying to outdo, whether they knew it or not. Merle had been a tad better at the sex thing than she recalled him being way back when. Not as good as Denny, but Denny was younger and stronger. And, sadly, now dead.

She by no means took any responsibility for what had happened to Denny or, by the domino effect, for what had happened to her son's best friend Leo. While a less narcissistic woman might have felt some sort of cause-and-effect guilt from the tragic event, Lindsey simply thought it was wonderful the poor young man was able to have sex with such a skilled lover only hours before he died. She lacked the empathy required to make the connection between Leo's death and her seduction of Denny. Even if she had made the connection, guilt would not have factored into the equation. With the exception of his best friend, it looked as if the entire twenty-two hundred citizens of Watermill had showed up to pay their final respect and say their good-byes to Leo. Those who couldn't fit into the small Catholic Church quietly waited outdoors. They scuffed their feet on the sidewalk and whispered to each other and tried to wrap their heads around the idea that a drunk reporter from Miami had killed one of their favorite sons. Denny, of course, would forever be remembered in Watermill as some sort of demon from the outside world. And Watermill would not be remembered any more fondly by his family back in California.

The sermon was of course about the senseless loss of life of a young man in his prime and the difficulties of understanding God's reasoning and will. The truth was no one could understand or wanted to understand the reasoning. They just wanted Leo back. The chorus sang songs, the organ reverberated, and the family and friends sat in numb silence. Many cried, but most reached deep into their inner spaces and handled the loss in whatever manner best suited them. After the service, they all caravanned to the cemetery and stood on the soft green grass under the blue breezy sky and said their final farewells. Most of them passed through the Schnell home at some point over the next two days to shake hands, give hugs, and eat cold cuts and casseroles.

Avis stayed away from the funeral out of respect for Tina and her family. In fact, Savannah had put the word out that he wasn't going to be there, so there was no need for the press to swarm the mourning and services for Leo Schnell. Of course some of them still showed up and lingered around the steps of the church while the service went on. None of them had the nerve to stay on the same side of the street when Leo's casket was carried out of the church and loaded into the hearse and driven off to be buried in the Watermill Memorial Cemetery.

* * *

At a little past 2:00 in the morning Avis strolled down the long crushed-rock path with his head hung low and his hands stuffed deep into his front pockets. A twelve-pack of Pabst Blue Ribbon was stuffed under one arm. He had never been in the cemetery at night and didn't find it to be a particularly haunting place. Instead he found it to be peaceful, with a soothing quietness and a strong smell of fresh-cut grass and springtime flowers lingering in the air. Cricket chirps and the crunch of rocks beneath his feet were the only sounds to be heard. No fishing stream splashing in the background. No stream of endless questions from Leo. No breeze rustling the leaves. Nothing but the crickets, the rocks beneath his feet, and a constant whirl of thoughts filling his head.

Finding the grave should have been easy. Watermill was a small place and it had a small cemetery. Avis knew Leo's grave would be the new one with the fresh dirt. It would be the one without rooted grass or perennials springing back to life. The stone would be shiny with sharp edges, as people's hands and the weather, had not yet run over it year after year. The tears in the soil would be plentiful and fresh. The grave would be the one where sorrow hung heavy in the air. It would be the place where the body of Avis's best friend was stored while his soul soared through the universe like light released into darkness. Avis was certain of it.

He wandered around the stone garden looking at names and dates of bodies that had been buried beneath the green grass of Watermill for the past three hundred years. He was surprised to find that Herbert Schnell, Leo's great-great-great-something or other, had one of the oldest headstones to be planted in the ground and set into its final resting place, way back when.

Herbert R. Schnell
Born – 1717
Died – 1768

For some reason, he hadn't known Leo's family was one of the founding families of the town. He squatted down and ran his fingers across the letters on the headstone and wondered why, with all the books he had ever read, he had not read one book about the history of Watermill, New Hampshire. Then he wondered how much alike Herbert and Leo might have been. Three hundred years after the town came to be, it hadn't really changed all that much. The Schell's were all still living in the same place. They were good and decent people. The newest Schnell had just joined his ancestors.

He wandered around a bit longer and read a few more names on the headstones, not at all surprised to find Smiths and Harringtons and Sullivans and other names of families who still raised their children and grandchildren, and buried their elders, in Watermill. Forty-five minutes later he admitted to himself he was intentionally not looking for the one grave he had come to visit. When he'd climbed into his truck a couple of hours before, he thought he was ready, or at least as ready as he could be. Now that he was here, he was sure he was not. Then again, he probably never would be ready to visit Leo under these circumstances.

He had two joints tucked into his T-shirt pocket along with a wrinkled and tattered Powerball ticket that stuck with him like the Black Plague. And there was a slowly warming twelve-pack of PBR hanging from his hand. He took a deep breath and ran his tongue along his lower lip as he turned to the left and stared at the impossible. One of them, either Leo or Avis, was supposed to be doing this in another forty or fifty years. If they were unlucky maybe it would only be twenty or thirty. But to be doing this *this* year, was impossible, unthinkable, and unimaginable.

With nothing else left to do, Avis squatted down and opened two beers and set one of them on the fresh dirt. He sat down in the grass next to it. For ten minutes he sat and drank in silence; silence that would have normally been broken by a question from Leo. He finished his first beer and opened another and lit a joint. Finally, the question came from Avis: "Hey Leo. What's it like on the other side?"

There was no response, and Avis cried. He cried and drank and smoked and asked more questions that were always left unanswered.

"How could you leave me like this, man?"

Nothing.

"What the hell am I supposed to do now?"

Nothing.

"Who am I supposed to go fishing with?"

Nothing.

Five more beers later, and Avis continued to ramble an onslaught of questions. He asked Leo more questions than he had asked him in all the years he and Leo had hung out together.

"How could you possibly fish with me for over twenty years and still be the worst fisherman I've ever known?"

Nothing.

Two more beers. "Any idea if Agnes is still in my trailer? I need clean clothes, and there's no fucking way in hell I'm having a conversation with her this week. And I can't send Savannah by with that bat-shit crazy woman hanging around."

Nothing.

A couple more beers. "Can you believe Carmen is a lesbian? How did I not see that?"

Nothing.

One last beer. "What the hell am I supposed to do now, Leo?" he asked again. Then he cried some more.

As it was with all the questions, the only response Avis heard was the chirps coming from the crickets around the cemetery. He lit the second joint and took a long drag and then laid it on top of the full beer can sitting in the freshly dug dirt of Leo's grave. He drew a heavy sigh and fell back onto the grass and closed his eyes and hoped they would both be fishing on a riverbank when he woke up.

* * *

The New England sun began to peer above the trees around 5:00 in the morning. Two robins sat on a branch and looked down at Avis. He lay in the grass with his mouth wide open, snoring almost loud enough to awaken those buried around him. Eleven bent-up Pabst Blue Ribbon cans were scattered in the grass, and one full can still sat in the dirt on Leo's grave with a joint sitting on top of its rim.

"Hey Avis. Why don't you go see George? He'll know what to do," Leo said into the morning silence.

Avis bolted upright and looked around.

Leo's voice had been as clear as the birds singing in the branches above his head. Avis knew it defied logic, but he heard what he heard; he was certain of it. He twisted to the left and then the right, and repeated the twisting at least three more times, and looked everywhere for his best friend. The sun blasted on his face when he turned to the east and he closed his eyes and hoped Leo would blurt out another question. Thirty seconds later he was almost certain he had heard his voice, but not as confident as before. A minute later he lay back down on the grass and thought about what he had heard Leo say: "Hey Avis. Why don't you go see George? He'll know what to do." He thought maybe his friend was right, and he stopped wondering if he was hiding behind one of the headstones.

Half an hour later he strolled back up the crushed-rock path to his truck with a box of empty beer cans in his hand and drove away. The one full beer and the joint remained sitting right where Avis had put them before he fell asleep. He didn't want to wake up in the middle of the night with Leo accusing him of taking his last beer.

CHAPTER THIRTY-NINE

Savannah was up and dressed with a cup of coffee in her hand when Avis stumbled back into the camp an hour after he walked away from Leo's grave. His feet were heavy as he climbed the wooden steps and shuffled across the porch through the front door. He wanted to say something meaningful or caring, or at the very least appropriate, to Savannah when he saw her face; but he was stuck in that strange place halfway between drunk and sober and hung-over and alive and destroyed. They looked at each other and she kissed him on the forehead and rubbed his back.

"Go get some sleep. I'm going to run into town for the day. I'll bring dinner back later."

Avis nodded and headed to the bedroom without saying a word. He had taken everything in stride, up until the accident. But now, the old Avis Humphrey had begun to change under the pressure of the Powerball ticket and all the collateral damage that had come with it. She watched him go through the bedroom door as if the weight of the world was crushing him to the ground. He collapsed onto the bed without undressing or taking his boots off or even tossing his Red Sox cap off his head.

Twenty-five minutes later Savannah walked into the diner and went straight to the corner table and sat down without introducing herself or asking permission to join him. Tom peered at her from over the top of his coffee cup with his one good eye and took a long, loud sip, followed by, "Ahhhh. Good stuff."

She laid her phone on the table and stared at him without speaking a word.

"Savannah Gardener," he said, as he set his cup down. "Do you know, you're about the last reporter in town to sit at this table. I was beginning to think you had something against me." He grinned and fidgeted with his eye patch. Savannah sat and looked at him, straight-faced, and silent.

"I suppose you're not here to get a story from Avis's cousin, being that you've already spent a good amount of time with him. Least that's the word around town," he added, and tried to size up what was about to go down. She continued to watch him without talking. When the grin began to disappear from his face, she picked up her cell phone and opened an email from Steve with three attachments and slid it across the table. He glanced down at it and took a deep sigh and slid the phone back to her.

It was a picture of his driver's license, his faculty picture from the university, and his professional bio from LinkedIn.

"You want to go somewhere a bit more private to discuss this?" she asked, still showing no emotion.

He nodded and stood up and sauntered toward the front door with Savannah right behind him.

Ernie had watched her come in and sit down. Now he watched them, as best he could, as they strolled toward the empty bench in the park.

It was just over two weeks ago that Savannah had decided to kill herself. Her life had been so empty she couldn't find a valid reason not to go through with it. Then she came to Watermill and met Avis and Leo. It was all a blur after that. She fell in love with Avis and befriended Leo. Then Leo and a kid from Miami died in the car wreck. While all that was going on, it seemed like an entire universe of parasites had descended on Watermill, and she was ashamed to admit she had been one of them. They were all in search of Avis Humphrey, with hopes of sucking something out of him and his situation. She was all right with it at first, before she knew him, before she had kissed him and before she had wept with him. It was before she had become a part of the Schnell family or had been taken in by Ernie. And it was before she had sat with George and listened to him talk about eight-year-old Avis Humphrey. Everything had changed. Since the accident there had been almost no sleep and she was tired. And this Tom guy—it was time somebody ended whatever game he was playing.

Late in the afternoon, the day before Leo's funeral, Savannah stopped in to see Ernie and tell him enough was enough. It was time to find out just who this one-eyed clown might be and take him down if needed. Ernie said he always seemed to walk in from the north end of the street.

The next morning, four hours before the funeral, she parked and waited to see where he came from. A red Volvo station wagon pulled in at 8:30 and parked a quarter-mile up the road from Ernie's. A tall, lanky guy with an eye patch, ragged jeans, and a flannel shirt climbed out of the Volvo and strolled down the road toward the diner. After he had disappeared inside, Savannah took a picture of his license plate and sent it off to Steve and asked him if he could make some calls.

He was glad to hear she hadn't died in the woods at the hands of some New England vagrant. He made a couple of calls to get the initial information. After that it was as simple as typing in a name and city on Google. The unmasking of Pirate Tom had begun. When Savannah read the note and the attachments from Steve, she knew there would be some sort of confrontation in the morning. She hoped, against the odds, that something good would come from it. She wasn't optimistic, but she hoped.

They sat on the same bench Denny and Lindsey had sat on not many days ago. Tom looked around as if he were there to watch the birds and enjoy the fresh air.

"Not really any need for questions. Why don't you just tell me what's going on and precisely what you are up to," Savannah said in a monotone voice, and sat back and lit a cigarette. Smoking was a habit that had been quickly fading since she started fishing with Avis, but she needed one this morning.

"Nice park, huh?" Tom said without looking at Savannah.

She crossed her arms and breathed in a deep sigh and bit her bottom lip.

"Why should I tell you, and not go to someone else?" he added.

"Because I've already written my version of it and can have it online in less than an hour. You'd be a world-famous fraud," she answered, still in her monotone voice. "I assure you, you will come off as a strange parasite preying on Avis, even after his best friend was killed. If that's what you want, then it works for me."

He stared at her, as if he momentarily thought he might be able to play games and call her bluff. The thought only lasted a second. She had the look of a determined woman. He knew she wasn't bluffing.

"Do you really care about him, or do you just want the story?" he asked as he pulled off the eye patch. "I couldn't care less about the story. Avis Humphrey is a good man and it's time for all this nonsense to stop. Especially yours," she snapped back. "Enough is enough. So, start explaining what you're doing or I'm pulling up the story I've written and hitting Send. The current version ends with, 'When asked about all that had transpired, the fraudulent cousin said he had no comment.'"

CHAPTER FORTY

It was 6:00 in the evening when Avis finally crawled out of bed and worked his way toward the kitchen to brew a pot of strong coffee. The fog in his head was thick enough to slow his thought processes to a near standstill, but not so thick he forgot about drinking and smoking with Leo the night before. It was also not so thick that it kept at bay the memory of Leo not answering any of his questions—and not so thick he could forget there were things that needed to be taken care of and decisions that had to be made. Three cups of coffee later, the fog began to lift and he became acutely aware of his pounding headache. Avis smiled and thought about how much Leo would be complaining today if they had both drunk that hard the night before.

"I think I ate something bad last night," is what Leo would have said. Or "I think I've got a bug or something," he would have mumbled.

"Too bad you didn't drink more. Alcohol kills germs," Avis had told Leo at least a dozen times over the years.

"Next time," Leo had answered more than once. "Next time I'll drink enough to kill the germs."

As it was, Avis suffered by himself and wanted to tell someone, "I think I ate something bad last night." He had *eaten* his share, and Leo's to boot. But Savannah was gone to town and there was no one else to talk to. He hadn't spoken to anyone over the past two weeks except Leo and Savannah. He hadn't spoken to Tina Schnell yet to say how sorry he was, and he hadn't spoken to Alice Chen since she had gone underground. When he was camped out at the stream he had an excuse for not calling: no cell coverage. But that excuse was gone, and he knew it was time to reach out and connect with those who had been so affected by the winning ticket.

He looked at the phone for a long time before he decided not to call Tina. He knew she would understand why he was staying away for the time being, and he didn't want their first post-Leo conversation to be on the phone, with a hangover.

An hour and a half later Savannah walked in through the door carrying a small bag of groceries just as Avis was saying good-bye and hanging up the phone. "Yup. Same to you," he said, and then listened for a few more seconds. "Yup. I'll call you again soon, I promise." There was another pause as he held the phone up to his ear. "Yup. Same to you," he said again, and then pushed End.

Savannah walked past him without speaking and set the groceries onto the counter.

"That was Alice Chen," he volunteered without being asked.

"Did she call you? Or you call her?"

"I called her," he said as he quietly contemplated their conversation. She had said, "I love you, Avis" twice at the end of the call. His automatic response was, "Yup. Same to you." In his mind, it was the same as, "I love you too, Alice." It was just his way. Alice had known him forever. It was the same in her mind too.

"And how's she holding up?" Savannah asked as she began putting cans of soup into the cupboard.

Avis shook his head. "Sounds like I had more success hiding out than she did. Seems like the whole damn world has her email address. She said she's gotten thousands of emails and had to shut down her Facebook page."

"Oh, that's terrible," Savannah said without giving it much thought.

"Seriously!" Avis snapped, catching her attention. "She said she's heard from just about every charity that's ever existed. Environmentalists, dog shelters, kids' soccer teams, orchestras, hospitals, LGBT people, religious groups, politicians, cancer funds, cop funds, and a thousand more have all written and said they can't wait to get together with her and let her know how she can make their world a better place. She said a lot of them are pretty good at laying on the guilt as thick as peanut butter."

"You're not all that surprised, are you? Do I have to remind you, Avis? Nine hundred and sixty-seven *million* dollars?"

"And the Go Fund Me requests," Avis started in again. "My God, she said they're off the charts. Vacation funds. College funds. Please Pay My Taxes funds. New car funds. One lady is asking for money for boobs and some guy wants her to pay for his sex change." He rambled on and stared into his coffee as he contemplated the mess he had dragged Alice into. "She's heard from half the financial advisors east of the Mississippi and almost every realtor within the continental US and a few from beyond. And," he added and waved his hands in the air like a madman, "She said she never knew there were so many damn lawyers in our neck of the woods."

"Have any of them upset her?" she asked. "I mean, other than there being a million of them?"

"Alice said the people she knows personally have been the hardest to deal with. Friends and relatives," he added, and shook his head again. "Some of them are sharing some real personal shit she wishes she didn't know. I think she wants to un-know a bunch of it. And she's heard from relatives she's never even heard of. Doesn't even know if they're actually related."

"Has she considered shutting down her email?" Savannah asked, thinking it might be the obvious answer.

"Said she thought about it, but her husband suggested that maybe it was good everyone was concentrating on reaching her through her current address. He thinks if she changes it, they'll just find it again and it will start all over. Then she'll be getting it in two different places." He shook his head again. "Man. People suck," he mumbled.

"There are a lot of good people out there, Avis. Don't lump everyone into one pot. Things are just a bit crazy right now." She was trying to be positive, but even Savannah was having a hard time seeing the good side of most people lately. When she had first arrived in town, after her car broke down and after her first day of fishing, most of the locals were a bit standoffish, but polite. Once the rumors spread about her and Avis being in a relationship, half of the town had become friendlier and the other half turned into full-fledged shitheads. She was surprised at how many of them treated her like a gold-digging whore without ever having a single conversation with her.

"Do you know she said that one couple asked for money to pay for his and hers tattoos on their privates?"

"Get the hell out of here," Savannah said, and stopped putting the groceries away and turned and looked at him for the first time since the conversation started.

"She said they even sent pictures."

"Of the tattoos or their privates?" Savannah asked with a shocked, wide-eyed look on her face.

"Hell, I don't know. She was my third-grade teacher, Savannah. It wasn't a conversation I felt comfortable having with her. I just told her I was sorry and moved on."

Savannah sat down at the table without saying anything more and reached out and rubbed the back of his hand. He took a deep breath and blew his frustrations out into the air and closed his eyes. When he opened them up, he looked at her and wondered what she was smiling about.

But before he had a chance to ask, she started speaking. "I was just thinking about what Leo would be saying right now. 'Hey Avis. If you were going to have your penis tattooed, what would the tattoo be?'" She giggled.

"I'm afraid not." He smiled. "He wouldn't be thinking of my tattoo one little bit," he said and looked down at Savannah's lap. She blushed and they both laughed. It felt good.

"Alice said mayors from at least five different towns have written and offered to name their town after her if she would get them out of financial debt. One of them even said they would name their town Chen City." They both laughed again. Avis had made the same suggestion a few days ago, in jest. Neither of them had actually believed some small town in America would want to be named Chen City.

"Hey. You're the one who said you didn't care what she did with the money," Savannah reminded him.

"Chen City. Kinda has a nice ring to it, doesn't it?" Avis asked, with his words trailing off and his mind drifting on to other things.

Savannah smiled. She was glad they were having a couple of light moments, but she knew everything was wearing him down. She stood up and cradled his head against her breast and ran her fingers through his hair. "What are you going to do, Avis? You're going to have to deal with this pretty soon."

"Right now, I'm going back to bed," he said, and stood up and kissed her and slowly walked back toward the bedroom door.

"And after that?" she asked, implying that "after that" it was time to start having a serious conversation about the money.

"Hang out with you," he said with a wink as he closed the door behind him.

The truth was he had talked about a lot more than just the parasites with Alice Chen. They talked about Leo and the accident and how Avis couldn't go to his funeral. They talked about how Alice had to leave her sister's house and go hide out at another relative's home because reporters had found her. Like he had said, she wasn't as good at disappearing as Avis had been. Alice talked about Avis's childhood and his father situation. She had heard what was going on back in town and knew he wouldn't talk about it, but he would listen. She told him he was a good boy and he would have to forgive all these people one day. Alice was big on forgiveness.

Last but not least, they talked about Savannah, and for the first time in two weeks, Alice felt her heart warm and fill up with goodness. She was happy her little boy had found someone to love. Her eyes watered with tears of joy when she heard he wasn't going through all of this—the ticket, the parasites, Lindsey's return, and Leo—all by himself. She was happy to hear that it sounded like Avis was quickly becoming Avis and Savannah.

The last thing he assured her of before hanging up the phone was that the world would be told Alice Chen was out of the billion-dollar-giveaway picture before the end of the week. In another two or three days, she could return to her home on Sherwood Street in Watermill, New Hampshire and resume her uneventful and boring life as a third-grade teacher at the same school she had taught at for the past twenty-five years. She was giddy with excitement and overwhelmed with relief.

CHAPTER FORTY-ONE

It seemed like it had been months since Savannah had slept so late. In truth, it had been less than two weeks. That's how long it had been since two scraggly small-town New Hampshire men pulled off the side of the road and one of them, Leo, asked her what was wrong with her car. She lay half asleep, wrapped in a quilt, and wondered how she could have known co-workers and friends from college for so long without bonding, and then she met Avis and Leo and almost immediately felt like they'd been friends for their entire lives. She rolled over and rubbed her eyes and saw the empty space on Avis's side of the bed. She listened for a few minutes, but didn't hear him in the other room, nor did she smell the aroma of coffee drifting through the house. She half-dozed back to sleep with blurry thoughts of Leo drifting in and out of her semi-conscious brain. "Hey Avis. Who do you suppose invented toilet paper?" She smiled with her face buried deep in her pillow. "Hey Avis. What do you think the first guy who caught his penis in his zipper said?" That was one of the last questions she had heard him ask and it was one of the few times she had heard him laugh at one of his own questions. For once, he wasn't looking for an answer. He chuckled and answered the question himself and said, "I bet he said the same thing every other guy has said since then: 'Son of a bitch!'"

When the morning fog finally cleared from her brain, she rolled over and laid her bare arm and leg in the spot where Avis had been when she fell asleep late last night. Her hand rubbed where his back had been a few hours ago, and she drew in a deep breath and inhaled as much of him as she could find still floating in the air. Through half-opened eyes she gazed at the indentation in his pillow and the blankets that had been neatly pulled back after he had quietly slipped out of bed a couple of hours earlier while she was still sleeping.

Savannah had come to town to write a small human-interest story that to be honest, would have drawn pretty short-lived attention if things had played out in any sort of normal manner. But nothing had played out like she had thought it would. She hadn't foreseen befriending Leo and Avis and she certainly hadn't foreseen falling in love with either of them. Nobody could have predicted the deaths of Leo and the reporter from Miami. And nobody from outside of Watermill could have predicted the dozen or so men crawling out of the bushes to claim Avis as their possible son. Savannah presumed anyone who knew Lindsey wasn't surprised when she showed up, but she and Merle reuniting after two decades of infidelity and claiming they had done it for their son, was a bit of a surprise even to the people who knew them both. Now that Savannah had changed priorities and Avis had become more important than writing an article, she had begun to wonder if she would even write one at all. Steve would never give her another chance, but he would get over it.

She climbed out of the bed, picked up a flannel shirt Avis had left lying on the back of the chair in the corner, and took in one more deep breath of his scent before slipping it on and buttoning two buttons. She slowly strolled into the kitchen, wishing the coffee had already been made.

Sunlight streamed through the dirty camp windows and onto the dining room table where a note and an envelope were waiting for her. She walked past the table on her way to the front door without picking them up. She looked past the empty porch and past the driveway, where her car was parked and where Avis's truck had been parked when she went to bed the night before. She wondered if he had snuck off to some secret fishing hole where he and Leo used to go. Or maybe he went to pay a visit to Tina Schnell. If that's where he had gone, Savannah knew he was having another rough morning.

She opened the door and took in the fresh breeze that blew off the water and closed her eyes and wrapped herself in the smells and sounds of the nearly perfect New Hampshire morning. With one last deep breath of the crisp morning air, she opened her eyes and turned and walked back inside to the table and picked up the note that had been left for her.

The paper was from a yellow legal pad Avis had found stashed in one of the cupboards, and the note was written in pencil. Surprising discoveries are seemingly endless in new relationships, and Savannah realized this was the first time she had seen his handwriting. It was much neater than she had imagined it would have been. Not that she had given it much thought, but if she had, she wouldn't have expected this. Avis dressed in loose sloppy T-shirts and ragged blue jeans, drove a beat-up old pickup, and lived in a rundown trailer. She had presumed his handwriting would mirror his life. His writing however, was meticulous and flowing, almost artistic. The spacing was constant. The letters and words flowed flawlessly on the page and his signature looked as if it belonged on the Declaration of Independence. Her fingers ran lightly across the words written on the paper and she wondered how many pages, perhaps volumes, he had written and had stashed away where nobody would ever see them. She picked up the paper and smelled it before reading. It had no scent. At least it didn't have an Avis scent. With the note in hand, she sat down and began reading.

Savannah,

I have something I need done today. I'll be back in a few hours, but I need a favor from you. I know I'm being presumptuous to put this on you without talking to you first, but it's important, and given my current situation, I cannot do it myself.

As you can see, there is an envelope with "Jake" written on the front of it. I need this delivered to him today. It's for Jake Potter. You can stop by the All American and ask your girlfriend for directions to his house. I know I'm taking a chance, but I'll just have to trust you will not give into her charms. (Even though I'm not sure I could pass up the opportunity).

When you give the envelope to Jake, let him know I need an answer tomorrow morning. You'll also have to make arrangements with him to go back and pick up his response.

Please do NOT open the envelope. I'll explain more to you later. Jake is a unique guy, but he can be trusted.

* * *

Two hours later when Savannah walked into the All American,

Carmen's face lit up. Savannah quickly dispensed any hopes Carmen may have had of Savannah changing her mind.

"Morning, Carmen. Avis sent me on an errand and said you could point me in the right direction." She knew why Avis had sent her to Carmen instead of Ernie or anyone else in town. While Carmen may have recently dashed his romantic dreams, she would be loyal and discreet and wouldn't poke her nose into anyone else's business. The last thing Avis wanted was for reporters to swarm Jake's house. He was a private guy and a nice guy, but he was also a guy whom reporters could easily mock in their papers and online.

"What? No warm hello and friendly greeting? No little hug or kiss on the cheek?" Carmen sweetly asked Savannah with a wink.

"Good morning, Carmen," Savannah answered again with a warm smile and no hug or kiss. "No. I just need directions from you."

Twenty minutes later she knocked on the screen door at Jake's house and waited for it to open. Avis hadn't warned her about his version of English, but Carmen had. She presumed one way or another they would be able to communicate.

"How'sitgoing?WhatcanIdoforyou?" he asked through the screen after he opened the front door. She was pleasantly surprised that she understood what he had said.

"Hi. I'm Savannah Gardner and Avis sent me to see you," she said, but he cut her off before she continued.

"I'mafraidthatI'mnotgoingtodoanyinterviews,ifthat'swhatyourhere for," he slurred, and shuffled, and started to close the door.

"Wait! I've got something for you from Avis," she said, not in the least bit understanding what he had just said. "He asked me to drop this off to you and to pick it back up from you in the morning." She reached into her pocket and pulled out the folded envelope.

"Whatisit?" he asked and looked at the envelope with "Jake" written on the outside of it.

"I'm not sure. He asked me not to read it. So, can I come back in the morning and pick up your response?"

"Waithereaminute," he answered and hurriedly stepped away from the door, leaving Savannah standing outside the screen door. Two minutes later he returned with the envelope cleanly opened up by a letter opener and the letter was in his hand.

"I'llseeyouaroundtenoclocktomorrowmorning?" he asked, with his mood obviously lighter and more excited.

Five minutes later he sat down at his computer and began working on *The Avis Project*.

CHAPTER FORTY-TWO

Avis and George had been sitting at George's dining room table for at least two hours with neither of them saying much of anything. It was typical of their conversations when they got together. They were thinkers, more than talkers. Their conversations contained few wasted words. Avis had taken a day to rest and recover after his night at the graveyard, but he was determined to follow Leo's advice and see what George had to say.

George got up and walked to the counter and picked up the coffee pot and shuffled back to the table and poured more into both their cups. Then he shuffled back to the kitchen and returned the pot to its place. Once he sat back down in his chair, he broke the silence and began to speak.

"Do you remember the first question Leo ever asked me?" George asked Avis, who was pushing on the lip of his spoon, tapping the handle against the Formica tabletop. He chuckled and thought back to all those years ago. "Actually, there were two questions," George added.

"Yeah. I remember."

"You brought him fishing with you one day and he walked behind us all the way to the river without saying a word. The minute my hook hit the water, he said, 'Hey George. How come you're brown and I'm white?' Kind of caught me off guard a little, and I just stood there and looked at him as if there might be a right or wrong answer. Then he said, 'Want some jellybeans?' and he stuck out his hand full of jellybeans toward me."

"Yeah. He was pretty funny, even way back then," Avis said. He shook his head and continued to stare at the spoon as it clinked again against the tabletop.

"I still remember taking one green and one red one. He didn't stop talking for the next two hours."

"Yup. It was the first time we ever went fishing and came home empty-handed," Avis said. "Seems like I recall you being pretty irritated."

"Yeah. I took my fishing serious back then. The little guy was a chatterbox. I was worried you might want to bring him with you every day. Thought we might never eat fish again."

They both chuckled and then sat silently at the table and sipped on their coffee for another ten minutes.

"I met your friend in the park a few days ago. Savannah. That's her name, right?"

Avis nodded.

"Leo brought her and said you wanted me to talk to her. Figured you were either trying to pawn her off on me or you really liked her. Guessing it was the second one, hmm?"

Avis nodded again without saying anything.

"She seemed nice."

"I went to Leo's grave the other night, after the funeral," Avis said. "Didn't want any reporters following me to the church, so... you know." His words trailed off, but George understood what he was saying. This time George nodded and said nothing.

"This ticket, it's been more trouble than I can say," Avis sighed, bouncing from one burden to another without directly connecting the two, but George could see the connection without it being explained. Avis drew a deep breath and composed himself before he continued. "I took a twelve-pack with me to see Leo. Thought we'd drink it together. Didn't really take into account, I was going to have to drink both of our shares."

"Oh Lawdy! It's been a bunch of years since I ever drank like that. Guess I was young and dumb like you the last time I did it," George said and took another sip of his coffee.

"Yeah. I was in pretty rough shape yesterday. Fell asleep on the ground next to Leo. I gotta tell you, George, I never imagined I'd be sitting in a graveyard talking to Leo that way." They both sat and sipped in silence for a few more minutes.

"You're gonna be all right, Avis. Just gonna take you a while."

"I woke up when I heard Leo say, 'Hey Avis.' I swear to God, George, I heard him clear as day."

George stared into his coffee for a few seconds before he started sharing a story about his wife. "Don't know if I ever told you, Eve died the year before you started fishing with me." He rarely talked about Eve. She was his memory and he felt no compulsion to share her with anyone else, at least not until now. Even after all the years that had slipped away, it hurt too much to think about her being gone. She had filled up all the empty spaces in his life for over thirty years. Twenty-plus years later, he was still trying to fill them up as best he could. "For a few months after she left me, I woke up to the sound of her voice. Sometimes she was calling my name, like it was breakfast time or something. Sometimes she was saying something else. Sometimes I just heard her voice and I didn't know or care what she said. Just the sweet sound of her saying anything at all was good enough for me. To this day I don't know if she was real or if it was my brain playing tricks on me. Don't really care, either." He looked up at the ceiling with a smile on his face. "Good Lord, she sure had a beautiful voice."

This time, there was a longer silence. Maybe twenty minutes. Avis wondered what Eve was like. He wondered if George really heard her or imagined her. He wondered if he himself really heard or imagined Leo. Then he began to understand what George meant, when he said it didn't really matter. The sound of Leo's voice was enough to comfort him.

"He told me to come see you," Avis said matter-of-factly. "He told me to come see you and you would know what to do with the Powerball ticket."

"Sounds like Leo. Pain in my ass, even now," George said with a smile. He rarely swore. Even *ass* was not typical of his vocabulary. He presumed Eve was in heaven, and he had become much more godly since her passing. There were a lot of youthful sins to make up for and he wanted to see her again. "Did Leo really think I had the answer, or do you suppose he was just trying to get under my skin?"

Avis laughed out loud. "I hadn't really thought about it. I guess I presumed it was a spiritual message from above. Or maybe I was just hoping you had some sound advice about what I should do." The smile faded from his face. "I got this ticket and it's brought almost nothing but bad and I don't know what to do with it, George."

George leaned back in his seat and crossed his arms. "Leo. Quite a character, huh?"

"Quite a character," Avis whispered, nodding his head. "So?" he added.

"Rumor has it you and this girl Savannah have gotten pretty serious."

Avis nodded in agreement.

George grinned. "I drove by your trailer yesterday and it looks like Agnes is back. What are you going to do about that one?"

"Crazy Agnes," Avis said, just above a whisper. "Don't know about that one, George. I got to hit one problem at a time." He shook his head back and forth in mild disbelief that Crazy Agnes was back in his home and was likely preparing herself for some good times with Avis that would be followed by disaster, if she got her way.

"Well, let me give you the easy advice first. Stay away from her. You guys had your fun, but nothing good is going to come out of reuniting with that woman. Let her keep the trailer if you have to. It ain't that nice anyway."

Avis nodded in agreement again. This time the silence was less than five minutes.

"You believe Leo was reaching out to you? I mean, do you really think he was giving you a message to come and get big advice from a foolish old man like myself?"

"You're probably the wisest man I've ever met, George. And I don't know about any supernatural message or anything like that. All I know is I woke up to Leo telling me to come see you, and here I am."

George sat with his arms folded across his chest and his head slowly nodding up and down. His lips puckered as he lost himself deep in thought. As time went on, Avis presumed he was praying. George prayed over everything. Avis had asked him once while waiting for him to decide what he was going to order for lunch at the diner, "Damn, George, you've been looking at that one-page menu for like ten minutes. How long can it take to pick something?" George had answered, "I was praying over it. I'm torn between the BLT and the tuna sandwich. Letting God decide." Avis shook his head and never interrupted the man's silence again.

Ten minutes passed at the dining room table. Twenty. Twenty-five. Then George finally un-puckered his lips, stopped nodding, and looked at Avis. "I believe I know what you are supposed to do." Avis listened as his wise old friend instructed him. When he finished talking, Avis considered his advice without praying over it.

"I don't know about this, George."

"Well, I understand your reluctance. And you have to do what you have to do. I'm just saying Leo and me and God put our heads together and that's what we came up with."

"She's not going to like this," Avis said, shaking his head. George gave him a pat on the back as he walked out the front door. He had hoped another few words of wisdom would be offered, but none came. "Better say a prayer for me," he added just before the door closed. He knew it was an unnecessary instruction. George prayed for his young friend every day, especially over the past few weeks.

CHAPTER FORTY-THREE

The clouds and drizzling rain lingered for most of the afternoon, but as evening set in, the sunless sky was replaced with bright stars and a brilliant moon. Savannah sat on the front steps of Ernie's camp and listened to Avis's story about visiting the graveyard, and the graveyard message from Leo, and his conversation with George. And then she listened as he explained how George prayed a lot; and after thinking and praying about it for a really long time, this is what George and Leo and God had decided he should do with the ticket.

"Have you lost your mind?" she asked, with no sign of joking. "Seriously Avis, have you gone completely mad?"

"I don't think so," he answered. He already knew she would challenge his plan and his sanity. "I'm pretty sure I'm on the fringe of losing it, but I have not yet lost my mind. As a matter of fact, you know what?" he asked, sounding a bit like Leo, "I know you're probably questioning the whole God and Leo and George tag team process, but the solution sounds brilliant to me."

"To you? The solution sounds brilliant *to you?*" she snapped. "Of course it does. You're pawning the whole damn thing off onto me. You're taking *your* problem and making it *my* problem?" Everything she said sounded like a question and a proclamation at the same time. "You want to give the ticket to me? Just like that? Here, Savannah. Here's a few hundred million dollars that the whole damn town of Watermill, along with thousands of other greedy little bastards and god knows who else, is begging for. Handle it please."

"Yes. Me, George, Leo and God have all agreed you should take care of the ticket," Avis said, adding himself to the list of the *holy* men.

"Jesus Christ, Avis. It's nine hundred and sixty-seven million dollars."

"Careful. God's in on this conversation," he scolded, as if he had suddenly become a devoutly religious man.

Savannah sat and looked at the reflection of the moon shimmering off the lake and tried to absorb everything that had transpired over the past couple of weeks. She'd gone from making a suicide pact with Bruce her cat, to having to decide what to do with nearly a billion dollars, all because some small-town hick/genius had had the hots for a lesbian convenience store clerk. She started laughing and buried her face into her hands.

"What's so funny?"

"You realize this is the most unwanted Powerball ticket in history, right?" Avis just shrugged. "No. Really. Think about it. You tried to give it to Alice and look what happened. So, first you didn't want it, and then Alice didn't want it. That's two people. Then just a few days ago at the campsite, I was yelling at you and Leo because you didn't want the ticket and Leo didn't want the ticket. That's three people. Then you tried to give it to me, but you and your sidekick decided I was too high-strung to handle it. Now the same two guys, plus George, and God of course, have decided the suicide girl from Maine should be in charge of the ticket. And guess what? I don't want it either. Can you believe it? I don't want nine hundred and sixty-seven million dollars. That makes four people in one tiny New Hampshire town who do not want the winning Powerball ticket. I'm beginning to wonder if anyone wants it."

"Well, you own it now," he commanded. "You know... God, George, Leo; my blessed trinity; you can't say no to those three guys. I mean... there's a lot of wisdom there. If they say give the ticket to Savannah, then I'm giving the ticket to Savannah."

He reached into his T-shirt pocket and pulled out the tattered ticket and handed it to her. She looked at his outstretched hand and shook her head back and forth before snatching it out of his fingers. She flipped the ticket around in her fingers and inspected the front and the back, before stuffing it into her own shirt pocket, her safe place, and got up and headed back inside the camp for another cup of coffee, or perhaps something stronger. When she reached the front door, she stopped and turned back around.

"I'll tell you what I'll do Avis. I'll keep the ticket for a day or two and I'll decide what I think *you* should do with it. But in the end, it's your call. This is still your ticket. Deal?"

Avis shrugged again.

"Deal?" she snapped. "Either agree or I give the ticket back to you right now."

"Well then, I guess it's a deal," he answered, completely indifferent to whatever she decided to do with it.

Savannah walked into the cabin and slammed the door behind her and mumbled something all the way to the kitchen.

Avis smiled and looked out over the lake. "Thanks, Leo," he said quietly. "Good call."

CHAPTER FORTY-FOUR

It was a sleepless night. At 4:30 a.m., just a little before the sun rose over the lake, Savannah understood how Frodo Baggins must have felt, and the overwhelming burden the weight of the ring must have been on the little hobbit. Then she realized Avis was the real-life Frodo and her heart broke for him. The universe had rained down with its full force and he hadn't seen it coming. She pictured him flirting with Carmen and jokingly buying the ticket that would change the course of his life forever, and it nearly took her breath away. The weight of the ticket was crushing him, but it had not yet destroyed him. This small-town guy who had not gotten much of a break in life, this extremely smart and simple guy who never wanted anything more than to hang out with his friends, to have fun with a good-looking woman now and then, and to spend his days fishing in the local lakes and streams, had been hurled into a firestorm that had brought out the worst in so many people around him that it was tough to fathom. The ticket had resurrected ghosts from a past he thought had long ago faded away. And worst of all, it had taken the life of his best friend. It was only at that late hour, as Savannah sat on the couch with the ticket in her hand, that she could fully understand the ironic tragedy of it all. She thought if she listened hard enough and long enough she would hear "My precious" whispered in the dark by a cursed hobbit or some other unknown voice. Or even worse, from voices Avis would have easily recognized. The wolves had been howling at Avis's door from the moment someone at Fitzgerald's law office started gossiping and lit the fire that ravaged his world.

For one brief moment, she thought her eyes were going to tear up. Then something exploded into a moment of clarity. Back in Biddeford, when she spent weeks trying to justify killing herself, everything in her head had been constantly wishy-washy. And before that, when she first got engaged and after it ended, it was exactly the same. She thought she wanted to get married, but she wasn't a hundred percent certain; and then she wanted to call it off but wondered if she was just getting cold feet. And she thought she had wanted to be a reporter, but over time her commitment wavered, and she began to question what she really wanted to do with her life. Whispers of doubt *always* found their way into her life just enough to keep her from committing to... anything. Her engagement, her career, her family relationships and her friendships had all been good when they were good, but when things got tough and the road got bumpy, she always wavered and stumbled and caved in, while she searched for answers that never came. For the first time in her life she realized that whenever the real battles in her life, the battles that counted, got heated and tough, she always retreated and pondered and thought and considered and, finally, failed.

Not once in her life had anything stirred her strongly enough or deeply enough for her to stand and face the fire without flinching, without blinking, without questioning, and most importantly without slinking back into the shadows and letting it all just fall apart. But things had changed. Life had changed. *She* had changed. She didn't think of herself as the lily-white girl from suburbia any more. Or perhaps more importantly, she didn't think of her*self* all that much anymore. At the very least, she didn't think she was the most important person in her life anymore. For the very first time, the only thing that mattered to her was somebody else. The only thing that mattered right now was Avis Humphrey. So when the tears of defeat tried to sneak up on her, she reacted like a mother protecting her young from harm. Her protection came swiftly and decisively—and above all, it was laser-focused on the well-being of the man she loved more than anyone she had ever loved before.

In a strange sort of way, she was honored and humbled that George, Leo, God, and now Avis had all teamed up, and perhaps even conspired, to put this burden on her shoulders. She sat on the couch and looked at the ticket she had set on the center of the coffee table and lit a cigarette. Smoke streamed from between her lips as she continued to look at the ticket, as if it might try to escape or find someplace to hide while it planned another assault on Avis's life. Halfway through her cigarette, she stood up and slowly circled the table without taking her eyes off the ticket. Once around. Then again. And again, and again, until the cigarette had burned away.

It was still dark outside when she had first stood up and looked down at the ticket, but now the sun had risen over the lake and rays of light had begun to stream in through the windows. After hours of staring and pacing, Savannah was exhausted, but she still lacked the answer to her problem. Solutions came into her head, but none of them felt like *the* solution. She walked one final circle around the table and continued her standoff with the ticket. Then a smile cracked the corners of her lips and, just like that, she knew what to do. In the light of day everything, including the ticket solution, became clear. After hours and hours of self-reflection and soul-searching, she had the answer to more than just what to do with the ticket; but the ticket was by far the most important one.

Priorities suddenly became clear to her. Everything suddenly made sense. Growing up and doing what was expected; going to college; getting engaged to the *right* guy; becoming a journalist; and then more importantly, failing at all of it made perfect sense. Or, more to the point, *why* she failed suddenly made sense. For the first time in her life Savannah Gardener had passion. Deep down in her soul. Passion. It was the kind of passion she would fight or die for. It was the kind of passion she would put everything on the line for. It was the kind of passion that would give her the strength to do what was right, no matter what anyone, other than maybe Avis, thought about it. It was the sort of passion that convinced her she was not the most significant factor in the equation. It was the kind of passion that silenced the whispers.

Leo and George and Avis, and apparently God, had given her a task. And she was not going to let them down.

Earlier in the night she had sat on the couch and thought about Googling previous Powerball winners to read about what they had done, but she recalled hearing somewhere that a lot of lottery winners went broke within five years of winning and more than a few of them met tragic ends. She didn't see how that search could help her make a decision about what to do with *this* ticket. Her mind had raced, and she hopelessly grasped at ideas that streamed through her head faster than she could process them.

But that was before her epiphany. That was before she was reborn. That was before she snapped herself out of her childhood and realized that being a grownup, being a woman as opposed to being a little girl, was as different as day from night. It was a new day. Savannah Gardener was a new woman. Or perhaps she was finally a mature, passionate, loving woman.

Avis strolled in from the bedroom to the smell of freshly brewed coffee.

Savannah had wandered from the living room to the porch, to the lake and back to the living room, from midnight until a couple of hours earlier when she and the ticket faced off at the couch.

"What time did you get up?" Avis asked, as he rubbed his face and poured a cup of coffee.

"Haven't been to bed yet," she answered.

"Really. What have you been doing all night?" He looked around as if he expected to see something she had built or fixed, or walls that were freshly painted, or curtains that had been hung.

"What have I been doing?" she repeated, with a roll of her eyes. "In case you forgot, you pawned almost a billion dollars off on to me last night and said, 'Handle this, please,' and then you went to bed. I couldn't imagine getting much sleep until I figured it out."

"And?" Avis asked, in a long-drawn-out word as if he expected a brilliant plan to be laid at his feet.

"And.... I have a plan, thank you very much. But you're going to have to wait to hear it. I'm tired and I need sleep." With those words, she rose up from the couch, kissed his still-sleepy face, and headed to the bed that he had just climbed out of.

CHAPTER FORTY-FIVE

It was noon when Savannah finally woke up. She dragged herself to the bathroom and splashed water onto her face and stared into the mirror. She wondered if it were possible that she could have aged five years in the past few weeks. She splashed more water onto her face and looked again to see if her hyper-aging had diminished. It had not. Ten minutes later she sat on the porch drinking a cup of coffee before making the drive to Jake Potter's house to pick up Avis's big secret.

Jake opened the door and handed her the unsealed envelope with a scowl on his face. "Youweresupposedtobehereatten," he slurred.

She smiled and thanked him and headed back to her car with the envelope in her hand.

Yesterday, it had taken all of her willpower to not open the sealed letter Avis had written to Jake. Today, the urge to read Jake's response was even stronger when she returned to the car with the unsealed envelope he had just given to her. She picked up the envelope from the passenger seat three different times on the drive back to the camp. Each time, she fought off the temptation to accidentally make the letter fall out of the envelope onto her lap. When she finally walked into the camp, Avis sat at the table milling through an old magazine he'd found in the living room. She walked straight to him and stuck out her hand holding the message, as if she were a military courier delivering an envelope marked, Top Secret.

"What's it say?" Avis asked, without reaching for the letter.

"You asked... no, you *told* me not to read it," she answered, a bit irritated that he would presume she had read it anyway.

"Oh. I just meant don't read it before giving it to him. You can read it now," he said, motioning for her to sit, "And let me know Jake's response."

Savannah rolled her eyes and sat down and read the letter to herself.

Jake,

You and I have shot the shit a bunch of times and discussed just about everything under the sun over the past five years. We have talked about greed and charity and what people and societies have thought to be right versus wrong, or moral versus immoral, according to a lot of different people over the centuries. We have talked about crossroads in human history and the difference a turn to the left or the right may have made. And of course, we have talked about the advancement of technology—your religion, so to speak—and whether or not the world is a better or worse place because of it.

In the end, as entertaining and as enlightening as our sometimes-heated discussions have been, they have been mostly theoretical or historical. They have been, "what if" hypothetical discussions about events that may or may not come to be or rehashing and interpreting events which have already passed.

I'm sure you've heard of my current situation and the recent events that have spun off due to "the ticket." In keeping with the spirit of our discussions, I am interested, even intrigued, to hear what you have to say.

It's my understanding the Hindu religion largely believes wealth is a wonderful thing. Perhaps even divine. And it is also my understanding, from what I have read, that Muslims more or less believe everything on Earth, at least material things, is a mere illusion. A Jewish guy once said the test of wealth is a greater test than the test of poverty. And last but not least, my Christian forefathers covered wealth and greed in depth with my favorite view being, Be content with what you have.

Nietzsche pretty much viewed wealth with bitterness and skepticism and I recall reading something from Heraclitus which said, "No one that encounters prosperity does not also encounter danger." Last but certainly not least, in reference to material things, Homer Simpson said, "I'm not impressed easily. WOW! A blue car." I thought the significance of Homer's financial focus was somehow greatly relevant in today's world, since he is probably watched by more than all of the others who I mentioned, will ever be read again.

With all that said, let's do it again. Put all the stuff you believe to

be relevant into your computer and spit out your—or its—recommendation of what Avis Humphrey should do with a ticket worth $967 million. While I may or may not take the advice, I will certainly ponder it.
See you again soon,

Avis

Savannah read the letter silently while Avis sat at the table and waited for her to finish. She stopped at the end of every paragraph and glanced up at him as if she were trying to persuade herself that this scraggly-looking fisherman she had fallen in love with was the same guy who wrote the letter she was holding in her hand. If there had been any doubt he had actually read all the books in his trailer, those doubts were fading. When she finished reading, she set the letter in her lap and breathed in and out with a deep sigh.

"Holy crap. You're really as smart as Leo said, aren't you!" she said, restating what she already knew, but perhaps hadn't yet fully grasped.

"Well. I ain't dumb," he answered, with a shrug and a grin.

"I mean, who reads and references Hindu scripture, the Torah, the Koran, the Bible, philosophers, and Homer Simpson all in one letter?"

"Don't forget the computer god. Jake gets upset when folks don't consider his computer to be at least godlike, if not actually God. He's funny like that."

"Holy crap," she mumbled again and looked back down at the letter.

"So? So, what was his recommendation?" he asked as if he were simply asking, "So? What's for dinner?"

Savannah looked down at the two words scribbled on the bottom of the paper. She grinned wide, proud of herself, and blurted out, "Exactly the same as mine."

"Well?" Avis asked.

"Burn it!"

"Well then, let's light a fire," he said. He reached for the ticket and a lighter, both of which were lying on the dining room table. Savannah snatched the ticket off the table and slid it back into her pocket.

"Tomorrow. We'll burn it tomorrow. This has to be done right," she said as if there were legal guidelines that needed to be followed.

Avis shrugged and tossed the lighter back down onto the table.

"Besides," she continued, "I have another date with George this afternoon. We're meeting in the park to listen to the Sox play Cleveland." Avis shrugged again.

The truth was Jake's computer, or the program he had put the ticket into, had concluded that Avis Humphrey would be best served if the ticket were destroyed or simply went away. Then he immediately wrote another program to determine the best method of destroying or getting rid of the dreaded ticket. The program concluded that fire was readily available and inexpensive, and the destruction would be total. Hence, "Burn it!"

Savannah had paced circles around the ticket last night for hours before Leo flashed into her mind as clearly as he had spoken to Avis at the cemetery. She recalled Avis telling her and Leo, "I thought about throwing it into the fire a couple of times." When she had expressed her doubt that Avis would actually do that, Leo chimed in, "Oh hell yeah, he would. If Avis says it don't mean anything to him, then it don't mean anything to him."

That's when the light came on and it all took shape. Avis was struggling and suffering under the extreme weight and burden of a Powerball ticket that meant nothing to him. He wasn't doing it for himself. He didn't want the money. There was nothing he wanted to buy and there was nothing he wanted to do that cost any real money. He was concerned for others and how the money might help them, and all the while it was destroying him. Her life-changing moment came when she heard her own voice quietly whisper, as she looked down at the worn, wrinkled, despicable Powerball ticket.

"Burn it," she whispered to the universe. Then she smiled and quietly spoke the words only a little bit louder than a whisper. "Burn it."

CHAPTER FORTY-SIX

A few hours after reading the letter, and Jake's response to Avis, Savannah drove to George's house and spent the better part of the afternoon with him. Even though she did most of the talking, she didn't let on as to what she and Avis... and Jake had decided to do with the ticket. George mostly listened and nodded. He occasionally filled in the silence with a fishing story about himself and Avis. When she had nothing more to say, or ask, and George didn't fill in the silences any more, he walked her to the door. Halfway across the room she abruptly stopped and turned and wrapped her arms around him and gave him a big hug and buried her head into his chest. He patted her on the back and breathed in the scent of her perfume. When she drove off, he said a quick prayer and thanked God for sending her to Avis. Then he said another one asking one more time that he would hug Eve again one day soon.

She went straight from George's house to Ernie's diner and promptly took a seat in the corner. After discussing some details that needed clarification and feeling reassured she was making the right decision, she climbed back into her car and headed back to the camp with a red Volvo station wagon following her.

Savannah walked into the camp with a man Avis vaguely recognized. His face looked familiar, but he couldn't recall from where and didn't care all that much. He was sitting at the dining room table staring at an old picture of Leo that had been stuck above his visor for the past couple of years. In the photo, Leo was standing at the edge of a stream holding up a three-inch trout. Avis had written "Jaws" on the bottom of the picture and had given it to Leo to immortalize the big catch. They both got a good laugh out of it, and somewhere along the line, it ended up tucked under the visor where it stayed until Avis pulled it out last night when he sat in his truck with no place to go. Memories of Leo would never disappear, and it would be a very long time before they even began to fade. He could almost hear Leo's voice in the silence of the camp: "Hey Avis. Who do you think took the first picture ever?" He fought back tears again and set the picture down onto the table.

Savannah walked over and gave him a kiss on the cheek and he cracked a slight smile. With her lips still on the side of his face, he suddenly recalled where he'd seen the man standing in the doorway. He broke into a scowl so quickly, it was as if he smiled and scowled at the same time.

"He's okay," she said, while still leaning over him.

"Where's your eye patch?" Avis snapped. His head was half cradled in Savannah's arms and Tom shrugged and looked to Savannah for guidance.

"Avis. He's all right. You need to hear what he has to say," she said to soften the introduction.

Avis gave the pirate another dirty look. The guy had been lying to the whole world about who he was and how he was related to Avis for weeks. That wasn't exactly how Avis would have defined "okay" or "all right."

"Come sit down," she said to the Pirate, and motioned to the wooden chair directly across from Avis. Tom walked over and pulled out the chair and sat down at the table and nodded, not sure what to do or say. After all the searching and investigating and planning, this wasn't how he had envisioned it all playing out. He had imagined a much more amicable meeting taking place between the two of them. Of course, there wasn't hundreds of millions of dollars on the line, back when he was planning the details of their initial meeting. The money had changed everything.

"I'll pour coffee while you get started," she said to Tom, and he took the cue from her and breathed a deep sigh and began to speak. "My father died of cancer about a year ago," he mumbled, and hesitated, half-expecting a sympathetic response or condolences or something to come from Avis. There was none. Tom continued, "He was sick for a couple of years. Looked like he was making headway a couple of times, but in the end… you know… cancer. In the end, it's the end." He stopped again and looked at the table long enough that the silence became awkward. Avis still said nothing, and Tom remembered the uncomfortable silence when he had first met Savannah in the diner. He began to think she and Avis were a lot alike.

"Keep going," Savannah chimed in as she sat down with two cups of coffee.

"He was a pretty good guy, all in all. I mean, he wasn't the father of the year or anything like that, but he was a pretty normal dad to me." He stopped again. This time he looked like he wanted to take back the last sentence, but there was no way to unsay what had just been said. "Anyway," he continued, "A few months before he died, but after he realized it was coming, we started getting pretty close. He shared a lot of stuff, personal stuff he had never shared with me before. One day when he was feeling pretty strong and chatty, we sat on the front porch in a couple of rocking chairs. Out of the blue he blurted out, 'You have a half-brother over in Watermill.' I didn't know what to say, but it didn't matter, because once he started talking he didn't stop."

Avis sat up a little straighter and stopped slouching over his coffee and stopped thinking about Leo, but he still didn't speak. All that was running through his mind was this guy was weaving a pretty damned absurd web to get to the money. His jaw clenched, and he glanced at Savannah with a wrinkled forehead and wondered how she could have been so gullible and taken in by a story like this.

"I'm not sure how he knew, but he told me he was pretty sure my brother's name was Avis and he didn't really think there could be more than one Avis in Watermill."

"Funny this would all come to light after the Powerball thing," Avis said, making the accusation clear as day.

"I can see how you would think that, but you can ask Ernie: I was here in town asking about you, two or three weeks before the Powerball thing came about. The ticket actually complicated things for me a lot more than I would have imagined it could have. Besides, like I already told Savannah, I don't want anything from you. Be glad to sign something to make it official."

"The ticket complicated things for you?" Avis asked with a tone of sarcasm. "You've got no idea."

Tom looked uncomfortable once again; he was aware that in less than two minutes, he had put his foot into his mouth twice.

"So, if we're half-brothers, who was this supposed father of mine and how did he know my mother?" Avis picked up Leo's picture from the table and slipped it into his shirt pocket.

"His name was Mike Palmer," Tom began. "Back in the day he was a bass player in a jazz band. They played all over New England and a little beyond. He said they went as far as New York, Pennsylvania, and into southern Canada," Tom said, as if those locations were just a mile or two from reaching the Promised Land. "I guess they almost made it, but they never really got past being just another small-town road band."

Avis looked annoyed that Tom thought he cared about where some jazz band played twenty-something years ago or that they almost made it big. He didn't care that the guy across the table was pretending to be his brother. Just one more freeloader in a growing list of parasites, was Avis's take on him.

"From what I made of his story, I guess they came through Watermill and played for a few nights. Your mother and my father would have both been in their twenties back then. I guess they hooked up, and well, that was that. He told me he didn't know about you for a long time. Didn't say how he found out about you. He just told me you were here in Watermill."

"And I'm just supposed to take your, or his, word about all of this?" Avis said, as he pushed himself back from the table and leaned back in his chair with his arms folded across his chest. It was bad enough he had to hear the stories about all the might-be fathers who crawled out from under whatever rock they had hidden under for the past twenty-six years. And then, of course, there was Merle, who was his father for five years, then wasn't his father for twenty-one years, and now apparently was his father again. And how could he exonerate his mother? A woman who abandoned him almost twenty years ago, but somehow had the nerve to show up to lay claim to her son... and presumably the millions. Compared to that bunch, the reporters and the good folks of Watermill barely registered on the offensive scale, but Tom's claim was a new twist that caught Avis off guard even more than he was prepared for. "I mean..." Avis threw his hands up into the air in exasperation. He had heard it all and then some. Now this. "You've got to have something better than a long-lost-brother bullshit story," he finally said, and thought about getting up and leaving him sitting at the table with Savannah. Then he thought about grabbing Tom by the shirt and throwing him out the front door.

On the other hand, he trusted Savannah. She wouldn't have brought him here if there wasn't more to his story than what he'd heard so far. He glanced over at her for a cue, to see if she wanted him to put this guy in his place or hear him out. Avis was emotionally worn out and his instincts were frayed.

"Absolutely not," Tom said, in reference to the 'just taking his word for it' question. "I was a skeptic too, and I did a DNA test to confirm it. We're brothers, man. Or half-brothers, I should say."

"And how exactly did you do a DNA test without my participation?" Avis snapped. He was still leaning back in his chair with his arms crossed and a glare on his face. Tom was leaning forward with his elbows resting on the table and his coffee cup in his hand. There was no reason that Avis could have understood that this guy had unintentionally gotten caught up in the whole Powerball fiasco, or that he had no way of knowing the damn thing would have dragged on this long and gotten this far out of control.

"A few weeks ago, I came into the diner and waited for you to finish some pie and coffee. When you left, I took your fork and your cup. A friend of mine from the university salvaged some samples and we sent it off for testing. I was trying to figure out how to deal with the whole situation and how to break the news to you. Then you won the Powerball, and everything got pretty damn complicated."

"Pretty damn complicated," Avis mumbled, barely loud enough to be heard. He pulled out Leo's picture again and set it down on the table. His mind went numb at the thought of how his life had been turned upside down the past few weeks. "There's the understatement of the year," he added without looking up. He hadn't let his guard down yet, or bought into Tom's Jazzman story, but something about it rang true. Maybe it sounded so absurd that it actually made sense. And if Tom was being honest, if he was actually signing away any claim or desire for the Powerball cash, it helped his credibility. There could be no argument that banging a complete stranger sounded right up Lindsey's alley.

"So, I presume you're not a pirate in real life?" Avis asked, and leaned forward setting his elbows back down onto the table. The angry stare off at Tom had softened, but it hadn't yet disappeared.

Tom grinned. "No. I'm an English teacher at White Duck College over in Burlington. I'm also involved in the Drama Department. Hence the costume." He pulled the eye patch out of his pocket and tossed it onto the table next to Leo's photo. Avis half-smiled and shook his head back and forth.

"So why the eye patch?" he asked. His tone and scowl finally softening a bit.

"The truth? I was heading up here one day to look around to... I suppose, stalk you a little more. That's when I heard your big news on the radio. When I got here, the sleepy little diner I had gone into at least a half-dozen times before, was suddenly booming with reporters. I had some theater stuff in my car and I was just kind of goofing around and put on the eye patch. Not long after I sat down, the first reporter came along, and the stories just started rolling out of me. Once I told the first one, everything just started taking on a life of its own. After that, there was no turning back."

"So, what was the first eye-patch story?" Avis asked, his attitude now almost cordial.

"I think it was the pelican in Daytona. But to be honest, I've kind of lost track."

Avis looked at Savannah for some reassurance. She was a part of his life now and what she thought mattered a lot to him. "So?" he mumbled at her.

"He's okay. I think he's telling the truth. He said he'd be willing to take a DNA test with proper samples. And I believe him when he said he's not looking for anything other than his brother." Tom looked uncomfortable again as they talked about him as if he were not sitting in the same room with them.

"Any other family?" Avis asked, looking back at Tom.

"No. Dad died last year, and Mom died about ten years ago. No brothers or sisters."

"Cousins?"

"Nobody I'm close to," he answered, and wondered if Avis was curious about whether or not he had more relatives to meet or whether there would be more people seeking his money. Both were valid questions.

Avis wasn't sure whether he didn't know how to feel, or if he was just too worn out from feeling too much lately. Too much pressure, too much betrayal, too much pain, too much emotion altogether. This news, if it was true, should have been good news. Celebratory news. He had a brother! But Avis was emotionally flat lined, and any bonding and celebrating was going to have to wait.

"Does he know?" Avis asked, looking at Savannah.

"No. I told him he'd find out what was happening with the money when everyone else found out. Not that he asked about it," she added at the end.

"I don't need any money," Tom reiterated.

Avis drew in a deep breath and looked to Savannah for reassurance again. Then he looked back at Tom and reached his hand across the table. "Nice to meet you. Your timing is incredible."

"Nice to meet you, too, Avis," he answered, and squeezed his hand.

"The eye patch was a nice touch," Avis said with a sad smile. "Leo couldn't figure out who you were or what your angle was, but he kept telling me, 'You gotta see this crazy eye-patch guy telling everyone he's your cousin and he owns an emu farm.' I don't know which he thought was funnier, the eye patch or the emus. But he was really fascinated with you."

"I hear he was a really great guy," was all Tom could conjure up, and he wished he hadn't said anything... again. Savannah's eyes watered when Avis talked about Leo. Avis fell back into his silence and stared blankly out the window as he looked out over the lake.

Tom had known his brother for less than half an hour, and already he knew what it was to feel his brother's pain. It was bittersweet; and in a strange, albeit lesser manner, he felt the curse of the ticket hanging in the air. A billion dollars' worth of bad news.

Avis looked up at him and smiled. "I don't know your name."

"Eric. Eric Palmer," he said, and reached across the table to shake Avis's hand once again, as if the correct name made everything official. Avis stood up and walked around the table with his arms wide open. Eric stood up and the two brothers hugged for the very first time. It was more emotional than Eric had thought it would be, and more than Avis would have imagined it to be.

Savannah cried. Then she took a picture of the two men standing together in Ernie's camp.

CHAPTER FORTY-SEVEN

Last night was just one more emotional night in what had become a month laden with way too many emotionally charged days and nights. Tom/Eric the Pirate-Emu Farmer/Teacher had stayed until almost midnight. They talked about his life in Vermont. They briefly discussed their father, but it was too much and too soon for Avis to wrap his head around. They did not so much as utter one more word about the ticket, the money, or Leo. And they barely spoke of Avis's life in Watermill. Savannah was more like a fly on the wall than a participant in the conversation.

Around noontime the next morning Avis sat at the dining room table and fumbled through the chipped and dented tackle box he had pulled out from behind the seat of his truck a few minutes before he found the picture of Leo above his visor. Leo had stuck the box there about six months ago and had forgotten where he had put it. Avis left it there to see how long it would take him to remember where it was. Since the question had now been answered, Avis dug it out and started sorting through the hooks and lures and swivels to see just what else Leo kept in his beat-up old treasure chest. He found Leo's jackknife and picked it up and opened it and rubbed bits of rust and dirt off the blade and slid it into his pocket. A few seconds later he found his own knife that he had lost over a year ago. Leo had argued with him when Avis accused him of losing it. It was a classic Leo move to forget where he had put his own knife and then put Avis's in the same exact place and forget about that one, too.

Eric's arrival into his life hadn't lessened the emotional roller coaster he was living. If he was being honest with himself, Avis was pleased to learn he had a new brother, but it was too early to tell if that was a good or a bad thing. Or for that matter, if the story was the ironclad truth. Of course everyone, including Avis, had heard a version of the Jazzman story over the years, so there was a ring of truth to Eric's arrival into his life. That being said, if *everyone* had heard all or parts of the legend, it would have been easy for Eric to create the fictitious Jazzman from thin air. It was just too much to deal with. Avis continued to search through the tackle box and pull out odds and ends that Leo had stuffed into it.

If he could have wound back time and burned the ticket before anyone knew he had it, the ticket would be long gone, and he and Leo would be on a riverbank fishing while Leo rattled off one question after another. "Hey Avis. If we evolved from polliwogs, then why are there still polliwogs?"

Avis drew a deep sigh and closed the box. He presumed if Savannah were destined to be with him, it would have happened one way or another.

"You're going to have to wait until tonight to burn it," she said, when he stood up as if he were heading outside to put a match to the ticket—and then get on with the rest of his day as if burning it was a nothing event.

"How come?" he asked, with a look of disappointment.

"Because people know you have it. If we don't document it correctly, they'll never believe you burned it and the hounding won't let up. No. We..." She stopped and corrected herself. "*You,* need to do this right." It felt too awkward for her to claim partial ownership of the billion-dollar ticket, even if Avis and the Trinity had given it to her. As far as Savannah was concerned it was still Avis's ticket and she was just assisting in the process. As far as Avis was concerned, it was her ticket and he was just helping her with what she had decided to do with it.

"We," he responded.

"What?"

"You said '*You* need to do this right.' We're in this together Savannah. Technically speaking, I gave it to you, and I'm just including myself as a courtesy."

She closed her eyes and wearily shook her head back and forth and decided she was arguing with twelve-year-old Avis, not grown-up, genius Avis. "Just wait until tonight, please. I'll take pictures and then we'll need to decide how we're going to let the world know what you did."

"We did," he clarified again.

"Okay," she snapped. "We. And we're still going to need to talk about how to move forward."

"Nothing to talk about," he answered, as he walked into the kitchen and opened the refrigerator. "Is there any ham?" he called out with his head stuck inside.

"And why don't we need to talk about how we're moving forward?"

"Never mind. I found it," he said, holding the package of ham up while he searched for the mustard and cheese. "Because you're going to write your story and your little e-zine in Maine is going to break the wonderful news to the world. *Crazy Avis Burns A Billion!*" he said, as if those words were going to be the headline.

"Crazy Avis with help from Crazy Savannah," she mumbled, just to remind herself of the harassment that would be coming her way, too.

"Well, you work out the details on how you want all this to go down and we'll do it after the sun sets, okay?"

"Sounds good," Savannah said. "I'll just jot down a few notes on how to get rid of a billion in three easy steps," she said aloud with a tone of sarcasm. The more she talked about it, the crazier it sounded.

"Light fire. Pick up ticket. Toss ticket into fire," Avis said as he spread the mustard and threw a couple of slices of ham and cheese onto his bread. "You want a sandwich?" he asked, with a bite already stuffed into his mouth.

Savannah watched him chomp away on his sandwich and sip his beer. She began to waver. The same old whispers were creeping in. The seeds of doubt once again began to sprout and root. That calm, comforting voice that never led her to anything good, the voice that only steered her away from whatever it was she was headed toward, had slipped into her head and begun nudging her resolve. *Is this really the smart way to go? Are we, or am I, out of my mind for doing this? Maybe the pressure is clouding my judgment and we should just slow down a little bit.* They were all the same questions that always came, and they came because they were the savior questions. They were her parachutes. They were the safe-place questions. They were the words that always kept her mundanely between the lines and prevented her from doing anything risky or dangerous... or passionate. They were the words that always kept her from taking the giant leap into places that could be her destruction—or her salvation. Avis took another bite and wiped some mustard off the side of his mouth.

"Well. Do you want a sandwich?"

"We're really going to do this, aren't we? We're really going to burn a billion dollars?" she asked, and a wave of nausea swept over her.

"Damn sure are," he said, and started making her a sandwich without getting an answer from her as to whether she wanted one or not. When he finished making it, he handed it to her and said, "You're going to need your strength. I would think it's a pretty tough job to burn nine hundred and sixty-seven million dollars. Want a beer?" he asked and winked at her, already opening one and handing it to her. She wished she had one of Leo's joints right now.

"That's the last beer until after we do this," she said as she reached for it.

"How come?" he asked. He walked to the corner and picked up his fishing rod with the hand not holding his beer.

"Because we don't want to have anyone saying we were the two morons who got drunk and burned a winning billion-dollar Powerball ticket."

"Damn," he mumbled and headed for the door. "Carmen would never put all these rules on me."

"There are a lot of things Carmen wouldn't do to you," Savannah said. She laughed at the absurd idea that Avis hadn't completely rid himself of his infatuation with Watermill's sexiest lesbian.

"Good point."

"And you're going fishing?" she asked, more as an irritated statement than a question.

"Absolutely. It's beautiful out. What else would I do?"

It sounded to Savannah like a Leo question.

"You could help me figure out how we're going to do this. That's what else you could do." She was far and away more stressed out over this than he was. Whether he ever wanted the ticket or not was irrelevant. It was a lot of money they were about to get rid of. One way or another, the Avis Humphrey life path was about to change in a drastic way. She couldn't help but hear the whispers speaking louder than before. *Are you sure this is the right thing to do?* whispered from somewhere deep in her head.

"Okay. Here's my master plan, so pay attention," Avis started. "I'm going to catch some fish. Then I'm going to clean the fish and light a fire in Ernie's fire pit. After that, I'm going to cook the fish. If you're not too busy planning how to drop a ticket into the fire, I hope you're going to join me and we're going to eat the fish. You following the plan so far?" he asked with the screen door held open with his foot.

"Haven't lost me yet, smart ass."

"Then after we eat the fish we're going to quite unceremoniously burn the ticket, so I can have another beer or three before the whole damn night slips past us. Sound good?" He asked without caring whether she thought it sounded good or not, because that was how it was going to go down. Unless of course, he didn't get to the water to catch at least a couple of fish.

Savannah looked down and drew a deep breath and began to talk. "But—" That was as far as she got before she heard the screen door bang closed. Her head jolted up as she watched Avis walk across the porch toward the water. *Maybe the pressure is too much. Maybe you should wait a few weeks or months before burning the ticket. Give it some time.* The voice was getting louder.

A half-hour later she strolled down to the water with a fishing pole in her hand. "Figured we'd probably go hungry if I left it up to you," she said while baiting her hook with a worm.

"Just don't come down here and start jabbering and scaring the fish away. Don't want to have to start calling you Little Leo," he added, and they both smiled and felt a twinge of pain and the warmth of his memory. Just as the words left his lips he got a bite and began reeling in his first trout of the day. His good luck charm had arrived. She was nothing like Leo, other than she had become his best friend.

The sun set quickly over the lake. It had gone from bright in the sky to an orangish ball glittering over the glassy lake, to a brilliant pink-and-orange haze shining above the white pines on the western shore a mile or so away. Avis sat on an old log bench Ernie had made beside the fire pit while

Savannah flipped the fish in the cast-iron frying pan. Butter spattered and popped, and Avis reached over to take a piece of trout from the pan. Savannah slapped his hand without looking up.

"Man, I got yelled at when I slapped your hand last week," Avis said.

"Yeah. Well, the fish aren't cooked, so hands off," Savannah replied.

She knew Avis had been right. Sitting around and waiting all afternoon for the sun to go down and worrying about the pointless details, would have been unbearable. They had spent the afternoon fishing and talking and laughing, mixed in with a couple of nearly tearful moments.

It was dark when they finished eating, Avis stood up and headed back toward the camp. "I'll be right back", he said.

Savannah felt her heart jump into her throat. *My God. Are we really going to do this?* one of the voices screamed inside her head. *It's not too late. Do something. Stop this madness!*

A few seconds later Avis came back with two beers in his hand. "Let's drink a toast and then let our journey take us where it will," he said, and handed her a can of PBR. They popped their beers open and he sat down beside her.

"Well. What are we drinking to?" she asked with her beer held up toward Avis.

"To Leo," he said and clinked his can against hers. They both took big gulps. "I suspect we'll be toasting him for a long time." Avis gulped because he was thirsty. Savannah gulped because she was scared to death and the voices were getting louder. "Damn guy was responsible for saving the lives of hundreds of fish over the years," Avis added as he thought about all the trout Leo had scared off with his questions or just his general banging around.

"Leo said you'd burn it if that's what you wanted to do. I sure didn't believe him."

Avis took a smaller drink and looked at the fire for a few seconds and carefully considered what he wanted to say. "I love you, Savannah." The voices in her head suddenly fell silent. She stared at him and tears filled her eyes.

"I love you too, Avis."

"I've never told anyone that before. Never said 'I love you' to another person in my life. You've changed everything, Savannah, and—"

She stood up and kissed him and stopped him from talking any more. He had said everything. He told her everything she needed to know, and more. They kissed a long slow kiss and then both sat down and watched the fire. The sun was gone, the moon was up, and the stars were bright. It was time.

"It's only money, you know? If a man's no good without money, then I doubt he's any good with it. That's the way I look at it." He stood and pulled the ticket out of his pocket. It had become more crinkled and wrinkled with each passing day. If he kept it in his pocket a bit longer it would be rendered worthless without burning it. "Let's get this over with."

Savannah stood up and pulled her iPhone out of her pocket and opened the camera. "I suppose we should get a few pictures of the ticket before it's burned, just to prove you actually had it," she said and pointed the camera at him. Avis shrugged. "I'm going to take a bunch to make sure I have some useable ones." Avis shrugged again. She took a dozen close-ups with the ticket in his hand and then looked at them to make sure she had some good ones with the numbers and date clearly visible. The world needed to know he actually had the winning ticket and, more importantly, he actually burned the winning ticket. She stepped back and took a dozen or so more with him holding the ticket up, a look of indifference on his face. After she decided she had taken enough pre-burning pictures, she stopped and looked at Avis and shrugged without saying a word. Avis's shrugs were of indifference. Savannah's were *holy shit* shrugs. She was scared.

"How about you take a couple pictures of me pulling it out of my pocket? Then I'll hold it over the fire, so you can take some more. Then... poof!"

She nodded, but still couldn't believe what they were about to do.

He stepped closer to the fire and the camera app began clicking away again. He slowly pulled the ticket out of his shirt pocket and held it between two fingers. There was no smile on his face. He didn't want anyone thinking this was some sort of moronic white-trash joke. He had considered all angles of what to do with the cursed piece of paper. In the end, he had turned to his dearest friends and asked them what they thought he should do with it. He trusted them. His arm slowly extended over the fire with the ticket at least three feet above the flames. Everything, Avis, the ticket, and the fire were all frozen in time in the pictures. Even at this late stage of the game, there was something in Savannah's head that whispered he wouldn't really burn almost a billion dollars. The camera kept clicking and small puffs of smoke swirled into the air and gave a haunting image of Avis and the ticket in the photo. Then the corners of his mouth rose ever so slightly and a faint smile appeared. Calm filled the air the moment she knew he was really going to do it. Avis Humphrey was going to throw away almost a billion dollars in hopes of getting his life back. It was a crazy thing to do. It was a bold move. It was the right thing to do. For the first time in her life, when she reached a critical crossroad, the voices in her head fell silent. Savannah smiled and nodded at him. His fingers barely separated and it all seemed to happen in slow motion as the camera continued a rapid series of clicking. The ticket slipped away in the air and floated through the smoke and into the fire, with her camera documenting it all. It clicked on the way down. It clicked when the ticket landed. It clicked when it was half-burned. It clicked when the entire ticket was engulfed in flames. And it clicked when there was nothing other than the ghost of a ticket in the fire that had only an hour ago cooked their dinner.

They both stood over the fire and looked down at it. Avis was relaxed and almost indifferent, other than he was relieved that it was done. Savannah was in a mild state of shock.

"You just burned almost a *billion* dollars Avis," she said, without breaking her trance from the fire.

"We," Avis answered. "We just burned almost a billion dollars," he said with a grin and slapped her on the backside and kissed her forehead.

"Holy crap," she whispered, still staring at the fire. "We just burned almost a billion dollars." Then she looked at him and felt as if she were going to be sick. "*I* just burned almost a billion dollars," she said as her stomach knotted up.

"We," he said and pulled her close to him and gave her a hug she would remember for the rest of her life.

She pulled another all-nighter. An hour before the sun came up she emailed her article to Steve along with some pictures and instructions of how the story and pictures should be laid out. There was a picture of Leo showing off Avis's library. There were a couple of pictures of Avis and Leo standing on the edge of the stream with their fishing poles in their hands. And of course, there were several pictures of *The Burning*. The article did not mention that she or Jake had been instrumental in its destruction.

Her headline read, *The Ticket Is Gone!* Steve left almost the entire article just as she had written it, except for the headline. The headline had to be changed to something that grabbed the world's attention. It only took him a few minutes to come up with the new one.

BILLION DOLLAR BONFIRE!

"Three weeks ago, the New Hampshire Lottery Commission announced there was a single winning ticket sold in Watermill, New Hampshire. A few days later, news leaked out the sole winner was 26-year-old Avis Humphrey and he intended to give the money away. Last night, after struggling with the decision of what to do with the ticket, Mr. Humphrey came to a decision and then promptly tossed it into his campfire."

The story continued on for several paragraphs and recapped the events that Savannah thought appropriate to publish. Her main concern with each and every word she wrote was one thing and one thing only: Avis.

Steve had the story posted on Down East eNews by 7:00 a.m. By 7:00 p.m. the story had gone worldwide viral. It was picked up by every paper and news outlet nationwide. Google, Facebook, Twitter, LinkedIn and dozens of other sites blasted the story on the Internet. If Avis was seeking less attention this might have been the wrong way to go, but he knew what he was doing. He was well aware that with no money to be extracted from him, the story would first blow up—and then, like smoke from an exploded bomb, it would drift away.

Three mornings later, he and Savannah walked into Ernie's for breakfast and it was empty, except for a few locals. The reporters were gone. The cameras were gone. The Pirate was gone from the corner table. And all the guys who wanted to be his dad had slinked back to their old wives and old lives. Well, except for one who had come in for breakfast and nothing more.

"Hey. Welcome back. I missed you, son," Ernie yelled when they walked into the diner. "You missed all the excitement," he added and tossed a menu in front of him.

"Bacon and eggs and black coffee," Avis said and pushed the menu back and reached out and shook Ernie's hand. "Thanks for the camp."

"I hear Agnes is gone already," Ernie said while pouring coffee.

"Yeah. Tina said she left before sunset on the day the article came out. Guess she doesn't love me after all," he added. They both chuckled. He and Savannah had already moved back into the trailer. A very clean and organized trailer.

CHAPTER FORTY-EIGHT

Almost eight months to the day from the *Billion Dollar Bonfire*, Tina Schnell came downstairs wearing her purple chenille robe over her flannel nighty. Both the nighty and the robe reached almost to her ankles, which were covered with wool socks tucked into her fake-wool-lined slippers. Despite the staggering amount of warm clothing that covered nearly every inch of her body, she still reeled back and almost fell over when the sub-zero February air bit her face as she opened the front door.

"Jesus, Mary and Joseph!" she called out to nobody. "Who in their right mind would live in New Hampshire in the wintertime? If I were of sound mind I would pack up and head south." The truth was her family had been in the Watermill area for over three hundred years for good reason. They loved it. It was where their friends lived. It was where most of their family lived. It was where their history was. It was their home, and she wasn't going anywhere.

But on this particular February morning, her commitment to friends and family and her home were wavering somewhat as she pulled the collar of her purple robe up tight around her face. She battled the gusting blast of snow and bitterly cold wind on her way to the mailbox at the end of the driveway. She pulled the plastic bag containing The Concord Times out of the box and slammed the frozen lid closed. Then she tucked the paper under her arm and turned back toward the house. It was then that she realized as cold as it felt on the way to the mailbox, it was even colder on the way back. The wind was blowing from the east, coming from behind her on the first leg of her journey. Now that she was retreating, it was blasting razor-sharp gusts almost directly into her face. She lowered her head and plowed forward. The snow crunched under her feet; each step drew her one step nearer to the pot of hot coffee sitting on the counter in her warm kitchen. When she finally reached the porch, she was forced to take her hand out of her fuzzy robe pocket to turn the frozen doorknob. She grabbed the ice-covered knob, twisted it, and stepped forward, slamming her shoulder against the old wooden door. The door didn't budge. A million degrees below zero and the door was stuck. A moment of panic set in as she thought she might have locked herself out. It was too cold to fiddle around with anything, so she turned the knob as far as it would go and kicked the bottom of the door so hard that it nearly broke her big toe. The door crashed open and she leapt through and quickly closed it behind her and tried to ignore the pain in her toe and her shoulder and her ice-bitten hand.

"Good God Almighty. Why would anyone live here?" she asked herself once again. "One day I just might move away." A shiver ran through her, as she shook off the brutal morning cold in the warmth of her home. She walked into the dining room and set the paper down on the table. Then she walked over and put her face almost against the picture window in an attempt to read the thermometer hanging outside. It read seventeen degrees below zero Fahrenheit, but the wind was blowing at least twenty miles an hour. The chill factor dropped it somewhere in the neighborhood of thirty below.

She shivered again at the mere thought of the outside temperature and went into the kitchen and poured herself a cup of hot coffee. She grabbed two powdered sugar doughnuts from the box on the counter and dropped them onto a small plate. With all of her preparations completed, Tina sat down at the dining room table and slipped the paper out of its plastic bag.

Before opening it up, she knew what the headline would be on this particular day. She might not know the exact wording, but she knew the message: RECORD COLD HITS NEW HAMPSHIRE or ARCTIC BLAST ROCKS NEW ENGLAND or something along those lines. Small-town news was almost always predictable. An article would recap last night's lows, and the expected lows to follow over the next day or two, and then the story would recap brutal weather from years or decades gone by and compare them to today's weather. There would be some input from NOAA and maybe from one of the local universities, likely chiming in about global warming. After reading the article, the only thing she would know was that it was damn cold, it's been colder before, and everyone was talking about how cold it might be tonight.

She slipped the paper out of its bag and opened it flat on the table and began to run her hands across the open paper to flatten it out some more. That's when she saw it.

ANOTHER AVIS HUMPHREY SURPISE: HE DIDN'T BURN IT!

Tina momentarily froze, this time from mild shock and not the frigid outside temperature. She stared at the headline again. Then she calmly picked up her coffee cup, sat back in her chair, and smiled. She began to take a sip and scan the article before reading it.

* * *

He hadn't told anyone. Not Tina. Not Alice. Not George. And for the first few months, not even Savannah. Avis had bought the ticket in early June. Within a week, the news leaked out to the universe. On July 1st, Savannah sent her article to Steve, so he could in turn inform the universe that the $967-million Powerball ticket had been destroyed. Ashes to ashes. Dust to dust. Everyone could now leave the poor guy alone. And surprisingly, they pretty much did exactly that. He and Savannah settled into a simple small-town life in his trailer. Avis went back to work at the Rusty Wrench. Savannah wrote a few freelance articles, but nothing that compared to *The Billion-Dollar Bonfire*. Every once in a while, they wandered up to the cemetery and had a beer with Leo. And they stood on the edge of streams around Watermill and caught more fish than Leo would have caught in ten lifetimes. The Watermill trout no longer had a guardian angel named Leo.

On October 16th, Savannah turned twenty-five. After cooking her a dinner, fresh-caught brook trout of course, and sharing a glass of wine with her, Avis went to the kitchen and returned carrying a cupcake with a burning candle in it, and a birthday card in a sealed envelope.

"Aw. You shouldn't have made that for me," Savannah said, knowing damn well he had stopped by the All American and picked up a six-pack, a bottle of cheap wine, and a package of Hostess cupcakes. Avis shrugged and handed her the card and sat and took another sip of his wine. "Make a wish," he said, and set the cupcake in front of her.

Savannah closed her eyes, made a wish she did not speak out loud, and then opened them back up and wiped a tear away. She blew out the candle. He hadn't forgotten after all.

She flipped the envelope around and looked at both sides. It was blank. Then she slipped her finger under the edge and carefully opened it and slid the card out. Her face scrunched in confusion when she looked at the solid black card with a big orange jack-o'-lantern on the front with Gothic letters that screamed "Happy Halloween" above the pumpkin's face. She looked up at Avis for an explanation.

"They didn't have any good birthday cards at the All American. Carmen thought you'd like this one."

"So, you think Carmen is still looking out for your best interests?" Savannah asked and looked back down at her card. "You're not a fast learner, are you, Mr. Humphrey?" she added, without looking up at him before opening up the card to see if he even bothered to write a note inside.

"You like it? It's a funny face, huh?" he asked again and then smiled at her blank expression.

Savannah shook her head back and forth in mild indifference as she opened the card and stared at it for a long time without saying a word. After the initial shock wore off, her brain finally kicked back into gear and all she could do was mumble a question slightly louder than a whisper.

"What is this?" she asked.

"It's a Powerball ticket," he blurted out.

"It's *the* Powerball ticket!" she whispered with her eyes still glued to the ticket lying inside the card.

"You like it?" he asked one more time.

"Avis. What the hell is this?" This time she looked straight at him, and she looked angry and confused. He had burned the ticket. She saw him do it. He had burned it and she took pictures of him doing it. Then she wrote a story about it and sent it to Steve.

"Just something special I thought you'd like," he said with a grin that told Savannah he was quite proud of himself. "Although it's going to be tough to top this one next year. I don't want you to think this'll be happening every birthday."

"But you burned the ticket. I saw you do it. Then you told the whole world you had burned it." Savannah felt as though she was on a hidden-camera show, and she didn't think it was amusing at all. She knew what she knew, and she had seen what she had seen. Whatever this ticket was in front of her, it couldn't be the real one. She looked back up at Avis and waited for the punch line.

"Yeah well. I kind of faked the burning thing. And technically, *you* told the world I burned it. I didn't tell anyone."

"Excuse me?" she snapped, shocked he was implying he was innocent in spreading the news about the ticket being burned.

"I'm just saying," he defended. "I didn't tell the world I won. I didn't tell the world I was giving it away. And I didn't tell the world I burned it."

"Let me tell you something, Avis Humphrey." She raised her voice, and suddenly the whole thing was not going quite as smoothly as he had envisioned. "You may not have told the world you won or that you were giving it away, but you damned sure let them know you had burned it." She wasn't about to get lumped in with all the other gossip hounds who had come to town wanting a piece of the ticket, one way or another.

Avis smiled at her and got up and kissed her on the forehead. "Happy birthday, baby. Want another glass of wine?"

She looked back down at the ticket and sat in shock. "Yes, please," she whispered. The overwhelming reality of having almost a billion dollars back in her hand was hitting her. "But... I saw you burn it," she added.

"Yeah. You left a ticket in the truck. I think it was the one you bought from Carmen when you were there with Leo. After you took a bunch of pictures of the winner, I slipped the winner into my back pocket and pulled out the other. It wasn't too hard." He set a glass of wine in front of her. "I mean, it wasn't like you were watching for it or anything," he added.

"But you said you were going to do whatever I said to do with it," she said, still staring at the winning numbers.

"I didn't think you'd burn the damn thing. I mean, who in the hell burns a billion dollars, Savannah?" he said shaking his head back and forth.

"But I thought..." Her words trailed off.

"And I gotta tell you. I had to wonder if I should be dating someone who would do something like that. A billion dollars, Savannah. You don't just burn something like that. What were you thinking?" He said all of this with a tone of seriousness, as if he had never really considered burning it. As if he hadn't waited until the very last second to decide which ticket to toss into the fire.

"But what about Jake? You asked for his input and he said the same thing as me," she defended.

"You're not helping your case, Savannah," he said. "Jake spends sixteen hours a day creating games where hot chicks with forty-inch boobs and sixteen-inch waists kill dragons with swords and magic wands. I mean that's not exactly who I'd put in charge of what to do with that kind of money."

"Then why did you ask him?" she snapped with a tone of disgust.

"Hell, I thought the two of you might actually come up with some sound advice. You know, I thought you might come up with some good ideas, like buying everyone in the United States a beer, or something along those lines. But burn it? Even Leo wouldn't have suggested that," he said, shaking his head back and forth.

"And George? You said George told you to let me decide what to do with it. What happened to that?"

"To be honest? I think George thought you'd suggest something like giving the money to St. Judes. Or you'd tell me to keep the money and buy Vermont or Northern Canada. But there ain't no way he thought you'd say, *Burn it*."

Savannah sat and stared at the ticket. She looked at the tattered paper with all the wrinkles and then she examined each number. She flipped it over and looked at the backside, then flipped it back and looked at the bar code. Her brain had gone numb. She didn't know whether to be devastated or elated. She had questioned her own advice a hundred times since that night, but what was done, was done. The ticket was gone. Avis had burned it. She saw him do it. She accepted it as done. And her new life with her new love had begun to take shape. Now this.

"So, what about God?" she asked, once again trying to understand how this came to be. "You said George and Leo and God had all gotten together, and you knew they were your trinity, or something like that." She was still trying to comprehend what was going on. Other than deciding to kill herself, which she didn't follow through on, burning the billion-dollar ticket easily ranked up there as the single most Earth-shattering decision she had ever made. It was bigger than quitting her journalism career, another decision she had gone back on. It was bigger than calling off her wedding, a decision that seemed trivial compared to this. Savannah Gardener had taken on the burden of being the woman who had been responsible for burning Avis Humphrey's fortune, or so she had thought. But it had all apparently been some kind of a hoax.

"What happened," Savannah said, "to all that divine message bullshit from George and Leo... and God?"

"Just a test, I guess," he answered with a shrug.

"Stop shrugging like this is no big deal, Avis. This is huge, and—and I'm..." She trailed off again. And Avis shrugged again.

"What now?" she asked, holding the ticket up to the light as if that would somehow verify that it was a fake.

"We've got an appointment with a lawyer in Boston on Friday. A real one, this time. Not like Fitzgerald. Then we figure it out from there."

CHAPTER FORTY-NINE

HE DIDN'T BURN IT!
ANOTHER AVIS HUMPHREY SURPISE

Last spring, twenty-six-year-old Avis Humphrey became famous for a whole list of events. First, he allegedly won the 967 million-dollar Powerball jackpot. Then he allegedly gave the ticket away to his one-time teacher and dear friend, Alice Chen. Once the press got ahold of the news, Mr. Humphrey went into hiding and finally, he allegedly burned the ticket in hopes of getting his life back to normal.

Last Friday, February 9th, at 2:45 in the afternoon, Mr. Humphrey, along with his fiancée, Savannah Gardener, and his legal representative Belinda Bart, from the Boston law firm of Bart, York & Desouza, walked into the offices of the New Hampshire Lottery Commission, at 14 Integra Drive, Concord, New Hampshire, and presented the winning Powerball ticket. Mr. Humphrey claimed an amount of over 500 million dollars, opting for a one-time payout.

Merle and Lindsey, who were now Mr. and Mrs. Humphrey again, sat in their kitchen and read the article. Their hearts raced at the thought of having another shot at the Avis fortune. Of course, since confirming The Jazzman was in fact Avis's real father, Merle had no real claim; but Lindsey was still family. She was still married to the greediest man in Watermill, and she still had access to a lawyer. Their greed fueled their dreams; and even though there was no chance in hell they would ever get a penny, it wouldn't stop them from trying.

Neither Mr. Humphrey nor Ms. Gardener gave any public statements other than to say their lawyer would put out a statement and all questions would go through the law office. According to Ms. Bart, the reason Mr. Humphrey decided to go public with his winnings as opposed to remaining anonymous, which is allowable in New Hampshire, was because, given his history with this ticket, he felt the information would likely leak out anyway. He wanted to make the announcement and be done with wondering if the world was going to find out again. He also wanted to provide answers to questions individuals might have about what was going to happen with the money.

Alice Chen sat in a rocking chair in her living room with the paper sitting in her lap as she read the article. Halfway through reading it, she stopped and sat back and gazed up at the ceiling. She wasn't surprised. Avis was the son she never had, and she loved him. She never fully believed he had burned the ticket, although she was all right with it if he had. She closed her eyes and imagined what he was doing, or had done, with the money; and she was certain he would do good things with it. While most of Watermill was buzzing with excitement, Alice sat and felt a warm surge of satisfaction. Avis was going to be all right. Despite what his family had done to him, and despite the onslaught of attacks he weathered after winning the jackpot and then supposedly destroying the ticket, he was going to be all right. He was a good boy.

While a full accounting of all the winnings was not released by Bart, York and Desouza, they did provide a short list of charities that would receive substantial donations. First on the list was St. Jude Children's Research Hospital. Ms. Bart said Humphrey and Gardener were both strongly committed to helping children in need. She said they are excited to help in any way they can. Next on the list was the Gary Sinise Foundation. Mr. Sinise is famous for his role as Lt. Dan in the movie Forrest Gump. His foundation is committed to helping US Military veterans. Again, according to Ms. Bart, both Humphrey and Gardener have a strong desire to help military members who have given so much to defend our nation. While no other charities were listed by name, Ms. Bart said several charities tied in with libraries, schools, and river and lake conservations are going to be supported. "Most importantly," Bart emphatically added, "There is no need to contact either Mr. Humphrey or Ms. Gardener about supporting your charity. Mr. Humphrey has committed the vast majority of his winnings to a Charitable Trust Fund Board who will designate where the money is to be given. They will keep in mind Mr. Humphrey's original wishes, but he will not be an active member of the board."

George sat at his dining room table with the paper spread in front of him and his head bowed in prayer. He thanked God for taking care of Avis and Savannah. He thanked God that Avis did not listen to his advice and let Savannah decide what to do with the ticket. He momentarily lifted his head and shook it back and forth. "Who would burn that much money?" he mumbled to himself and shook his head back and forth some more and then returned to his prayers. He thanked God for life and asked him to take care of Eve. Lastly, he asked one more time to let him be reunited with her one day. That was always the last request he had every time he spoke with God. "Please God, let me hold Eve's hand and hear her voice one more time." It was what he wanted more than anything in the world.

As to how much of the winnings Mr. Humphrey has kept for himself, all that was said by Ms. Bart was, "It was a modest amount. The overwhelming majority of the 500 million dollars was turned over to the board and slated for charities." When asked if Mr. Humphrey would be remaining in Watermill, Ms. Bart stated, "Although he has made no immediate plans to leave, Mr. Humphrey humbly requests he be allowed to return to his normal life."

Eric, aka Tom the Pirate, had become a minor celebrity at his small college. The combination of being Avis Humphrey's brother and being the world-famous Emu Farmer Pirate fit perfectly into his life as the director and teacher in the university theatre department. With that said, he wanted nothing more from Avis than to have a relationship with his new brother. He sat at his desk in his study and carefully clipped out the newest article and put it into a folder he had made of everything written about Avis over the past few months. He was certain one-day he would write a play about the entire escapade.

The article continued on and on as they usually do. It was filled with names of Lottery Commission personnel who verified the lottery processes. And it listed information about the Charitable Trust Fund Board. Mostly, it just rambled. Avis won it. Gave it away. Burned it. Claimed it. And gave it away again. All facts other than those paled in comparison.

And of course, there was a recap of the wannabe fathers, the return of his mother, and a few words about Leo; but America knew those details by heart. All that mattered was Avis hadn't burned the ticket, and he had given the money away again.

Below the headline, off to the right of the article, was a picture of Avis fishing in a stream somewhere in New Hampshire. The picture, the headline, and the article were all provided by Bart, York and Desouza to multiple media outlets just a few minutes after they walked out of the Lottery Commission office.

CHAPTER FIFTY

Everything had changed for Avis Humphrey since the winning numbers popped up on his TV screen. Before it all went down, he had never been out of New England. His big journeys in life had been going to Boston three times to watch the Red Sox play, and to Foxboro once to see the Patriots. He had never flown in an airplane, or even gone far enough away to need to fly in one. Now, with most loose ends cleaned up and the remaining ones being handled by people he could trust, he was not only leaving the state, he was leaving the country. And he was not only going to fly for the first time, but he and Savannah were traveling on a chartered jet. Despite his reluctance to live the rich life, he had been advised that slipping away beneath the radar of the press was a difficult thing to do if they were going to fly on a commercial airline. As much as he disliked it, Avis was taking a lot of advice from his legal team this time around. Even with almost every detail being taken care of, there were still occasional wolves lurking outside his door. In fact, as Savannah and Avis sipped coffee and ate bagels in a hotel in Concord before heading to the airport, there were three reporters camped out in the frozen driveway in front of his trailer, hoping they could ambush him with a few questions. Another half-dozen, who the first time around had become familiar with the only place to get breakfast in Watermill, were hanging out at Ernie's, showing little hope of actually making contact with the ever-elusive multi-millionaire.

At 9:00AM on the bitterly cold February morning, the same morning Tina Schnell had hiked her way down to her mailbox to get the newspaper, Avis and Savannah climbed up the steps of the Dassault Falcon, slipped off their coats and handed them to the flight attendant. They wouldn't need them again anytime soon. They were the only two passengers on a plane that could comfortably seat nine. Avis passed on the coffee he was offered and looked out the window at the snow banks on the edge of the runway and the de-icing truck preparing to spray down their jet before they taxied away. Savannah sat beside him and took his hand, breaking his gaze out the window. He leaned over and kissed her.

"Quite a mystery, don't you think?" he asked, and looked around the plane.

"What's that?"

"Life. Quite a mystery, don't you think? I mean, neither of us could have predicted this a year ago. It's amazing how we get comfortable in life, as if we have any idea of what each new day will bring."

Savannah smiled and listened. *He's right. Quite a mystery.* "Can you believe I almost married an accountant in my old life?"

"Damn. An accountant. That would have been horrible," Avis mocked.

"You never know, though. Life is a mystery, right?" she argued, defending a life she had thrown away—although it really did seem horrible to her, even back then. "You never know what might have happened." She didn't believe her own silly argument. She and Mack, her ex, would have bought a house near Portland, Maine, where he took a job with a big accounting firm. She would have gone to work for a local paper. A couple of years later they would have had a kid or two, and a puppy, and their parents would be proud grandparents. And then, blah, blah, blah. She actually thought those words, "Blah, blah, blah," in her head, and started to laugh out loud.

"So, are you ready to become Mrs. Avis Humphrey?" Avis asked with an ear-to-ear grin and looking as if he were daring her to do it.

"The question is, are *you* ready to marry me? And more importantly, how are you going to handle it when your wife becomes a better fisherman than you?" Savannah asked, with one eyebrow raised and her head cocked to one side. He looked forward to the possibility of finding out.

Avis smiled at her. She was beautiful. She had become his best friend. She loved him, and she loved going fishing with him. That last fact had sealed the deal, not that it was required. She was like Leo, except she was smart and sexy and could catch fish. "I think I can handle it… if you ever catch more fish than me."

They had started doing a funny thing shortly after Leo died. It wasn't planned and neither of them had given it much thought at first, but with more and more frequency one of them would blurt out, "What do you think Leo would be asking today?" or, "What do you think Leo would say about that?" It was their version of *What would Jesus do,* except they had their own funny little holy man to turn to.

"So, what would Leo be asking this morning?" Savannah asked as the de-icing truck began to spray the plane.

"Well, the logical questions would be, 'Hey Avis. Why do they call them jets?' or 'Hey Avis. What does that stuff they're spraying on the outside of the plane do?' But you know Leo." He stopped talking and glanced around the inside of the plane for a couple of seconds and then looked outside the window to consider all the questions Leo wouldn't have asked. Then he blurted out, "Hey Avis. Who decided the North Pole was at the top of the world and the South Pole was at the bottom?"

They both laughed. Leo almost always asked about irrelevant things that had nothing to do with logic. Even the penis in the zipper question came out of the blue when he had asked it. He hadn't gotten his penis caught in his zipper and neither had Avis. And none of them had heard of anyone else recently doing it or heard anyone talking about it. Only Leo could reach into the thin blue air and come up with, "Hey Avis. What do you think the first guy to get his penis caught in his zipper said?"

The nonstop flight from Concord to Anguilla took just over four hours. Avis spent most of it with his face pressed against the window, looking to see what he could see. For the most part, all he saw were the tops of clouds, but they amazed him. He nudged Savannah periodically and said, "Look at that!" almost every time he saw through an occasional break in the puffy white pillows below and caught a glimpse of land or water. She was happy for him the first couple of times and humored him the next couple. When he elbowed her for about the twelfth time and said, "Look, there's water again," she elbowed him back.

"Hey! Stop waking me up every time you see something."

Avis looked at her and wrinkled his forehead. "Does this mean the honeymoon is over?"

"Oh baby. Let's see if you survive the honeymoon before you start whining about it being over," she answered, with her eyes already closed and going back to sleep.

The jet had left the cold of New Hampshire and climbed to the cold of high altitude, but within a couple of hours, whether it was cold outside or not, it began to look warm. Avis no longer disturbed Savannah as she dreamed away the flight. He continued to watch in amazement as the clouds gave way to the dark waters of the Atlantic, which in turn gave way to the aqua blue waters of the Caribbean. Tiny islands began to pop up sporadically like white and green flowers floating in a bowl of blue water. Pictures and movies hadn't done it justice; and Avis wondered, with the water being this blue and magnificent, what the fishing must be like.

The white and green flowers began to pop up with more frequency, and of varying sizes, until the jet began to descend in a wide banking circle as they approached the long, skinny, flat island of Anguilla. Ten minutes later the plane came to a full stop on the taxiway. The flight attendant opened the door and lowered the stairs. Standing just outside the plane, a local island woman with long dreadlocks and dressed in a dark-blue uniform smiled and shook both their hands and welcomed them to the island of tranquility wrapped in blue. She explained the Custom and Immigration processes and then let them know that Avis's cousin, Pellet, was waiting for them just outside the fence. Her hand motioned in the direction of a white guy standing on the outside of a chain-link fence that separated the airport from the parking lot.

Pellet grinned and waved at them. Savannah thought he looked exactly like one might expect of a small-town guy from Maine who came to the Caribbean to work and then never returned to his homeland. His hair was long and scraggly and was topped off by a dirty and faded old Red Sox cap. His cargo shorts looked as if they had been new a long time ago. And his T-shirt—well, Savannah wondered if his T-shirt had ever been new. Avis waved back as they headed toward the terminal entrance.

"He looks a little like Leo on the first day I met him," Savannah said, not meaning it as a compliment.

"That's cool. Could be worse, right?" Avis answered.

"What am I getting myself into?" she mumbled and squeezed his hand tight.

A warm gust of air blew across the runway and carried a shadow of soft Caribbean sand an inch or so above the pavement. Avis watched. He waited for a dust swirl to kick up and remind him that they would never be far apart from each other, but it didn't happen. The sand skirted over the pavement like a whisper of snow being blown across a New Hampshire field and then silently disappeared into the trees and flowers as it settled down into its new home in the soft tropical grass.

"Quite a mystery isn't it!" He squeezed back and smiled.

"HEY AVIS."

"YEAH, LEO."

ABOUT THE AUTHOR

B.M. SIMPSON was born in rural Maine. He joined the Air Force at 18 and lived and moved across the U.S. and Europe. After retiring from the Air Force, he spent nearly a decade living and working in the Caribbean. On the islands of Anguilla, St. Kitts and Grand Cayman, he discovered a passion for island life and formed friendships second to none. In 2015 he released his first novel, *Island Dogs*, and he followed it up with his second, *Avis Humphrey*.

Today Simpson calls South Sound, Grand Cayman home, as he continues to travel to and work in the Caribbean. Despite his blue water passion, he holds onto old friendships and cherishes his New England roots. He is currently writing his next novel, *The Bella Vita*.

www.BMSIMPSON.COM

www.facebook.com/BMSimpson.author

Made in the USA
Columbia, SC
13 October 2018